THE FALKLANDS WAR

Twentieth-Century Wars
General Editor: Jeremy Black

Published titles

Gerard DeGroot	*The First World War*
Spencer C. Tucker	*The Second World War*
Peter Lowe	*The Korean War*
David L. Anderson	*The Vietnam War*
D. George Boyce	*The Falklands War*

Twentieth-Century Wars
Series Standing Order ISBN 0–333–77101–X

You can receive future titles in this series as they are published. To place a standing order please contact your bookseller or, in the case of difficulty, write to us at the address below with your name and address, the title of the series and the ISBN quoted above.

Customer Services Department, Macmillan Distribution Ltd
Houndmills, Basingstoke, Hampshire RG21 6XS, England

THE FALKLANDS WAR

D. George Boyce

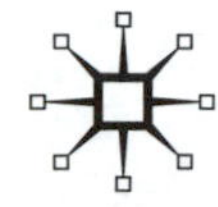

First published 2005 by
PALGRAVE MACMILLAN
Houndmills, Basingstoke, Hampshire RG21 6XS and
175 Fifth Avenue, New York, N. Y. 10010
Companies and representatives throughout the world

PALGRAVE MACMILLAN is the global academic imprint of the Palgrave Macmillan division of St. Martin's Press, LLC and of Palgrave Macmillan Ltd. Macmillan® is a registered trademark in the United States, United Kingdom and other countries. Palgrave is a registered trademark in the European Union and other countries.

ISBN-13: 978 0-333-75395-8 hardback
ISBN-10: 0–333–75395–X hardback
ISBN-13: 978 0-333-75396-5 paperback
ISBN-10: 0–333–75396–8 paperback

This book is printed on paper suitable for recycling and made from fully managed and sustained forest sources.

A catalogue record for this book is available from the British Library.

A catalog record for this book is available from the Library of Congress.

10 9 8 7 6 5 4 3 2 1
14 13 12 11 10 09 08 07 06 05

Printed in China

Contents

Acknowledgements vi
Map 1 The Falklands: the campaign vii
Map 2 The South Atlantic viii
Chronology, March–July, 1982 ix

Introduction 1
1 Sovereignty and Self-determination 8
2 The British Response 39
3 The Armed Forces 61
4 Diplomacy and War 79
5 From the *Belgrano* to San Carlos 98
6 From the Bridgehead to Goose Green 116
7 Victory 133
8 The MOD, the Media and Public Opinion 148
9 War and the state of 'Thatcher's Britain' 171
10 War and the Falklands 191
11 Retrospect 208
Conclusion 221
Guide to Further Reading 224
Bibliography 227
Index 240

Acknowledgements

I am grateful to the Leverhulme Trust for awarding me a fellowship from January to September 2001 to enable me to work on this book; and to Val and Roy Anthony for carefully typing my manuscript.

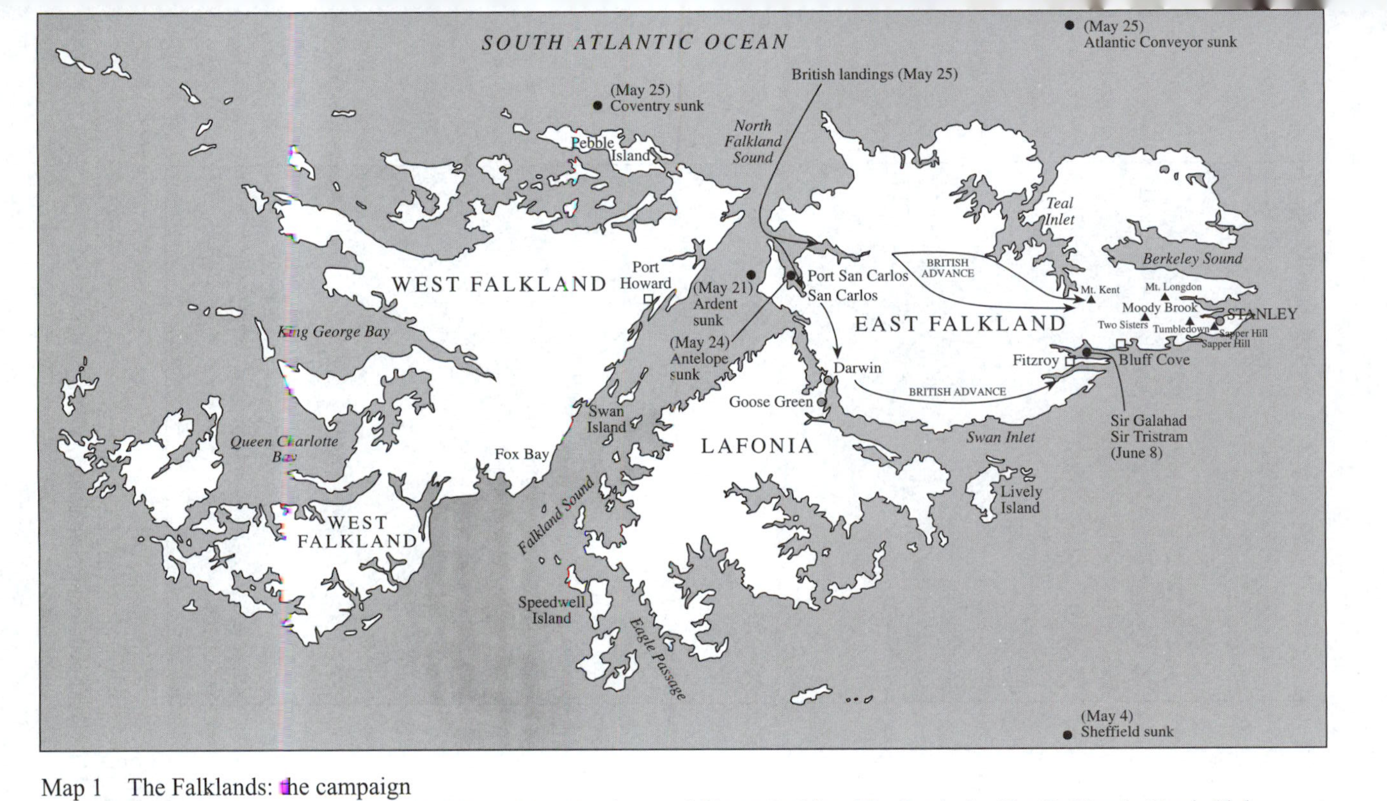

Map 1 The Falklands: the campaign

1) The Falklands: the campaign. Adapted From Max Hastings and Simon Jenkins, *The Battle for The Falklands* (Book Club Associates Edition, London, 1983), Frontis Piece

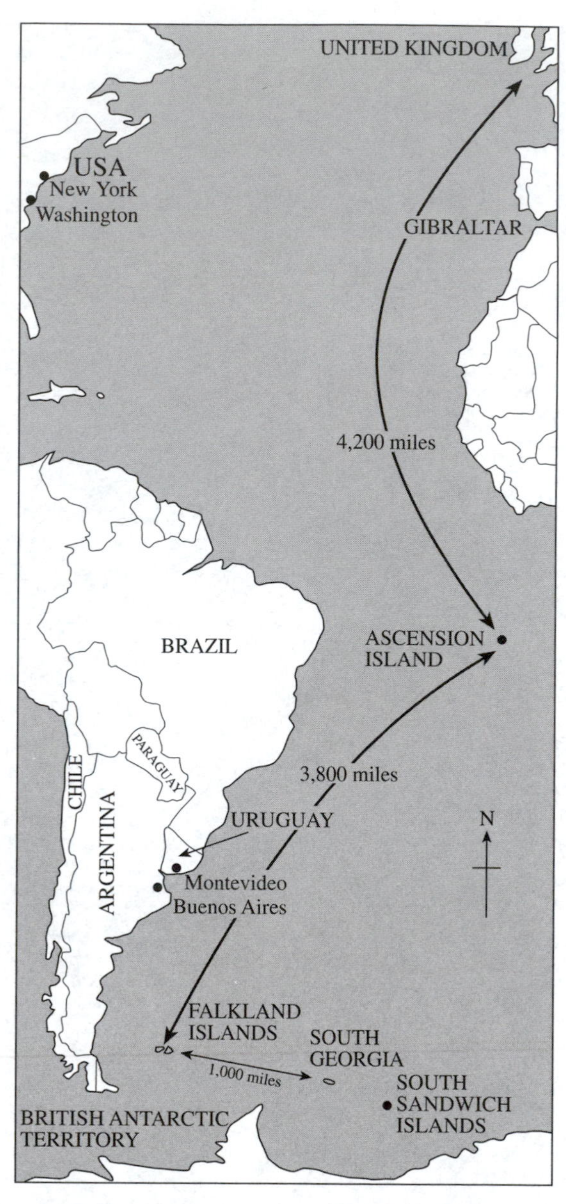

Map 2 The South Atlantic
2) The South Atlantic. Adapted From Derek Oakley, *The Falklands Military Machine* (Spellmount, Staplehurst, 1989), p. 108

Chronology, March–July 1982

19 March	Argentine scrap merchants land at the disused whaling station at Leith. Raise Argentine flag.
22 March	*Bahia Buen Suceso* leaves Leith harbour. 48 scrap merchants remain behind.
25 March	*Bahia Paraiso* lands Argentine marines at Leith.
31 March	British Intelligence warns that Argentine invasion is under way. Navy tells Mrs Thatcher that it can prepare a Task Force.
1 April	Royal Marines deploy in defensive positions around Stanley.
2 April	Argentine troops invade Falklands. Governor Rex Hunt orders Royal Marines to surrender after a three-hour fight. British Cabinet approves sending Task Force to the South Atlantic. UN passes resolution 502 calling for withdrawal of armed forces by both sides and renewed negotiations for a peaceful settlement.
3 April	Emergency debate in Parliament. 22 Royal Marines captured at Grytviken, South Georgia. UN Security Council approves Resolution 502.
5 April	Lord Carrington resigns. Succeeded by Francis Pym. Task Force sails from Portsmouth.
7 April	President Reagan approves Haig's peace mission.
8 April	Haig and his team arrive in London. Mrs Thatcher accepts principle of independent inquiry into the Government's handling of the dispute.
10 April	Haig in Buenos Aires. EU approves sanctions against Argentina, with strong French lead.
12 April	British Government declares 200 mile Maritime Exclusion Zone. Haig again in London.
14 April	Argentine fleet sets sail. Haig in Washington to brief President Reagan.
15 April	Haig returns to Buenos Aires. British destroyer group takes up position in South Atlantic.

16 April	Task Force vanguard sails from Ascension Island.
17 April	Admiral Fieldhouse in conference with Admiral Woodward and 3 Brigade on Ascension Island. Haig presents Argentine Junta with five point plan.
19 April	Argentine response to Haig's plan conveyed to London.
21 April	SAS and SBS troops land on South Georgia.
22 April	Pym in Washington with British response to Haig's plan. SAS lifted from Fortuna glacier.
24 April	Admiral Woodward's Task Force Group rendezvous with destroyer group.
25 April	South Georgia recaptured.
27 April	Haig's final peace plan sent to London.
28 April	Britain announces Total Exclusion Zone to include aircraft and ships of all nations.
29 April	Task Force arrives at Exclusion Zone.
30 April	TEZ comes into force. General Moore and Brigadier Thompson confer in Ascension Island. President Reagan declares US support for UK.
1 May	Pym returns to Washington, declaring that US is now an 'ally'. SAS and SBS land on Falklands. First Vulcan raid on Stanley Airport. Sea Harrier raids and naval bombardment. *Conqueror* trails the *General Belgrano.*
2 May	*General Belgrano* sunk. Pym in New York with UN Secretary General de Cuellar. Peruvian and UN peace initiatives launched.
3 May	General Galtieri rejects Peruvian initiative.
4 May	*Sheffield* hit by Exocet missile.
5 May	British full Cabinet accepts Peruvian plan.
6 May	Argentine again rejects Peruvian plan.
7 May	UN Secretary General discusses peace plan with Argentine and British delegations. TEZ extended to 12 miles from Argentine coast.
11 May	Argentine declares whole of South Atlantic a 'war zone'.
12 May	QE2 sails from Southampton with 5 Infantry Brigade. Argentina says sovereignty is not a precondition.
14 May	British ambassadors to UN and USA return to London for consultation. War Cabinet draws up final British proposals for de Cuellar.
18 May	Junta rejects British proposals. San Carlos landings plan goes to full Cabinet.

19 May War Cabinet authorises Woodward to proceed with landings at San Carlos.

20 May Mrs Thatcher tells House of Commons of collapse of peace talks.

21 May San Carlos landings. *Ardent* sunk. 16 Argentine aircraft lost. UN Security Council debates crisis.

23 May *Antelope* sunk. 7 Argentine aircraft lost.

24 May EU renews sanctions, Ireland and Italy opting out.

25 May *Coventry* badly damaged and *Atlantic Conveyor* sunk. UN Security Council debate ends.

26 May War Cabinet questions lack of movement out of the San Carlos beachhead. UN resolution 505 bids de Cuellar to seek settlement.

28 May 2 Para battle at Goose Green/Darwin begins.

29 May Argentine forces surrender at Goose Green/Darwin.

31 May 42 Commando fly to Mount Kent.

1 June 5 Brigade disembarks at San Carlos. War Cabinet debates peace proposals.

2 June 2 Para fly to Bluff Cove. Argentina says she is ready to accept UN trusteeship of the Falklands. Mrs Thatcher says she can see no role for Argentina 'in anything related to sovereignty'.

3 June Western summit at Versailles. Britain under pressure to seek peaceful end to conflict. Reagan gives five-point peace plan to Britain.

4 June Britain vetoes ceasefire resolution in the UN Security Council. US vetoes also, then says it would like to change its mind.

5 June Scots Guards embark at Fitzroy in *Sir Galahad*.

6 June Scots Guards land at Fitzroy. Welsh Guards embark for Fitzroy on *Fearless*.

7 June UN Security Council announces peace plan.

8 June *Sir Galahad* and *Sir Tristram* bombed at Bluff Cove. 51 killed. Major General Moore finalises plans for attack on Stanley.

11 June Battle for Stanley begins. 42 Commando attacks Mount Harriet. 45 Commando attacks Two Sisters. 3 Para attacks Mount Longdon.

12 June All attacks successful by dawn. *Glamorgan* hit by Exocet missile. 5 Brigade moves into position.

13 June	2 Para attacks Wireless Ridge. Scots Guards attack Tumbledown. 1/7 Gurkhas attack Mount William.
14 June	All Argentine forces surrender. British do not demand 'unconditional surrender'.
6 July	Mrs Thatcher announces appointment of Lord Franks to chair a committee of Privy Councillors to review Government policies leading up to the conflict (Reports 18 January 1983).
12 July	Argentina announces 'de facto' cessation of hostilities.

Introduction

I

Military historians today generally hold that their subject involves not only the study of armies, weapons, supplies, clothing and tactics, but also issues of legitimacy (as the United States and British Governments are discovering in the Iraq crisis of 2003–4). Lack of legitimacy does not necessarily lose a war, but it makes it hard to win it, or to enjoy the fruits of victory. My method in writing this account of the Falklands War of 1982 is to try to combine what might be called the traditional (and vital) aspects on the conflict – arms and the men – with the kinds of values, national and international that in part (at least) shaped its outcome. I have therefore included many quotations from speeches, broadcasts, books, plays, poems and reports to illustrate the characterisation of the war. This is particularly important, given that the Argentine armed forces had never fought, except for engagement in security/repressive duties, and yet was given the momentous task of recovering the Malvinas and healing the wound of history; while the British, whose army had certainly experienced and was experiencing internal security conflict, had not engaged in 'regular' warfare between state and state since the Korean War of 1953, and (more ambiguously) the abortive Suez Campaign of 1956.

Behind the Argentine military expedition to recover the Malvinas lay a military junta which calculated rightly that its just war would arouse public support even in a country in which political opposition was suppressed by brute force. For the British the predicament was unusual. The Falklands certainly absorbed, from time to time, British Parliamentary attention; but there was no long-standing desire on the part of the nation to preserve the heritage of British nineteenth century expansion in the South Atlantic. Moreover, Professor Jeremy Black has pointed out that, in the contemporary world, there are places where 'audiences as well as soldiers will have to be "blooded"'.[1] What was significant in 1982 was that the 'blooding' of their fathers' generation in World War II resonated with the generation that confronted the Falklands crisis. Much was therefore expected from the British army, navy and air force; defeat was, as Mrs Thatcher the British Prime Minister put it, 'unthinkable'. Words and phrases out of history were deployed again to the surprise of many and the disgust of some.[2] I have tried to encompass the varied dimensions of the Falklands War for it is my contention that words were as of as much significance as the bayonet of the soldier. Indeed this contention is itself flawed. Words in warfare are weapons; and weapons are words, because they shape public response to the legitimacy of a campaign: the expression 'collateral damage' is a good example of this interaction, summing up both the inevitable consequences of the use of air power in warfare, and the way in which its description has discredited its use. Fortunately for both sides, their efforts in the Falklands/Malvinas war reconciled words and weapons, with the exception for the British of the sinking of the Argentine warship, the *General Belgrano*, and enabled them to continue the conflict until victory should be won, or defeat acknowledged.

II

In her commemoration symposium, *Ten Years On: the British Army in the Falklands War*, Linda Washington described the campaign as 'a war that the British took very personally'. [223, p. 95] No other conflict in which the British armed forces have been engaged since the Second World War – not even the internal war with the Irish Republican Army; not even what was regarded as the seminal Gulf War of 1991 – had the same impact. This helps explain the 'personal' character of the Falklands War: the Northern Ireland conflict was perceived, from the beginning, as one of great complexity. The politics of the province, the Civil Rights issue, the Unionist-Nationalist confrontation, the way in which the British Government and its armed forces were drawn into the crisis, all deprived the long-drawn out struggle of a clear moral foundation on which the British response could be based. The Gulf War saw British forces engag-

1. Jeremy Black, 'Determinisms and Other Issues', in *Journal of military History*, 68 (Oct. 2004), pp. 1217–32, at p. 1232.
2. See Chapter 9.

ing a clearly defined foe in regular battle; but as part of a wider coalition assembled by the United States of America. The Falklands War, by contrast, saw the British armed forces (albeit with international diplomatic and intelligence support – as well as some opposition) engage a regular army in what appeared to the bulk of political and public opinion as a 'just war'.

It was this that set the Falklands conflict apart from these other contemporary or near contemporary military campaigns. The war can be set in another, less 'just' context: that of imperial retreat, of the war as a kind of last gasp of British imperial policing; only this time the result was not a piece of imperial retreating, but of imperial reassertion, since the Falkland Islands were, as a result of the war, not given away, but retained. The Suez crisis, to which politicians engaged in the Falklands crisis referred on occasion, seems nearer to the Falklands War, raising as it did questions of Britain's own character and her position in the world. But even here the comparison was not quite exact: the Middle East was, as the then Foreign Secretary Ernest Bevin put it, 'In peace and war…an area of cardinal importance to the United Kingdom, second only to the United Kingdom itself'. [122, p. 109] It was for this reason that, in 1956, the Conservative Government of Sir Anthony Eden embarked on a military intervention to retain the British hold on the Suez Canal and the Egyptian oil industry. This intervention was regarded by the British as a strategic and economic necessity; but by the world as a colonial military adventure. It proved divisive both at home and abroad; and it never attained the 'just war' status that the Falklands achieved – for most British people at any rate.

The various wars of imperial withdrawal did not strike the chord that the Falklands War sounded. It may well have been, as one senior soldier put it, that the counter-insurgency wars in Malaya, Kenya, Cyprus, Aden and the like turned 'the gormless young man…from a comic-strip reading callow youth into a self-reliant, tough, useful member of a military society'; [122, p. 143] but, although the press in particular stressed that the British Army was engaged in fighting a cruel and ruthless enemy, these 'brush-fire' campaigns did not catch the public imagination. The whole idea of empire, as well as the British presence in these far off regions, was in decline; indeed, it was almost something of an embarrassment. It might be suggested that the Rhodesian affair, when Ian Smith declared unilateral independence rather than hand power over to the African majority, has some resemblance to the Falklands question: a 'British people' was making a stand against loss of power. But no-one could describe Ian Smith's adversaries – the African people of Rhodesia – as an alien, unwanted invader; some preferred to ascribe this more appropriately to the white Rhodesian minority. And in any case the Labour Government of Harold Wilson was determined not to send a single soldier to Rhodesia on anyone's side; though he was prepared to close his eyes to 'sanction-busting' efforts by oil companies.

The Korean War of 1950–1953 might have been expected to arouse great public engagement. Here was a military intervention characterised as the free world making its stand against the spread of communism and tyranny. The Labour Government despatched a 'Commonwealth Brigade' to the Peninsula, and the fighting saw heroic 'last stands', for example by the Gloucester Regiment at the battle of the Imjin River in April 1951. But as the war then reached a stalemate, it lost its impact, and, even in the United States of America, ended with the heartfelt desire to end the war and 'bring the boys back home'. Britain defended the sovereignty of the newly emerging state of Malaysia; but this, though pursued with determination and success, did not engage the British public with the same intensity as the Falklands, whose people were seen as British, kith and kin of the home nation, speaking in familiar accents; moreover there was (to coin a phrase) no selfish economic or strategic British interest in the Falklands as there were in other colonial lands. This was reflected in the orientation of British defence policy in the years before the crisis became acute. The Labour Defence Secretary, Roy Mason, concluded in his pamphlet *Our Contribution to the Price of Peace* (1975) that 'Britain's security…is indivisible from that of the NATO Alliance'. [122, p. 257] The Conservative Defence Secretary, John Nott, reflected Mason's thinking when in 1981, in his *The Way Forward*, he outlined Britain's four main defence roles: 'an independent element of strategic and theatre nuclear forces committed to the (NATO) Alliance; the direct defence of the United Kingdom homeland; a major land and air contribution on the European mainland; and a major maritime effort in the Eastern Atlantic and Channel'. [122, pp. 257–8] None of these roles could be said to include a military campaign in the South Atlantic for what President Ronald Reagan called an 'ice-cold bunch of land'. [90, p. 154]

The Falklands War engaged parliament, the media, the public with a surprising intensity. This could be explained in terms of political theory. As Peter Calvert put it in his quickly written, but incisive analysis *The Falklands War: the Rights and the Wrongs,* 'the

Falklands crisis is first and foremost a dispute about sovereignty. Sovereignty is the fundamental concept on which the entire world order of the twentieth century is based'. [36, p. 1] But the sovereignty of what is arguably an integral part of the United Kingdom, Northern Ireland, never aroused political or public involvement, except, perhaps, as to the best means of ridding the Kingdom of this troublesome region.

Explanations for the 'very personal' nature of the Falklands War must be sought elsewhere. They are not monolithic: personal political ambition (and survival); pressures from the Falkland Islanders themselves; the desire of Service chiefs to show that their particular arm was still indispensable to the nation (and more importantly to the politicians), all played their part. But underlying these, and at times driving them, was a strong and sustained public surge, one that drew upon notions of national pride, obligation, history, tradition and – at times – xenophobia. Some claimed that the British people had at last rediscovered themselves, redefined themselves after decades of defeat, decline and disappointment. The very lack of a clearly discernible economic or for that matter strategic advantage to be gained from going to war seemed not to lessen the intense public involvement, but rather to enhance it.

There were, or course, dissenting voices. The *Guardian* denied that the issues were clear-cut, that this was a just war. It saw what it called the 'deep emotional hiatus' between 'the vision of the great ships steaming south and the fine bargaining about the small type of withdrawals, condominiums, referendums', a history that 'made it all the more difficult to risk hundreds of lives in so muddied a case'. [78, p. 189] The doubts that surfaced during the war were to reappear in more deeply critical and even savage form in the decade after the war's end, when playwrights, novelists, poets, cartoonists, a plethora of dissident voices condemned the war as exemplifying all the worst aspects of what they characterised as 'Thatcher's Britain'.

But this was later; the war was launched, pursued and won, and all within a context of the most complex diplomatic manoeuvrings and initiatives, involving shuttle diplomacy, United Nations' resolutions, the poring over the small type of possible compromises, and – not least important – hard fighting and risky military choices. Even the Task Force – especially the Task Force – anticipated a negotiated settlement rather than actual war, and some soldiers, sailors and airmen could hardly believe that the crisis would end in shooting. [208, p. 167] The experience of war – what the great military analyst, Carl von Clausewitz called the 'friction' of war – would also play its central role in interacting with diplomacy and public opinion: for there was that 'remarkable trinity'

> of primordial violence, hatred and enmity, which are to be regarded as a blind force of nature; of the play of chance and probability within which the creative spirit is free to roam; and the element of subordination, as an instrument of policy, which makes it subject to reason alone.

For Clausewitz, 'the first of these three aspects mainly concerns the people; the second the commander and his army; the third the government'. The 'passions that are to be kindled in war must already be inherent in the people; the scope which the play of courage and talent will enjoy in the realm of probability and chance depends on the particular character of the commander and the army; but the political aims are the business of government alone. [48, p. 27]

This 'trinity' of violence, chance and reason emerged as the significant directors of the Falklands War. But it is their inter-relationship that gives each conflict, including the Falklands War, its special, if not unique, character. It is not only generals who fight the last war; historians do so as well. And the search of themes, patterns and the like, which are the historian's business, must always be subject to an awareness of contingency. For example, the way in which British losses occurred; their description and justification; their timing, all might have been different and might have provoked a speedy disillusionment for the war. Public opinion remained supportive of the war; but it was not unconditional, and 'chance' and 'reason' played their part in sustaining 'violence'.

The war was also very personal for Argentina; it was an attempt to end the 'illegal occupation' of Argentine sovereign territory. The military junta and armed forces were transformed into the heroes of the hour. But the most surprising aspect of the war remains its resonance with the British public and politicians: British children were not taught (as were Argentine children) that the islands were rightfully theirs. It seemed indeed to be a special kind of war. Hugo Young described the war an 'an impressive, if appalling, spectacle'. [78, p. 42] That this 'spectacle' took place for far off and under-populated islands raises the question of what Colin S. Gray has called 'the geography of space, distance, time terrain, and weather'. [101, p. 162] These factors all warned against a British military expedition to recover possession of the Falkland Islands. But there is also the 'geography of the imagination'. Physical geography places the British Isles 'unambiguously' in the column of European terrain and European politics; but 'within those British Isles, however, "Europe" is a continental phenomenon, "over there" beyond the moat'. This contrast between the geography and space, distance, time, terrain and weather, and the geography of the mind, helps explain why the British Government's confident assumption that it had closed down the world-wide imperial theatre of military commitment and operations, was misjudged. The Falklands was both a war imagined and a real, violent and destructive experience. To explain why these two did not cancel out, but, rather, reinforced each other is the primary purpose of this book. To understand why they were, a few year, presented as inimical to each other is the second purpose. Both explorations, it is hoped, will help explain why the British saw the Falklands War as one the British took 'very personally', and why what was by most standards a very small war raised and raises profoundly significant features of what Trevor Wilson calls the 'myriad faces of war'. [232]

1

Sovereignty and Self-determination

Two of the most commonly used concepts in modern political and diplomatic history are also two of the most problematical: sovereignty and self-determination. As Roger Scruton has warned, 'It is now unclear what is meant by sovereignty, and the concept seems to focus disputes in political science and philosophy which no dictionary article could possibly resolve'. [194, p. 441] Scruton identifies two main aspects of sovereignty: the external (the recognition of state as having rights of jurisdiction over a particular people and territory and being solely answerable for that jurisdiction in international law); and the internal (the supreme command over a civil society, with legal and coercive powers over the members of that society). Self-determination, by contrast, is more easily defined (the right of a people of common cultural, linguistic, racial, ethnic or other identity to live in their own sovereign state and govern themselves); but is almost impossible to apply in practice: for the idea of self-determination presupposes some prior, identifiable national or racial or ethnic group; and yet such a group might be as yet only in the process of formation (as most 'nations' invariably are) or will contain minority peoples who reject the claim of the predominant 'nation'.

There are further complications to the application of these concepts to any particular case: as John Stuart Mill wrote in 1861, at a time of the making of nation-states in Europe,

> Nobody can suppose that it is not more beneficial for a Breton or a Basque of French Navarre to be...a member of the French nationality, admitted on equal terms to all the privileges of French citizenship...than to sulk on his own rocks, the half-savage relic of past times, revolving in his own little mental orbit, without participation or interest in the general movement of the world. [239, p. 10]

'The same remark', he continued, 'applies to the Welshman or the Scottish highlander as members of the British nation'. Yet Mill also acknowledged that 'where the sentiment of nationality exists in any force, there is a prima facie case for uniting all the members of the nationality under the same government, and a government to themselves apart'. [239, p. 41] The latter claim – a kind of forerunner to the idea of self-determination given international support at the Versailles Peace Conference of 1919 – might then conflict with the former. And even President Woodrow Wilson's enunciation of the principle of self-determination in his Mount Vernon speech of 4 July 1918 contained the qualification that 'every territorial settlement in this War must be made in the interest and for the benefit of the population concerned': the interest, not necessarily the wishes of the population. [65, p. 416] And so self-determination would be subordinate to the subjective and over-riding consideration of how useful or productive it is to the group of people who demand it: a consideration which (it can be assumed) the larger nation is entitled to make (the 'British' or perhaps the English in the case of Wales and Scotland).

The second difficulty lies with the concepts both of self-determination and sovereignty, when they are combined in the idea of the nation state and its legal and political role as the fundamental building block of internal and international politics. These ideas gained common parlance and legitimacy long after the world had been shaped and regulated by other, older considerations: by the rise of colonial empires; by dynastic transfers of what were, in the medieval and early modern age, regarded as the family or personal property of monarchs and princes; by the fortunes of war, even by chance encounters. Thus when some British sailors kicked out some Argentines in 1833 (with the Argentines in no position to resist) their boldness was followed by the British declaration of Crown Colony status on the Falklands Islands in 1841. [15, pp. 29–45] The Argentines, for their part, could lay claim to the Islands on the basis of their inheritance of Spanish rights, as the empire of Spain in the new world disintegrated. But the British could and did respond with the claim of discovery of the Islands by English navigators in the sixteenth century. There was a further complication: 'Argentina' as a sovereign nation-state did not exist until the latter part of the nineteenth century; and the Argentine claim on the Islands, asserted in 1820, was made on behalf of the Municipal Government of the province of Buenos Aires. [38, p. 412] The settlement on the Falklands of people of British origin in the nineteenth century might be regarded as a sound basis for the application of the principle of self-determination; but then it could be said that a small, diminishing population, 'sulking' on their rocks, revolving in their own 'little mental orbit' would surely benefit from close and ever-closer association with a wider nationality. And that, since the nationality of their origin (the British) were thousands of miles away, while the nationality they might be persuaded to join (the Argentines) were in close proximity, and were developing ties of communication and holiday visits, this mutuality should decide the most profitable way in which the Falkland Islanders could 'determine' their own future. Thus 'self-determination' would be rightly subject to the consideration of the real, as distinct from their own perceived, best interests.

But there is yet another complication which could not be lightly set aside: the character of the sovereign state to which the Falkland Islanders might be assigned. Argentine's history in the twentieth century was a far from reassuring one from the point of view of any prospective entrant into her sovereign territory (and from the point of view, too, of the Argentine people). Argentine claims to the Islands were stated most forcefully in 1946, when Peron was elected President for the first time; [146, pp. 391–4] his regime was hardly a model of democratic government. When Argentine claims were most persistently renewed, in the 1970s, the country was under military rule, and was suffering a brutal civil war, with the Government taking action of a highly illegal kind against its left-wing enemies. The consideration that Argentine citizens were themselves the 'Disappeared Ones', enemies, opponents or critics of the regime who were kidnapped and murdered by the military junta, was not an encouragement for the notion that less than 2,000 islanders 'on their own rocks' would benefit from attachment to a wider, citizenship-based state. It was, however, encouraged by the fact that the 1981 British Nationality Bill deprived the Falkland Islanders of full British citizenship [13, p. 432], and by what the Foreign Secretary, Lord Chalfont, in what he called a 'philosophising' mood, suggested in 1968: that the views of the United Nations might take precedence over those of the islanders: 'the very fact of membership of the United Nations implies that countries that belong to it derogated a certain amount of sovereignty to it'. [150, p. 465]

This set the scene for a further complication on the question of the future of the Falkland Islands: that their ownership was not, as in the past, merely the business of the state that happened to hold them, and the state that happened to claim them; it was now, since 1945, very much the business of a supra-national organisation, the United Nations. Thus whereas in 1952 the British Ambassador in Buenos Aires could write comfortably to the Foreign Office that President Peron was 'comparatively mild and even resigned' over his claim to the Falklands [146, pp. 391–4] (and the British could think in terms of defending the Islands through raising a force of local special constables) [201, 4 Feb. 2001] the world had now changed, and in directions less likely to occasion British complacency. The decolonisation of the European empires was, by the late 1960s, all but complete. The United Nations of the last quarter of the twentieth century was very different from that of the immediate post Second World War organisation, numbering as it now did new, post-colonial states, highly critical of their former masters. Resolution 2065 of the United Nations General Assembly, passed on 16 December 1965, referred back to a previous anti-colonial resolution (1514) of 1960, calling for 'self-determination of all peoples' and an end to colonialism in all its forms, 'one of which covers the case of the Falkland Islands (Malvinas)'. The contending parties to the dispute were invited to find a peaceful way of resolving their differences through negotiation, though 'the interests of the population' were to be borne in mind. This resolution was carried, with the United States of America and the United Kingdom abstaining. In 1975 the 'non-aligned' states took the issue up as simply one of decolonisation. [133, pp. 9–11] And although the British Government, for its part, always claimed that it had 'never admitted the validity of the Argentine claim to sovereignty over the Falkland Islands and Dependencies', yet in 1910 a Foreign Office memorandum acknowledged that it was 'difficult to avoid the conclusion that the Argentine Government's claim is not altogether unjustified and that our action has been somewhat high-handed'. [136, pp. 23–4]

If Britain had an Argentine problem, then Argentina felt that it had a more pressing British problem. Argentina was, comparatively, a new nation, one comprised largely of immigrants from southern Europe. It was easy to sneer at the spectacle of an immigrant nation seeking to make good its claim to the Falklands on anti-colonial grounds; and certainly there was, to say the least, a degree of inconsistency in Argentina's approach to the Falklands dispute. Argentine history was not a success story; and nationalism, as the Welsh historian Gwyn A. Williams noted, is a tale of 'half-memories, folklore, traditions, myths, fantasy'. [228, p. 197] Dr Guido di Tella, Under-Secretary of Economics in the last civil government in Argentina in 1975, described Argentine attitudes to the Falkland Islands as one where 'the knowledge is not very deep. I would think of many schoolboys not answering well that question' (on how many Argentines were living in the Falklands in 1833, when the British staked their modern claim to the Islands). [116, p. 268] But there was another kind of knowledge, and one that Argentine governments took pains to refresh. In January 1966 the government created the 'Instituto y Museo Nacional de las Islas Malvinas y Adyacencias' to 'stimulate the national conscience', and demand the return of the Islands to Argentina and to collect and disseminate information on the question. This worked only too well. On 28 September 1966 twenty young Argentines of the 'New Argentine Movement' staged 'Operation Condor', a 'symbolic seizure' of the Islands (to the annoyance of the Argentine President). [150, pp. 463–4]

It was this mixture of 'Argentina irredenta' and yet apparent acquiescence in the status quo, that was the most dangerous aspect of the Argentine approach to this historic dispute. The Argentine claim to the Islands was long-standing, and, in its view at least, irrefutable. Yet there was no sign that it would do anything other than pursue its claim by the slow and stately means of diplomatic pressure. The inauguration of a military government in 1975 did not, apparently, alter that procedure; even the populist government of Peron in 1946 did not go beyond acceptable political pressure in its attitude to the dispute. [146, pp. 391–4] The British problem in defining an attitude to the Falklands was the opposite to that of Argentina. Here there was no propaganda to arouse public opinion, and no strong desire to retain control of the Islands; but prescription exercised a hold on British official attitudes to the Falklands. In March 1967 the British Government for the first time stated formally that it would be prepared to cede sovereignty over the Islands, but that certain conditions must be met and the wishes of the Falkland Islanders must be respected. A 'Memorandum of Understanding' was prepared by August 1968 under the watchful eye of the Falkland Islands Executive Council which stated that the Government of the United Kingdom 'as part of such a final settlement will recognise Argentina's sovereignty over the Islands from a date to be agreed'. This date, it went on, 'will be agreed as soon as possible after (i) the two governments have resolved the present divergence between them as to the criteria according to which the United Kingdom Government shall consider whether the interests of the Islanders would be secured by the safeguards and guarantees to be offered by the Argentine Government, and (ii) the Government of the United Kingdom are then satisfied that those interests are so secured'. [77, paras. 22–3; 45, pp. 16–17] This statement left open the question of what the definition of the 'interests' of the Islanders was and who would make it. The 'unilateral statement' which accompanied the publication of the memorandum contained tantalising language. It stated that the British Government would be willing to proceed to a final settlement with

Argentina involving the transfer of sovereignty; but that this was to take place 'only if and when they were satisfied that the transfer of sovereignty, and the basis on which such a transfer should take place, were acceptable to the people of the Islands'. [77, para. 24] The 'critical reception' afforded to this document in the Press and in Parliament obliged the Government 'not to continue to attempt to reach a settlement on the basis of the Memorandum of Understanding', since Argentina was not prepared to accept either that the memorandum should include a statement that any transfer of sovereignty would be subject of the wishes of the Islanders; or that the unilateral statement, enshrining this safeguard, should be specifically linked to the memorandum. Thus the Foreign Secretary, Michael Stewart, found himself at one and the same time announcing that negotiations would continue; and conceding that one of the greatest obstacles to the proposed transfer of sovereignty, the wishes of the Islanders, should be 'paramount'. [77, para. 25; 45, pp. 24–5]

There was another possible way forward, and that was to leave the vexatious sovereignty issue aside, and develop instead a procedure that had been tried elsewhere in the search for co-operation and settlement. This was to give priority to issues of more immediate and practical concern which would reduce the barriers between states and nations, and, hopefully, lead more slowly and less dramatically towards a resolution of the more philosophical issues. In 1971 the Conservative Government of Edward Heath, and the Argentine Government, agreed on a 'wide range of communications matters' of which the most important was the establishment of an air and sea service between the Islands and the Argentine mainland, the guarantee of freedom of movement within Argentina for residents of the Islands, and travel to the Islands by citizens of Argentina. Other 'harmonisation' measures were put in place. [77, para. 26] Argentine tourists began to arrive in 1972. The English-born naturalist, Tony Strange, in his *The Falkland Islands*, first published in 1972, described the communications agreement as having 'lifted a veil of uncertainty. There is a better understanding within the public sector, both in the Islands and in Argentina of each other'. [32, p. 60]

There was, unfortunately, little sign of this in the formal diplomatic context, where the Argentine Government in 1973 took the issue to the United Nations. A Special Committee adopted a resolution which formed the basis for a further resolution by the General Assembly calling on both sides to accelerate negotiations for a resolution of the sovereignty issue. [77, para. 29] Behind these negotiations, however, significant developments were pushing Argentina forward. She felt, with some justification, that the communications agreements benefited the Falkland Islanders more than Argentina, which was in effect subsidising the air service between the Islands and the mainland; the Argentine state company which supplied fuel guaranteed lower petrol and diesel prices than had previously existed. Moreover, the Islanders had obtained access to Argentina's health and education services. [32, pp. 65–6] This grievance fuelled Argentine nationalism, which was now given a sharper political edge by the Peronist Party election victory in March 1973, and the swearing in of Peron as President in October. The Argentine Government's formal approach to the United Nations still kept well within the boundaries of normal diplomatic procedures, and was no more than an irritant to the British Government. But this irritation was increased by the mass circulation newspaper, the *Cronica*, which in December 1975 launched a campaign advocating an invasion of the Falklands, which, however, the Argentine political analyst, G. Makin, ascribed to an attempt to boost circulation and corner the popular market [32, p. 66; 146, p. 396] (though this ambition and the way in which it was pursued was in itself instructive).

Argentina now entered on a volatile and unstable era in her history, as military rule was fastened on the country. In these circumstances the best that the British could do was, it seemed, to weigh up the key variables: the objections of the Falkland Islands Executive Council to participation in any talks that might lead to the United Kingdom ceding sovereignty over the Islands; Argentina's determination fuelled by nationalism, to pursue its claim to the Islands; and the acknowledgement that, for Britain to agree to talks that touched on sovereignty would arouse the hostility of the Islanders and of British parliamentary and Press supporters of the Islanders. [77, para. 31] But to refuse to discuss sovereignty might invite Argentine military action: and this at a time when the Argentine Government was equipping and training its navy to European standards. [45, pp. 43–4]

The British Intelligence Services believed that 'official' military action by the Argentine Government was unlikely, but that there was a continuing risk of 'unofficial' action. The British Government now reverted to the offer of economic co-operation, with the sovereignty issue set aside, but Argentina insisted that this must be linked to sovereignty: possibly a transfer of sovereignty with simultaneous leaseback for a period of years. [77, paras. 32, 33] The dispute had come full circle yet again, but Argentine nationalism was rekindled when the British Government, alerted to the accelerating economic decline of the Islands, commissioned a survey of the long term implications, led by Lord Shackleton. Argentina protested that she had not agreed to the survey, which was announced in October 1975. The ease with which tension could be generated was revealed when a small force of British Royal Marines on the Islands was alerted to guard the Islands' airstrip when a large airplane that had not been scheduled to fly to the Islands seemed intent on landing. London and the British Embassy in Buenos Aires decided to ignore the incident so as not to increase the already hostile mood in the Argentine capital. [32, p. 75] Argentine anger was expressed in the United Nations on 8 December 1975, when her representative warned that 'the limits of our patience and tolerance should not be underestimated if we shall have to face an obstructive and unjustified refusal to negotiate by the other party'. [77, para. 35] This was revealed in February 1976, when the *Shackleton*, an unarmed British research vessel, engaged in scientific work in the South Atlantic, was intercepted some 78 miles south of the Falkland Islands by an Argentine destroyer and commanded to stop. The *Shackleton* protested that

> 'We are not in Argentine waters; we are more than 200 miles from the Argentine mainland and the British Government does not recognise these as Argentine waters. I have no intention of stopping.' [15, p. 3]

An Argentine Press campaign in early 1976 was dismissed by the British Embassy in Buenos Aires as a 'usual' affair; the Argentine Government was anxious not to let the 'anti-British bandwagon' get out of control. [77, para. 38] In March 1976 a military junta took power in Argentina without resistance, promising to restore national security; this, it transpired, involved purchasing significant quantities of small-arms and also aircraft and helicopters from the United Kingdom. Radio and radar equipment for use in coastal patrol vessels were also bought. [32, pp. 90–92]

The Callaghan Government was anxious to reduce its commitments in non-NATO areas, and considered taking HMS *Endurance*, which had been stationed in the Falkland Islands since 1967 as a guardian and scientific vessel, out of service. But the Secretary of State for Defence, Roy Mason, agreed to one further deployment; this was renewed on an annual basis until 1978, and then again under the Conservatives in 1979–80 and 1980–81. [77, para. 44] It seemed, therefore, that Argentine claims would not be pressed to the point of war; and that British prescriptive rights would not involve going beyond taking sufficient steps to remind Argentina that Britain maintained, and would maintain, a presence in the region. A report on the defence situation by Mason stressed limitations rather than possibilities. The Chiefs of Staff advised that air reinforcement was excluded because of the deficiencies of the Stanley airstrip, and the weather conditions there; the distance from Ascension Island (an essential base for any air operations); and the 'likely unavailability' of South American airfields in the event of a conflict. An amphibious force which embarked troops would be needed to dislodge an Argentine force from the Islands. It would not be practicable to provide transport and support the force necessary to ensure that a determined Argentine military assault could be repulsed. To recover the Islands by military means, while far from impossible, would be a major operation at this very long range, including a sizeable Task Force and the aircraft HMS *Ark Royal*. In these circumstances, with both sides (to say the least) apparently averse to placing themselves in a confrontational predicament, a diplomatic solution seemed the logical way to proceed, and the British Government decided to open a fresh dialogue with Argentina, including what it disingenuously called 'the nature of a hypothetical future constitutional relationship'. [77, para. 47, 48] British Intelligence believed that if this initiative failed then Argentina would react aggressively, but that she would do so without resorting to military action. The dispute would revert once again to an Argentine appeal to the United Nations. [77, para. 50]

It was just this sense of rather weary familiarity that forms the essential background to an understanding of the last years of diplomacy over the Falkland Islands issue. It was felt by the British that when negotiations, however unlikely to succeed, were reinstated, then Argentine excursions and alarms would diminish; if, or even when, negotiations proved fruitless, then Argentina would step up the pressure; but in a way unlikely to lead to serious military confrontation. This was shown in December 1976. HMS *Endurance* descried an Argentine presence on Southern Thule in the South Sandwich Islands. British Intelligence reported that it had probably been there since the previous month, with the approval of the Argentine Naval commander-in-chief. Argentina replied to British demands for an explanation that the personnel were there to establish a station with a view to scientific investigation, and that their presence need not be permanent. The British Government formally protested on 19 January 1977, but did not make the issue public; it was not known in the United Kingdom until May 1978. The

British assessment was that this was a 'probe', and a 'physical demonstration of Argentine sovereignty over the Dependencies', and a 'bargaining counter' in the forthcoming discussions over the Falklands. Intelligence held that Argentina had indeed a contingent naval and air force plan to invade the Falklands, but reported on 7 February 1977 that this plan had been 'shelved'. [77, paras. 53, 54–7] When tension rose again in 1977, with Argentina becoming more concerned that the British were prevaricating, the British Government responded to Intelligence reports that Argentina might take a more belligerent attitude by establishing a military presence in the area, consisting of one nuclear-powered submarine and a frigate standing about a thousand miles away. Rules of engagement were drawn up, but the force, it was agreed, should remain covert, [77, paras. 64–9] and could hardly therefore have been a deterrent though James Callaghan later claimed, after the Falklands War, that he had told the head of M16, Maurice Oldfield, that he would 'not be unhappy if the news of our deployment reached the Argentine armed forces'. [32, pp. 111–12]

The world of diplomacy is an odd one: it is at one and the same time inhabited by professionals, closeted in their rooms or engaged with their opposite numbers in discreet negotiations; and yet it is occasionally exposed to the fierce blasts of media and public criticism, criticism compounded by the belief (not without foundation) that diplomats live in a kind of moral-free zone, willing to bargain away the rights of, in particular, troublesome and unfashionable peoples: like, for example, the Falkland Islanders. Lord Chalfont, Minister of State in the Foreign Office, and a man with the closest possible connections with the United States Government and especially the Central Intelligence Agency, held that in 1966 the Foreign Secretary, Michael Stewart's decision to visit Latin America conveyed 'the impression that the British national interest transcended the Falklands' issue'; he felt strongly that British relations with the Americas 'overall' demanded that British foreign policy should not be disturbed by the wishes of the Islanders 'any more than the inhabitants of Wales and Scotland'. [45, pp. 15–16] When he visited the Islands in November 1968 he recollected that he informed the Islanders that 'what we were talking about was a future, an indeterminate future perhaps, but a future in which sovereignty would be handed over'. [45, p. 23] The Foreign Office had, by the mid 1970s, decided that the most promising road towards a settlement of its quarrel with Argentina was to cede Argentina's sovereignty claim and then (possibly) leasing back the Islands for a period of 70 years. But this clever, and, on the fact of it, reasonable solution was hard to attain in the face of political pressures from the Islanders, some sections of British political opinion, and the British media.

There was always an inherent contradiction in the British position, in that it conceded that the wishes of the Falkland Islanders should be 'paramount' [77, para. 25; 45, pp. 24–5], but this word did not necessarily imply that they should be definitive. British governments were aware of the danger of seeming to abandon British people to a foreign power, especially if that power were an undemocratic one; and the Falkland Islanders, alive to the danger of what they would call a 'sell-out', were active in seeking to win the attention and sympathy of, in particular, Conservative Members of Parliament. Ted Rowlands, Minister of State in the Callaghan Government, felt obliged to ask a question which events proved rather more vital then he perhaps expected, when he acknowledged that the Falkland Islanders numbered only 1,800 people, but pointed out that 'if they're only eighteen hundred people will you sacrifice three thousand people? What is the level of population that is required before you decide to fight for a people?' [45, p. 57]

This was not a question that anyone wanted to answer, or even pose. There was no inexorable drive towards war between 1979 and the Spring of 1982, but rather a series of events, some insignificant in themselves, that precipitated the final crisis. It is misleading to claim that because the British were stubborn, or even that they prevaricated, the Argentines looked to military action to make good their claim to the Falklands. On the contrary, it was because the British became more anxious to make progress that their diplomacy lost coherence. On 7 November 1980 Nicholas Ridley was authorised by the Defence and Overseas Policy Committee to visit the Falkland Islands in order to ascertain what degree of support there was for a leaseback agreement. Ridley made a parliamentary statement on 2 December that leaseback was one way of pursuing a negotiated settlement, while repeating the promise that any agreement must be acceptable to the Islanders. [63, p. 2] Labour and Conservative MPs alike warmed to the theme that there must be no surrender of the Islands or the Islanders. [90, pp. 15–16] On 21 January 1981 pressure on Ridley and the Government was maintained. Nicholas Winterton asked for an assurance that 'without the wholehearted support of the people of the Falkland Islands there would be no sell-out to Argentina'; [114, cols. 297–9] the emotive words 'sell-out' were repeated by Sir Ian Gilmour, who sought to assure critics that the leaseback proposal was 'not on the agenda at the moment'. [114, 21 Jan. 1981, cols. 297–8] On 30 June

1981 the Foreign Office 'beseeched' its Minister, Nicholas Ridley, to bring matters to a head by implementing the preferred option of 'lease-back'; this, it was argued, would be in the best interests of the Islanders. There was no doubt that, in the event of further delay, 'Argentine retaliatory action' could be expected 'early in 1982'. [126] The Joint Intelligence Committee warned on 9 July 1981 that if Argentina thought that Britain was no longer serious about the transfer of sovereignty, then the situation would become dangerous, and Argentina might resort to 'more forcible measures…swiftly and without warning'. [126] The Foreign Secretary, Lord Carrington, received this report in September 1981, but he was faced with two difficulties: he did not want to confront his Cabinet colleagues with this warning; and he felt that he was in no position to do anything about it anyway. As he wrote in his memoirs, 'the Chiefs of Staff considered the matter in September 1981 and, once again, assessed the requirement of complete deterrence as a huge one. It would take time to assemble such a force: it would mean our other priority commitments would be neglected…and – a factor given weight in intelligence assessments – it might provoke the very adventure it would be intended to deter'. [41, p. 359]

While the Foreign Office weighed up the lack of possibilities in the early years of the Conservative Government of Margaret Thatcher, the Argentine military government was encountering serious internal difficulties. The euphoria generated by the Argentine football team's victory in the 1978 World Cup competition in Buenos Aires was by 1980 becoming dissipated by a rise in foreign debt, the decline in the purchasing power of Argentine salary and wage earnings (which fell by 40 per cent), and interest rates rising to 'ruinous levels'. It was in these circumstances that the Argentine military government would take 'spectacular and unprecedented action' over the long-running Falklands dispute, to rid itself of political and economic embarrassments. [146, pp. 398–9] And all this took place against a background of a rise in tension between Chile and Argentina over the Beagle Channel. In November and December 1978 a propaganda campaign was organised by the Argentines, with Army, Navy and Air Force units prepared to fight a just war against Chilean territorial encroachment. On 8 July 1979 the two governments pledged themselves not to go to war, and the crisis passed. [32, pp. 112–15] But an important by-product of this tension was that the Argentine Government spent billions of dollars on arms procurement, including 40 A-4 Skyhawk aircraft and five Chinook helicopters bought from the United States of America, and

42 Dagger aircraft purchased from Israel. [32, p. 90] The Argentine armed forces were therefore mentally and physically prepared for war to defend or retrieve Argentine territorial ambitions.

The British Government in 1980–81 made what must have seemed to the Argentine Government a familiar move of advance, retreat and stalemate. Nicholas Ridley's recommendation of the policy of Argentine sovereignty combined with a leaseback agreement was rejected by Parliament in December 1980, a rejection that was itself symptomatic of the growing influence of the Falkland Islanders' lobby. Lord Carrington wrote in his memoirs that 'His [Ridley's] reception was hostile. He was told that any lease-back proposals weakened our title in international law. He was told that the FO had wanted to get rid of the Falklands for years – a mischievous misrepresentation (sic). He was told that there was a considerable British interest at stake – an implausible exaggeration. He was asked, in effect, that we should break off negotiations with Argentina, "to advise the Argentine Government that the matter is closed". He was asked why the FO could not leave things alone'. [41, p. 356]

The parliamentary debate on Ridley's proposals foreshadowed the celebrated debate of 3 April 1982. When Ridley spoke up for 'common sense', and for the 'long-term interests of the Islanders' he got little support. 'Hostility mounted on the one hand from the Labour Left, which expressed outrage at suggesting concessions of any title to a right-wing dictator', wrote Carrington ruefully; and 'on the other hand, from the Conservative right which regarded it as unthinkable that any British territory should ever be ceded to anyone, if British subjects lived on it, regardless of the guarantees given'. The former, Carrington complained, were 'remarkably bigoted', while the latter were 'narrow and nostalgic'. [41, pp. 356–7] But the distinction was less clear-cut. For Peter Shore, for example, the Falkland Islands was an issue that had wider implications: if the Argentine assumption were accepted 'we would have had trouble in a number of other parts of the world almost at once, and most certainly in Gibraltar'. When he was asked about 'Ulster' he replied 'Perhaps in Ulster too'. [45, p. 95] The former diplomat, Ray Whitney, spoke without exaggeration when he described the reaction to Ridley's speech as the 'roof' falling in: 'It was a day that made me feel ashamed...I had thought to myself – no point going to Nick's rescue because he's sunk already'. [32, p. 123]

On 3 December the Government's Defence Committee considered the House of Commons' reception of Ridley's statement of 2 December. The Cabinet discussed it the following day. It agreed that this was a highly emotive issue for parliamentary and public opinion, while noting that the Islanders' hostility to Ridley's appeal seemed to have been exaggerated; and concluded that it would be 'tragic' if the Islanders' chances of escaping from economic blight were to be dismissed by the attitude of their champions at Westminster. [77, para. 82] This was not quite to appreciate the depth of the Islanders' feelings, which were expressed by the Governor, Sir Rex Hunt in a meeting held at the Royal United Services Institute in 1986. There Hunt claimed that the leaseback option was rejected by the Islanders, even on a 99-year basis; and the notion that there could be a distinction made, as the Argentines wished to make, between the 'interests' of the Islanders and their 'wishes' was 'the height of arrogance'. The Islanders were, Hunt said, 'mature, intelligent, law-abiding people, not a bunch of impossible schoolchildren who need to be told what is in their best interests'. [119, p. 12] But this was not just what the Argentines wanted to believe; the British Government, for its part, was edging towards that distinction also, and might have pushed it further but for the hostile reception given to Ridley in Parliament and the Press. The notion that the Islanders might be suffering from a kind of false consciousness was rudely upset in January 1981 when the Falkland Islanders Joint Councils passed a motion that

> While this House does not like any of the ideas put forward by Mr. Ridley for a possible settlement of the sovereignty dispute with Argentina, it agrees that Her Majesty's Government should hold further talks with the Argentines at which this House should be represented and at which the British delegation shall seek an agreement to freeze the dispute over sovereignty for a specified period of time. [77, para. 83]

Two perceptions now began to deeply influence the diplomatic process; or, rather, one perception and one reality. The reality was that, as Richard Luce, Minister of State in the Foreign Office put it, 'we were boxed in; all we could do was buy time. We had run out of any innovating ideas'. [45, p. 183] It was this, rather than what the Argentine Foreign Minister Dr Oscar Camilion suggested after a meeting with Lord Carrington in the Autumn of 1981 that was the core of the impasse. Camilion believed that Carrington had what he called 'a very superficial grasp of the problem', and that 'he was in some ways thinking, "why is this fellow questioning, and with such a marginal problem, such a busy man as I?"'. [45, p. 106] This reality invited an important Argentine perception, that might be characterised as this: 'if not now, when?'. If the British had indeed let the Falklands' issue slip down their list of priorities – if indeed it had ever gained a place on that list at all – then Argentina can be forgiven for thinking of means other than the merely diplomatic. It was not surprising that a military dictator like General Galtieri should describe the failure to resolve the dispute as 'becoming more and more unbearable'; [77, para. 88] what was more significant were the words of the professional diplomat, Camilion, in September 1981, when he admitted to a journalist on the *Clarion* newspaper that 'Carrington left me with no doubt that resolving the Falklands is still way down the list of priorities as far as the British Government is concerned'. [32, p. 132] But Carrington was more aware of the danger than Camilion supposed. While making allowances for the benefit of hindsight, there is little reason to doubt what Carrington wrote in his memoirs: that a considerable shift in the dispute had taken place as a result of Nicholas Ridley's debacle. There was, he noted, 'little risk of outright military action against the Falklands provided Argentina supposed there was a chance that the British Government would ultimately be prepared to negotiate about sovereignty', but 'it must be increasingly difficult for Argentina so to suppose, since we were faced with apparent immobilism among the islanders, an immobilism which could not fail to draw encouragement from the Government's critics at home; while the Government, faced with this, had always made it clear that we would do nothing without the islanders' consent'. The outlook, he added (again with hindsight) was 'stormy'. [41, p. 357]

Carrington was not as far-seeing as he liked to claim; but he was right about the difficulties now facing the Government. British officials and ministers resisted Ridley's proposal that the Government should launch an active campaign to 'educate' the Islanders and British public opinion as a whole about the need to reach an agreement with Argentina. [32, p. 131] But their negative attitude to pressing on with negotiations – or rather their inability to see how they could do so with any realistic prospect of success – must have an effect on Argentina and this was an Argentina that was from December 1981 ruled by General Leopoldo Fortunato Galtieri and his junta of 'Military hard men, determined to sort Argentina's problems out'. The British took no notice of the coming of the new men: the Latin America Current Intelligence Group met 18 times between July 1981 and January 1982 but it seems that at no time was the Falklands on the agenda. [118, p. 287]

Two other factors edged the military government towards a bolder policy, one that would (at least) give diplomacy the firm backing of military support. One of these (and one the significance of which escaped the British Government) was a debate on an 'early day motion' in the House of Commons on 15 December 1981, which was taken as evidence by Argentina that the Falkland Islands pressure group was working hard, and successfully, to demands that sovereignty be excluded from the agenda in any discussion with Argentina. The early day motion which drew particular attention in Argentina was

> That this House declares its determination that the Falkland Islands and Dependencies shall remain under British Rule in accordance with the wishes of the Islanders and the British interests in the South Atlantic and in British Antarctic Territories shall be protected and advanced; draws attention to the importance of preserving the international co-operation enshrined in the Antarctic Treaty with particular regard to the conservation and protection of natural resources; and calls upon HMG to demonstrate its commitment to maintaining a tangible presence in these areas by ensuring that the ice patrol ship HMS *Endurance* continues in service after she returns from her current deployment in the spring of 1982 and to achieve these objectives by making the necessary modest savings in public expenditure in other areas which must have a lower order of priority than that of keeping HMS *Endurance* on active service. [198, p. 117]

The Argentine historian, Virginia Gambia, also draws attention to a debate in the House of Lords on 16 December which caused more anxiety in Buenos Aires. [94, pp. 108, 112] Here members of the Upper House spoke darkly of what they saw as the British official mind's willingness to compromise. Lord Morris declared that British policy reminded him of A. G. MacDonald's novel *England their England*, 'wherein your Lordships will recall the personal assistant of the United Kingdom's delegate to the League of Nations was sent to elucidate from the Permanent Representative H.M. Government's foreign policy on a particular matter'. The officials looked in total amazement when he asked this question, and answered: 'His Majesty's Government do not have a foreign policy other than, of course, that we must be nice to the French'. 'If one is to substitute "the Argentinians" for "the French" I think one has the message'. The attitude of successive administrations to the Falkland Islands was 'who will rid me of this turbulent priest'. Morris complained about the Government's lack of response to the report by Lord Shackleton on the economic future of the Islands; and warned of the dangerous implications of removing HMS *Endurance* from active service: 'The decision has been greeted with unalloyed joy in the Argentine press' where it was seen as a 'relaxation' of Britain's vigil in Antarctica. [117, 16 Dec. 1981, cols. 208–9] Lord Shackleton intervened to point out that he had been approached by friends on the Argentine side 'who have asked whether [the withdrawal of the *Endurance*] meant that the British were thinking of changing their posture generally'. The Falkland Islanders were 'unquestionably British…very British, very proud', indistinguishable from the inhabitants of the British Isles. The population of the Islands was now in decline, but for 23 years up to 1973 they had effectively contributed to the United Kingdom exchequer. Oil might be exploited in Antarctica; the white ensign should be there. Lord Hill-Norton agreed that the decision to withdraw HMS *Endurance* was a grave mistake. Lord Mottiston drew attention to the illegal occupation of Thule since 1978. 'When we possessed vast territories it was not necessary for each and every corner of the Empire…to be so watched over, because people knew that there was a force on the high seas keeping a watch for us which could come when required'. But now that Britain's horizons had narrowed it had become all the more important that the remaining territories should be watched over. [117, cols. 210–14]

For the Government, Lord Montgomery of Alamein contrasted the fervour with which the Argentines saw the Falkland Islands dispute ('an article of faith') with the British lack of interest: 'I think the importance of the issue is to a certain extent underlined by the small number of people who are here this evening'. It was imperative to work with Argentina; the land on which the Islanders lived 'is a subject that we have to consider philosophically'. This seemed to mean that the Islanders must be made aware of what the real situation was 'because this issue can never be resolved until the islanders themselves freely and willingly realise the advantages that will accrue from closer association with the mainland, whatever form that close association may take'. The Argentine presence on South Thule, 1,200 miles from Stanley, he dismissed as not a matter of 'great preoccupation' to the Falkland Islanders. [117, cols. 224–5] Lord Skelmersdale warned that the continued uncertainty over the Islands' future meant that private enterprise would not be willing to help their economy. HMS *Endurance* had, he added, only a limited military capacity; but a Royal Marine garrison on the Falklands would remain as a 'tangible' demonstration of British intentions to defend the Islands. The Argentine claim 'simply will not go away', but he assured critics that 'the wishes of the islanders themselves are paramount. No solution could be approved which was not acceptable both to them and to Parliament'. [117, cols. 231–4] To which assurances Lord Morris replied (in a somewhat mixed metaphor) that 'the cold hand of Government deciding what is in the best interests of the people of the Falkland Islands has raised it head again'. [117, col. 237]

The spectacle of anyone, let alone the Argentine military government, paying attention to a sparsely attended debate in the Lords seems unlikely; but a nervous and exasperated Argentine could take two, equally troubling, messages from the Lords: one was that the British Government was less than enthusiastic about keeping its grip on the Islands; the other was that it was nonetheless under considerable pressure to do so. The indecisiveness of the British was revealed later by Sir Anthony Williams, British Ambassador in Buenos Aires, when he summed up the dilemma: 'Giving them (the Falklands) to the Argentinians would mean our surrendering the Islands. That clearly was not on politically. Our keeping them would mean moving into a Fortress Falklands situation, and government after government in Britain has felt that this would be desperately expensive'. One way forward, he added, would have been to convince the Islanders that the Argentines did not 'have cloven hooves', and break down the Islanders' isolation. [19, pp. 7–8]

The debate in the Lords raised the question of the Government's decision to withdraw HMS *Endurance* from service in the South Atlantic; and this was a second important piece in the diplomatic-military jigsaw that the Argentines were assembling. Few decisions, relating to a single, far from modern vessel, of no significant military capability (but with a very important intelligence one of signal intelligence and warning listening suite) [118, p. 284] have aroused such controversy; indeed it has come close to being regarded as the occasion for the Argentine decision to invade the Falklands. But, at the time, and despite warnings from some MPs and Peers, it appeared to be an uncontroversial and indeed rational decision. It was a case of a micro decision taken against a macro background. This broader context is explained in Paul M. Kennedy's article 'British Defence Policy: an Historian's View', which he published in 1977. Here Kennedy presented his thesis that technological change, which the layman could not keep up with or easily relate to the political and diplomatic scene, combined with change in national consciousness of priorities (the call for a welfare rather than a warfare state), and relative economic decline, meant that a British war must be a NATO war; and he questioned whether defence cuts were serious if they were measured in the context of NATO's overall capacity. [131, pp. 14–16]

It was in this NATO defence system that John Nott, the Secretary of State for Defence, reviewed British commitments in his 1981 plan. It was altogether unremarkable, merely confirming the direction of British defence policy since the 1960s. Defence costs had to be carefully assessed, and if possible reduced. There was accumulating defence expenditure on new weapons; an increase in fuel costs; a substantial increase in the pay of the armed forces; and the delivery of many contractors' bills earlier than expected. The Ministry of Defence responded with deep cuts in procurement of ammunition, fuel, oil and spare parts. John Nott's task was to take the existing programme apart, and 'then reassemble the parts in such a way that the new whole became more effective and dynamic'. The Royal Navy bore the brunt of the reductions in spending, but the idea behind those cuts was that there would be fewer vessels afloat, but those vessels would be kept in a more effective state of readiness, with up-to-date weapons, and with fuel and stores sufficient to enable them to have a 'presence at sea', rather than in port. There would be a smaller but better equipped operational surface fleet, with British participation in NATO and the NATO deterrent role as the key to British defence policy: [96, pp. 124–8] Britain would be 'a forward base for operations in the Channel and North Sea and a rear base for operations on the Continent'. [35, p. 36] Admiral Sir Henry Leach described John Nott's defence review as 'ill conceived and ill conducted'; but Nott defended it on the grounds that the main British defence priority was against a Soviet threat and this threat would be the only 'realistic' one for the next ten or 20 years. [45, pp. 149–50]

This assumption was a fair one. But the problem was not that the British ruled out a threat from Argentina over the Falklands, but that they found it hard to see how such a threat could be realistically countered. Early in 1981 the Foreign Office asked the Ministry of Defence to update the assessment prepared in 1977 of what could be done to meet Argentine military action. It was acknowledged that the Argentine armed forces were the most efficient in South America; and that Britain's military capability was very limited. The conclusion was that if Argentina were to occupy the Islands there could be no certainty that even a large-scale military force could retake them, and then the logistical problems of such an operation would be formidable. [77, paras. 109–12] This report coincided with the 1981 defence review which concluded that HMS *Endurance* should be withdrawn from the area. Lord Carrington protested against this decision, but it was confirmed in Parliament on 30 June 1981. [77, paras. 114, 117, 118]

This decision was greeted in the Argentine media as evidence that Britain was 'abandoning the protection of the Falkland Islands'. [32, p. 139] And it is possible to describe the *Endurance* affair as the case of the little ship that started, or at least helped to start the (small) war. But there were other equally important considerations playing on the Argentine official mind. There was the increasing Argentine rapprochement with the United States of America, and the growing certainty on the part of the Argentine military rulers that the United States was what General Galtieri described as an ally in the 'march…in the ideological war that is being fought in the world'. [32, p. 143] The United States denied making any hint that it would remain neutral in the event of an Argentine invasion of the Falkland Islands in exchange for Galtieri's support of her interests in Latin America, but Argentina felt that the United States would at any rate decline to become involved in the Falklands affair, and would certainly not ally itself against Argentina. [32, pp. 143–4] Instinctive Latin American solidarity would determine that states (with the exception of Chile) would find it hard to vote against Argentina if she adopted a forward policy and this consideration was reinforced by the pragmatic belief that the Anglo-Argentine dispute had implications for the various territorial disputes in the region. The countries that would come out in strongest support for Argentine were those engaged in territorial claims against their neighbours, or, in the case of Panama, in dispute with the United States. [147, p. 13] Moreover, the United States' request for co-operation in protecting shipping lanes in the South Atlantic convinced Argentina that she possessed 'significant leverage' in Washington. [147, p. 18]

In January 1982 the Argentine Press began to talk in terms of anticipating more positive action to recover the Islands; an ultimatum would be followed by more frequent talks and a firm timetable for the return of the Falklands. [146, p. 399] In February the publication *Convicción*, regarded as the Argentine Navy's mouthpiece, reflected this growing certainty that some major progress would be made in the dispute. On 2 March the Argentine Press again stressed the need to resolve the dispute, and reserved the right to take action commensurate with the interests of Argentina. On 12 March the *Latin American Weekly Report* spoke of Argentine exasperation with 15 years of fruitless negotiation, and warned of her right to 'choose the procedure which best suits its interests'. On 19 March it reported that an Argentine Hercules aircraft had made an undetected landing at Stanley, amid rumours that the 'Argentine flag will soon fly over the Malvinas'. [146, pp. 400–1]

Yet all this could still be dismissed as Argentine bluster. The Argentine Government seemed intent on doing nothing much more than asking for monthly rather than yearly meetings on the subject of sovereignty over the Islands. But this was now being supported by certain contingency plans: that preparation should be made for a military option, which would in turn be a means of preparing for two possibilities: that the Falkland Islanders would work to ensure that the British Government would break off negotiations altogether; and that the British would be moved to establish a permanent naval force in the South Atlantic. [94, p. 115] These stark developments, if they took place, might indeed set off direct military action; but so far they were more of an adjunct to an increased diplomatic offensive.

British procrastination elicited from the Argentine Foreign Minister, Dr Costa Mendez (a pro-western and flexible diplomat) a communiqué on 1 March calling on the United Kingdom to engage in good faith negotiations, and warning that Argentina reserved the right to resort to 'other mechanisms' if its message was not heeded. [94, p. 119] The Argentine historian, Virginia Gambia, denies that this was a threat of military action: 'mechanisms' were not the same thing as 'means'. But the distinction is a fine one. Still, there was no sense that means or mechanisms would be taken out of the Argentine diplomatic locker and used against the United Kingdom. Thomas Enders, the United States Assistant Secretary of State concerned with Latin America, was due to visit Buenos Aires, and Lord Carrington requested Secretary of State Alexander Haig that he use his 'good offices'. By mid-March Haig reported that the Argentines had not discussed the Falklands situation with him in terms of threats, and that he had not received the impression that they intended to undertake drastic action. Lord Carrington noted that 'we received the same impression from our Embassy in Buenos Aires, whence the telegrams referred always to the necessity and possibility of a "civilised solution"'. [41, p. 364] But at the same time the Joint Intelligence Committee warned that a 'slow build-up of tension' was developing and that there was a possibility of a 'swift, without warning attack'. [125]

Lord Carrington reviewed the Falklands dispute on 5 March. He was aware that Argentine patience was wearing thin; but he felt that he did not have sufficient evidence to persuade the Ministry of Defence to order a submarine (a much more effective deterrent to possible Argentine naval attack) to the South Atlantic; and he did not, as David Owen, Secretary of State for Foreign Affairs had done in 1977, go directly to the Prime Minister to force the Ministry of Defence's hand. In any event, Mrs Thatcher for her part had shown little interest in the dispute so far. [126] The British Embassy in Buenos Aires on 4 March sent a telegram warning that an Argentine newspaper was predicting an early invasion of the Falkland Islands, but although the Prime Minister suggested that 'we must make contingencies', nothing was done. A further memorandum from the Defence Attache in Buenos Aires on the same day warned of a threat of invasion, but was not acted upon. [126]

The rather unreal world in which Britain and Argentina were living in the Falkland Islands saga became almost surreal. On 19 March some Argentine scrap dealers landed on the even smaller island of South Georgia, disembarking from the Argentine transport ship, the *Bahia Buen Suceso*. The *Endurance*, still at its post, reported the sailing of this vessel, and its perhaps ominous radio silence, on 11 March at midnight. [126] It is now known that these scrap dealers, led by one Constantino Davidoff, were regarded by the Argentine military Government as a handy means of reaffirming the Argentine presence on all the disputed South Atlantic islands. [94, p. 121] This was not the first example of Davidoff's incursions into British territory. On 20 December 1981 he landed at Leith on South Georgia to inspect the scrap metal of disused whaling stations. The Governor of the Falkland Islands reported this to the Foreign and Commonwealth Office on 31 December and was told not to do anything that 'would risk provoking a most serious incident which could escalate and have an unforeseeable outcome'. A formal protest was delivered to Argentina, and duly rejected. [77, paras. 161–5] The second incursion, on 19 March, when shots were fired and the Argentine flag raised, took the British by surprise, not least because Davidoff had apologised for a previous similar incident in February, stressed that in his salvage operations he was anxious not to create difficulties, and asked for full instructions about how to proceed. [77, para. 167] The Foreign Office still regarded the incursion of 19 March as a minor incident, though the Falkland Islands Governor, Sir Rex Hunt, took the view that the Argentine Navy was using Davidoff as a front to establish an Argentine presence on South Georgia. [77, para. 169]

The continued presence of the scrap dealers on South Georgia began to cause concern. On 20 March Sir Rex Hunt told British scientists at

Gryviken that they were to contact the Argentines by radio, and insist that the Argentine flag be lowered and that one of the scrap dealers must come forward to seek a landing permit. He also informed London of the Argentines' failure to fulfil the necessary formalities, alleging (wrongly) that Argentine military personnel were present. [152, pp. 9–10] The British Ambassador in Buenos Aires protested against the incursion into South Georgia and called for an explanation; and the London Press and the House of Commons began to define the South Georgia incident as a major incursion into British territory. [94, pp. 117–18] But the Foreign office was still inclined to play down the incident, and Dr Costa Mendez played on their fears of escalation by warning that any British action taken against the scrap dealers would risk the danger that the British wanted to avoid: that is, escalation. But the likely repercussions of the debate in the House of Commons on 23 March persuaded the Foreign Office to warn Argentina that the *Endurance* had been ordered to proceed with the eviction of the scrap dealers after all. Argentina responded through Admiral Jorge Anaya ordering a frigate to escort and protect the *Bahia Paraiso*, which had been sent to South Georgia, and which removed some, but not (as the British Ambassador in Buenos Aires warned on 22 March) all of the dealers. [94, p. 119] The British Defence Attache in Buenos Aires warned on 24 March that any attempt at forcible removal of the merchants from Leith would be met by force, either from a warship at sea, or by a 'rescue operation' at Stanley if they were taken there; the latter could escalate into an invasion of the Falkland Islands, and escalation would suit the 'hawks' in the Argentine Government who were pressing the leadership to take advantage of the incident. [77, para. 192] Argentine nervousness revealed itself in the instructions given to the *Bahia Paraiso* that if it arrived too late to stop the scrap dealers being evicted, it should not give chase, but await further orders. [41, p. 365; 77 para. 188] On the same day Lord Carrington minuted his Cabinet colleagues that 'negotiations with Argentina might be at an end, and that we could not exclude the ultimate possibility of military action'. [41, p. 365]

In his account of the last few days of this mixture of fear and resolution, doubt and uncertainty, Rubin O. Moro identified the significant occasion that led to war: a meeting of the Argentine Military Committee (the 'supreme joint discussion-making body for the conduct of military strategy') which on 26 March considered the South Georgia affair. Their perception was that the Argentine work crew had 'raised their national flag at Port Leith…thereby triggering an overreaction (sic) by Great Britain, which may well have grasped this opportunity as an excuse for increasing its naval presence in the area'. [158, pp. 1–2] This perception was based on the movement of supply ships which serviced the British Antarctic Survey, and hardly amounted to a major naval deployment. This assumption, Moro explained, was supported by the announcement on 30 March in the British media that the nuclear powered submarine, *Superb*, had been ordered to the South Atlantic, and that the polar vessel, *Endurance*, was carrying Marines taken on board at Stanley to regain Grytviken. On 29 March a decision to send two submarines to the South Atlantic was indeed taken and, it appears, leaked by a Minister to the Westminster lobby to reassure backbenchers that the Government was preparing an appropriate response to Argentina; *Superb* was not one of them, but the media reported that she had set out on 25 March and was well on her way. [90, pp. 73–5]

On 26 March the Argentine Military Committee considered what to do. It identified three options: to pursue negotiations; to bring charges against the United Kingdom to the United Nations Security Council; or to take the Falklands by force. The first option would not prevent a British naval presence in the area, nor guarantee the achievement of Argentina's desires; the second was a 'dismal' prospect; the third was the most likely to force the British back to the negotiating table, 'while giving Argentina the upper hand'. It would also pre-empt the Islands' 'fortification' by the British. [158, pp. 1–27] In the Argentine view, the military occupation of the Falklands was 'in no way aimed at cutting off the talks or triggering a battlefield confrontation with a world power'; it was to 'encourage' the British Government to return to negotiations with a more 'serious minded' attitude to Argentina's claims. There was as yet no set date for any plan; the earliest date considered was 15 May. But, in view of the events in South Georgia, the Military Junta was forced with 'an option as crucial as it was flawed: either the date for retaking the Malvinas had to be moved forward in order to head off the arrival of the British vessels; or all hope of achieving any change in the course of the negotiations had to be abandoned for a long time to come'. Therefore, if operations were to be carried out, they must be initiated 'no later than early April' to achieve surprise; and they must be secret 'to lessen probable enemy response' – and completely bloodless. [158, pp. 1–2] Moro added another significant factor weighed in the balance by the Argentines: the apprehension that the British would grant priority to the Falkland Islanders' wish for self-determination. [158, p. 15]

The result of the Junta deliberations on 26 March was uncomfortable for the Argentines. They forfeited what Moro called 'the political elbow-room that would have allowed them to seek a diplomatic solution', [158, p. 31] which was what the action now to be taken was supposed to achieve. It is at least plausible to suggest that had Argentina waited, the steady decline in the population of the Falklands (from 2230 in 1953, to 1957 in 1972 and 1813 in 1980) would have eventually placed the Islands in her hands. Coercion might overtake diplomacy, and become its driver; and this risk was enhanced by the fact that the Junta now, and for some weeks and months, thought the unthinkable – the resort to direct military action. Once this possibility was seriously admitted to Argentine official counsels, then it would require clear and firm – and immediately successful – diplomacy if it were not to gain the upper hand. As Dr Guido di Tella (Under-Secretary of Economics in the last civil government in Argentina in 1975) put it, in understated but unmistakable terms: 'the lack of decision on the part of Britain and Argentina over a decade and a half of fruitless negotiations has some bearing on the decision of the Junta'. [116, para. 257]

Di Tella did not deny that the 'genuine and longstanding' desire to see the Falklands returned to Argentina was one factor in the crisis; the other was the 'internal troubles' besetting the country. The Junta, if successful in this last military/diplomatic push, would 'bolster their reputation'. [116, para. 259] With hindsight, he added, 'one can see that as early as in the middle of January (1982) there were signs given by Argentina and they can be read in the newspapers, and there were some utterances by some officials about the possibility of an invasion'. [116, para. 262] But he stressed that he would have doubted this 'if you had asked me maybe two weeks before about the possibility of an invasion'. [116, para. 262]

The Junta had drawn up 'contingency plans' for a possible invasion of the Islands by the last days of 1981, but the Commander-in-Chief Fleet, Rear-Admiral Gualter Allara, insisted that they were meant to 'put some dynamism' into negotiations; there was apparently even talk of a 'voluntary withdrawal' from the Islands after the event which would be sufficient to force negotiations to a conclusion. Plans for a landing on the Islands were ready by the third week in February and were presented to the Junta on 9 March, accepted by them, and forwarded to the Chief of the Joint Armed Forces Headquarters, whose duty it was to incorporate them into the broader 'national plan'. [152, pp. 2–3, 6] The deadline for the use of force was still a long way off

(Gambia estimated it as October 1982); [94, p. 117] it was meant to give what Admiral Anaya called a 'nudge' to diplomacy. [45, pp. 111, 119] But now the scrap dealer incident, and the British response to it, propelled the military plans forward.

On 27 March the British Ambassador in Buenos Aires was informed that Argentina was investigating the South Georgia incident and would punish any breach of the peace, and later in the day Dr Costa Mendez told him of the Argentine surprise at the British proceeding to such a grave action without exploring the diplomatic options; those, like himself, who wished to deal with the South Georgia incident in a moderate way would lose control of events. The Ambassador duly reported to the Foreign and Commonwealth Office that, seen from Buenos Aires, the British reaction to Davidoff's 'trivial and low level misbehaviour' could do lasting damage to the whole structure of bilateral relations. The British responded by ordering *Endurance* to Grytviken instead of Leith, but urging that the Argentines be removed without delay or they would be removed by other means. [77, paras. 182–4]

For Costa Mendez, this reaction was a signal: what he called British 'over-reaction' obliged Argentina to bring forward her invasion plans. He believed that the United States would only act as a mediator in the crisis, and would not want an armed conflict between Britain and Argentina – a shrewd and by no means ill-founded prognosis. [19, pp. 14–15] General Galtieri described the British determination to remove the scrap dealers as affecting 'the national honour and dignity' of Argentina, and thus forcing her to implement the decision of 26 March (to invade the Falkland Islands). The final decision to do so was taken on 30 March, but delayed by bad weather for two more days. The Franks Report put the decision at 31 March or even 1 April. [133, p. 63]

The British reaction to the last, confused and hectic days of peace (or at least the absence of war) in the South Atlantic revealed a mixture of disbelief and then unwilling suspension of disbelief. Lord Carrington placed much of the blame for British indecisiveness on the Treasury, which gave him a 'dusty response' when he inquired about the possibility of planning for military conflict; the result was that now there were no contingency plans to implement. [41, p. 365] This rebuff came on 29 March. On the previous day Carrington met the Prime Minister on the way to Brussels; their discussions appear to have been somewhat contradictory: the Argentine reaction to the British reaction to the South Georgia incident was 'so hostile that it was hard to believe that the situation wouldn't worsen'; yet 'there were no serious indications of military action being imminent'. [41, p. 366] The following day they agreed on a reaction that reflected their uncertain state of mind: they ordered two vessels to sail to the area, one nuclear powered submarine followed by a second 'in order to help counter any aggressive Argentine naval moves, still assumed not to be imminent'. [41, p. 366] On 30 March the Foreign Office was advised that 'some sort of Argentine military initiative might be expected, some time during April'. [41, p. 367] This, Intelligence suggested, might take the form of occupying some outlying island, not an invasion of the Falklands themselves. [77, para. 218] But the JIC Latin America Current Intelligence Group, at a meeting on the morning of 30 March under the Chairmanship of the Foreign Office, insisted that an invasion was not imminent. They quoted the words of the British Ambassador in Buenos Aires that 'the Argentines intend no move in the dispute, but to let matters ride while they build up their strength in the area'. [118, p. 291] Noting the now considerable Argentine naval deployment the British considered ordering a surface Task Force to the Falklands, but decided against. Carrington was once again caught between the need to do something and the desire to do nothing that would escalate the crisis: to put a Task Force before diplomacy might be useful in a major crisis, but had to be 'set against the possibility of their provoking a pre-emptive implementation of the action they were intended to deter'. If Argentina were contemplating an 'adventure' (the word itself contains all the diplomat's horror of such things) then 'a credible deterrent force will anyway have to be larger'. [41, p. 367] This desire to play the diplomatic game down to the last card was seen in Carrington's hope on 25 March that he could use what he perceived as the moderating influence of Dr Costa Mendez to 'persuade his colleagues to find a way out of the impasse'. [77, para. 195] Unfortunately, the Junta was more impressed by his added phrase that the British Government did not wish to escalate the military situation, but that the Argentine Government should be left in no doubt that 'we are committed to the defence of British sovereignty in South Georgia and elsewhere'. [77, para. 195]

On 31 March Intelligence reports were sent to the Ministry of Defence that the Argentines had set the early morning of 2 April for the day of action, [41, p. 367] though Intelligence still believed that the Argentine response was a 'negotiating ploy'. [126; 130, pp. 458–68] By then Carrington was in Israel, still equipped with the optimistic assessment of Argentine intentions. The fresh and accurate Intelligence reports provided, in the language of the Franks Report, 'a positive indication of an Argentine intention to invade the Falkland Islands'. [77, para. 233] Now, at last, the British Government began to gather itself for a concerted diplomatic and military counter-offensive. At a meeting of the Prime Minister, John Nott, Humphrey Atkins, Richard Luce and Foreign and Commonwealth Office and Ministry of Defence officials, with the Chief of Naval Staff (who had gone to the House of Commons to brief Nott), it was agreed to send a message to the United States President Ronald Reagan that an Argentine invasion of the Falklands might be imminent, and that the British Government could not acquiesce in this. Reagan was asked to mediate and to tell General Galtieri that the British would not begin fighting. The Chief of Naval Staff was asked to advise on the size and composition of a Task Force which could retake the islands and to prepare such a force 'without commitment to a final decision as to whether or not it should sail'. [77, paras. 234, 235]

There was still, then, the hope that the crisis could be, if not dismantled, then at least controlled in such a way that diplomacy, backed by the possible use of force, could prevail. The problem was that, as Galtieri himself put it, he 'judged any response from the English scarcely possible, indeed absolutely impossible'. [187, p. 378] He could be forgiven for his certainty.

On 1 April the Latin American Current Intelligence Group assessed that Argentina could launch an invasion on 2 April, but that despite these military preparations, there was no intelligence suggesting that the Junta had taken a decision to invade the Falkland Islands, even though the co-operation between the three Argentine armed services and their involvement in the Argentine Task Force now at sea was 'disturbing'. [77, para. 241] When the Defence Committee met later in the morning of 1 April the Prime Minister informed it that an Argentine Task Force could reach Stanley by the morning of 2 April, but that the Argentine Government's 'precise intentions' were not known. A diplomatic solution had to be found if possible. [77, para. 242]

It was not possible. On 2 April Argentine forces invaded the Falkland Islands; on 3 April Grytviken was seized. Argentina was certain enough that the crisis was resolved in her favour and for good that she flew the original 1,400 troops of the initial invading force back to Argentine by late evening of 2 April, leaving a force of fewer than 500 troops, which was later itself reduced. [94, p. 145] But on 3 April the British Prime Minister announced that a task force would be sent to recover the Islands.

The character of the last minute debates, and the language used, at least clear Mrs Thatcher of any instinctive warmongering desires. They reveal the fundamental dysfunctional nature of British policy towards the Falkland Islands dispute. It is not hard to understand that dysfunctioning. The words and phrases thrown up over the whole, long period of the issue bear witness of diplomatic efforts to find ways of resolving the conflict between sovereignty and self-determination: 'leaseback', 'interests' of the Islanders (as distinct from their 'wishes'); 'non-escalation'; 'deterrence', all spoke of attempts to resolve the conflict. The key issue – what right had the Islanders to determine their own future? – opened one of the most vexatious issues of twentieth century history. What were the criteria for deciding the group of people who could stand out against the wishes of their sovereign government? How could 'British sovereignty' make sense when applied to two small islands, with a declining population, thousands of miles away from the homeland? But how could Argentine sovereignty make sense if applied to a people wholly different from the claimants? Yet how could it not make sense when seen from a geographical perspective, as a couple of islands not far from the Argentine mainland? Thus, while in one way the Falklands dispute seemed to be the last, dusty remnant of the long gone British Empire, in another the issues it raised were central to the political theory, and indeed the political ethics, of two nations.

This is not to overlook the mistakes and inconsistencies in British policy towards the Falklands; nor to exculpate the Argentine military junta for its precipitate invasion of the Islands. For the British, the problem was the rise of a heightened political awareness on the part of the Falkland Islanders, and their determined lobby of British Conservative Members of Parliament. This placed the British Government in the awkward position of wanting a settlement with Argentina, but one that, in focusing on the sovereignty issue, presented the main obstacle to its own aspirations: for sovereignty was exactly what the Islanders did not want to concede, and certainly not over their heads. The British Government – all British Governments since the 1970s – were aware of Argentine frustration over what they regarded as the failure to take their claims seriously. This would suggest to the rational observer that the British should have made preparations to contain this frustration, and deter it from moving towards military action. But distance lent disenchantment to the view: the cost of a force sufficient to deter any Argentine aggression would be disproportionate; the British contribution to NATO must take precedence. And there was the real consideration, always uppermost in British diplomatic circles, that action intended to deter might instead provoke. The criticism here is that the balance, admittedly hard to get right, leant too far on the side of conciliation, and lost sight of the fundamental role of military force: to deter hostility; to defuse it so that crisis might be avoided; but to do both without surrendering advantages which might later be turned against one's own side.

There was another piece of conceptual confusion in British policy: that between defence and deterrence. As Ministers frequently asserted, the defence of the Islands against an Argentine invasion would be costly; and in any case any force dispatched 'would not arrive in time or in sufficient strength to resist an invasion'. [77, para. 242] The word 'resist' suggested that this would be a defence force, not a deterrent one. A deterrent force was one whose object was to make it unnecessary to 'resist' invasion in the first place. Arguably, the presence of one nuclear powered submarine might well have been sufficient to act as a deterrent, though not of course as defence against potential Argentine aggression. As the Franks report noted, 'Given the relative closeness of the Falkland Islands to Argentina, their distance from Britain and the absence of a substantial British deterrent force in the area, Argentine always had the capability successfully to mount a sudden operation against the Islands'. [77, para. 277] The question of how 'substantial' this force should be was left unanswered by the Franks investigation. It requires perhaps a different kind of answer. If Argentina believed that Britain would retain the Islands at whatever the cost, then a small deterrent was all that was needed; but if (as Argentina was increasingly led to believe by the unconvincing character of British policy) Britain had no such desire, then of course a large deterrent force was needed – and was one that Britain did not wish to deploy, especially given her 1981 defence review which placed the whole of her defence emphasis on the NATO front. As Sir Anthony Williams put it, the Foreign Office 'thought that this was a problem which it could let ride'; right up to the Argentina invasion 'there were no contingency plans in London for dealing with this situation'. [19, p. 9]

This raises the question of what was happening in the last few days before the Argentine invasion. The Franks report concluded that the British Government 'had no reason to believe before 31 March that an invasion of the Falkland Islands would take place at the beginning of April'. [77, para. 261] The evidence from the Argentine side supports this conclusion up to a point; the final decision to proceed with the invasion was occasioned by the Argentine fear that, if she postponed or delayed her plans, then the British would establish a deterrent force in the region sufficient to necessitate the loss of the initiative. Military action would, Argentina believed, not only prevent this, but would give her significant and indisputable advantage in the diplomatic wrangling that would follow the Argentine action: she would be negotiating from strength, and from the position of the occupying power. To delay now would forfeit these potential advantages.

But this raises the question, from the British perspective, of the role of Intelligence in discerning Argentine intentions. British Intelligence in South America had been reduced in scope and personnel and was overburdened. There was, as Professor Laurence Freedman explained, 'little capacity for monitoring military movements within Argentine'. No intelligence was available from United States' satellites. [88, pp. 312–14] Despite this, Intelligence reports on 31 March were sent to the Ministry of Defence that the Argentines had set the early morning of 2 April as the day of action; these, together with earlier reports, provided (as Franks put it) 'a positive indication of an Argentine intention to invade the Falkland Islands'. [77, para. 233] But still Intelligence held that no irrevocable decision to invade had as yet been made. It was at this stage that the British Government began to pull together some kind of concerted response to the Argentine threat.

But the Government's failure to anticipate such a threat sooner was not only because of Intelligence failures: a reading of the Buenos Aires Press from January 1982 onwards might have yielded some inkling of increasing Argentine impatience with British unwillingness to move negotiations forward, and even threats to use force to resolve the dispute. [146, pp. 399–401] The British failure lay, not only in the lack of co-ordination between Departments, not only in confusion between defence and deterrence, but, in the words of two authorities: 'No intelligence system or technology can compensate for policy level direction and senior management that does not seek, or cannot accept, warning that disagrees with existing policy'. [52, p. 270] In 1973 Israel had intelligence warnings of an attack; there had been earlier warnings; but Israel was reluctant to mobilise, fearing the strain on her economy: and yet her national existence was at stake. [92, pp. 339–61] The British failure lay in the incoherence of her policy, but also in the disbelief that Argentina would resort to military force. In this sense, then, some at least of the blame for the British failure to avoid or prevent war over the Falklands was a failure of the imagination.

2
The British Response

One of the most influential facts about the Falkland Islands is that they are some 8,000 miles from the United Kingdom. When this is compared to the distance from, say, continental Europe (which seems a far away place of which the British people still know comparatively little), then the British political and official response to the Argentine invasion was, on the fact of it, a surprising one: surprising perhaps even to the British themselves. When Argentina launched her invasion (code name Operation Rosario) she did in the hope that it would be bloodless, though in warfare the chances of such an outcome are rarely guaranteed. Her troops boarded their landing craft at 05.40 on 2 April and by 06.00 had reached Government House, which they attacked at 06.30. The Argentine desire that the armed encounter would be, as Rear Admiral Carlos Busser, commander of the Argentine marines put it, 'if possible, without bloodshed' [151, p. 23] was matched by the instructions issued to the British Royal Marine garrison commander Major Mike Norman by the Governor of the Falklands, Sir Rex Hunt that if the Argentines landed he was 'to arrest them – not to shoot them, but arrest them'. [90, p. 110] Since Major Norman commanded only 76 men, together with nine sailors and 23 members of the local Defence Force, it might be concluded that his only realistic option was to do neither.

Major Norman had anticipated that the Argentine landing would take place on landing craft in deep water, but the Argentines landed their troops on a different, shallow water beach. The Royal Marines were obliged to make their way back towards Stanley, and the Argentine landing force occupied the airport, launched a grenade and submachine gun attack on the Royal Marine Barracks at Moody Brook (knowing them to be unoccupied) and pressed on to Government House. There they called for the Governor to give himself up, but were fired upon by the defenders, some thirty in number. Several Argentine soldiers were hit, and one killed. The Governor met Rear

Admiral Busser and asked him to leave and take his men with him; Busser refused and called upon Hunt to surrender and avoid further bloodshed. Major Norman, for his part, could draw a proper distinction between an honourable, but essentially token resistance, and a stubborn and hopeless fight to the death. Terms of surrender were agreed by 09.25, and by 12.15 the Argentine flag flew in the garden of Government House. [90, pp. 110–16] The only blood spilt in this brief invasion was Argentine; but the victors made the mistake of allowing four British journalists, who happened to be on the Islands following the South Georgia affair, to take photographs of the Marines lying on the ground face down in front of Government House. These pictures were later released in Britain and around the world. [32, pp. 302–3] This was the first serious Argentine propaganda error: it seemed to depict a British military humiliation, and this was not a spectacle that the British Army and public was used to nor, to say the least, one that they could allow to go unremarked.

The second Argentine military invasion, this time of South Georgia, was ordered for 07.15 on 2 April, and was completed the following day, again without loss to the small Royal Marine garrison, whose commander, Lieutenant Keith Mills, was instructed by London not to co-operate with the Argentines, nor to surrender, nor to 'take any action which may endanger life'. [90, p. 118] His use of his own initiative resulted in the destruction of a Puma helicopter and the death of four Argentine marines near Grytviken, and serious damage to a vessel, the *Guerrico*, which manoeuvred close to Grytviken to offer distracting fire. Having offered as much resistance as he could, Lieutenant Mills surrendered on condition of good treatment for his men. [90, pp. 119–20] Thus, Argentine hopes for a bloodless victory were not realised, though there was the compensation that she had not taken British lives: itself an acknowledgement that this was as much a political as a military operation, aimed at gaining for Argentina the initiative in any diplomatic or military developments that must now take place. Argentina now held the Falklands, South Georgia, and the South Sandwich Islands; she had not created any British or Falkland Islander martyrs; and she had placed the British Government in a difficult and embarrassing position. Above all, the Junta was now riding on a wave of Argentine popular support and approval of the recovery of the Malvinas. The Junta's bold action, taken at the last minutes, had resulted in the accomplishment within a few hours of what had not come near to achievement over the past two decades.

The British response was decided by several factors working on different levels. These were a mixture of the political, diplomatic, military and, by no means the least, moral. The diplomatic response, as described by the Prime Minister, Mrs Thatcher, was predictable: there were the dangers of a backlash against British ex-patriots who lived in Argentina; problems about getting support in the United Nations Security Council; the lack of reliance that Britain could place on the European Community or the United States of America; the risk of the Soviet Union becoming involved; and the disadvantage of being seen as a colonial power. The Defence Secretary, John Nott, later described his exasperation at the 'never-ending feebleness' of the Foreign Office, and its 'demeaning role as a spokesman for foreign interests', though he did admit that it 'might have been its duty to warn of all these obstacles'. [172] They were certainly serious obstacles; and when to this list was added the considerable military and logistic test of waging war thousands of miles from Britain, the objection to any course other than the purely diplomatic was indeed formidable.

But the response need not be purely diplomatic. If deterrence had failed (or not been persisted with) then there was still the option that a Task Force could sap Argentine resolve and prove a vital instrument in the diplomatic offensive that the Government must initiate. This mixture of military and diplomatic pressure was fuelled by a combination of forces and interests. There was, to take the lowest (or depending on the point of view, highest), the survival or demise of the Government, and especially of the Prime Minister: as the Permanent Secretary in the Ministry of Defence put it, either Mrs Thatcher or Galtieri would survive this crisis, but not both. There was the unity of the Conservative Party, many of whose members had always been sympathetic to the Falkland Islanders' desire to remain under British sovereignty. There was Parliament, which, in this crisis, would play a more prominent role than in the everyday business of government administration. There was the Labour Party, whose definition of the crisis and its meaning would also give it a more significant voice than the normal wilderness of opposition. And there was the public, as yet under-informed, or uninformed, about the rights and wrongs of the crisis, seeking information and guidance, forming itself in that volatile and unpredictable way that this amorphous entity invariably did, as it turned its gaze on an issue that, a week earlier, it had not even dreamed of. And there was the Press, already partisan for the most part, and now driven not only by its own opinions, but by the opportunities to search for scapegoats, write stories, brand enemies and praise friends;

and the visual media, with its potential for encapsulating a complex predicament in a few pictures, and the radio, second to television, but still able to paint vivid pictures in words of great events.

The beginning of the British response was in the heart of government. When on 31 March the Prime Minister met the Secretary of State for Defence, together with Foreign Office and Defence officials, Admiral Sir Henry Leach, the First Sea Lord, who had come to see John Nott, found himself entering the room as the discussion was taking place. Nott, in his whimsical but convincing memoir, remarked that the sight of the Admiral dressed in full naval uniform ('a man in uniform always pleases the ladies') 'clearly impressed' Mrs Thatcher. [172] She must have been even more impressed when Leach said that it was possible to prepare a large Task Force that could be ready to sail early the following week, though she was surprised to learn that the Falkland Islands were three weeks' sailing, not (as she supposed) three days. [44] This, according to Nott, 'clearly boosted Margaret's confidence' but 'was met with some scepticism among the rest of us'. Nott had his doubts about the cerebral content of a sailor in the best Nelsonian tradition, whose philosophy was 'Sail at the enemy and do not hesitate about the consequences'. [172] This was to underestimate the First Sea Lord who had already made 'one or two discreet minor preparations' (such as recalling John Fieldhouse, the Fleet Commander, from Gibraltar) 'because I thought it was time he was back at his headquarters'. (200, pp. 17–18) It was said that Nott, for his part, 'whitened' at the prospect. [236, pp. 72–3]

Nott's doubts about the Admiral's advice were well-founded. A Task Force could be quickly assembled; the vessels were, so to say, in the right places, or nearly so, for their gathering together, though the loading of stores and equipment would have to be done too rapidly for logical access when in operation to be guaranteed. [90, pp. 127–8] The decision at this meeting went no further than to ask the Chief of Naval Staff to advise on the size and composition of a Task Force which would retake the Islands, and to prepare such a force 'without commitment to a final decision as to whether or not it should sail'. It was also agreed that a message should be sent to President Ronald Reagan that an Argentine invasion of the Falklands might be imminent, and that the British Government could not acquiesce in this. Reagan was asked to mediate and to tell General Galtieri that the British would not escalate the dispute or start fighting. [90, p. 123]

This was evidence that the Thatcher Government was not determined to go to war, without exploring all the possibilities of a peaceful settlement of the dispute, even at this moment of crisis. Moreover, even at this late stage the Latin America Current Intelligence Group's assessment was that Argentina could launch an invasion on 2 April, but that, despite their military preparations, there was no intelligence suggesting that the Junta had taken a decision to invade the Falkland Islands, even though the co-operation between the three Argentine military services, and their involvement in the Argentine Task Force at sea was 'disturbing'. [77, para. 241] When the British Government's Defence Committee met later on the morning of 1 April, the Prime Minister informed it that an Argentine Task Force could reach Stanley by the morning of 2 April, but that the Argentine Government's 'precise intentions' were not known; a diplomatic solution had to be found if possible. [77, para. 242]

By the evening of 1 April it had become clear that an Argentine invasion of the Falklands could not be prevented. Nott, his 'scepticism...replaced by mild, tentative optimism', [171] the Prime Minister, and Lord Carrington, now back from Israel, met and decided that troops should be put on the alert to be deployed in the South Atlantic. Sir Henry Leach issued a directive that the Task Force should be made ready for sailing. [90, p. 124] On 2 April, before the Government fully and publicly confirmed that the Argentine invasion had taken place, Humphrey Atkins in Parliament would go no further than warning of a 'real expectation that an Argentine attack...will take place very soon'. The debate moved on cautious lines. Atkins stressed that the Government assisted itself with a request from the United Nations Security Council that both Britain and Argentina 'should exercise restraint and refrain from the use or threat of force, and continue the search for a diplomatic solution'. The Government was taking appropriate military and diplomatic measures to sustain Britain's rights under international law and in accordance with the provisions of the United Nations Charter. [114, 2 April 1982, col. 571] John Silkin for the Opposition offered the Labour Party's 'full support' for the rights of the people of the Falkland Islands to stay British and it was 'our duty to defend the right'. The Government had been right to inform the Security Council of the threat to peace, but 'some questions' must be asked. These revolved round the question of whether the Government 'misjudged the situation': were there signs that it had been seen some time ago? Had not the 'scrapping' of *Endurance* and a large proportion of the surface fleet given a false impression that Britain might be willing to abandon her responsibilities in the area? Did the Government consult other members of the Security Council before advising the Security Council of the threat to peace, and had Britain any support in the Security Council? Atkins reaffirmed that the decision to take the issue to the United Nations was the proper course, noted that *Endurance* was still in the area, and informed the House that the Government had indeed consulted its friends 'before taking the matter to the Security Council', and had support there. Atkins claimed that the Government would defend the Falkland Islands to the 'best of our ability': [114, cols. 571–3] an expression which did not smack of too much enthusiasm or self-belief. Late that evening, when Argentine forces had established themselves on the Islands, the full Cabinet met and agreed, collectively and with (it is said) one dissentient, the Trade Secretary John Biffen, that the Task Force should sail. [90, p. 124] On that same evening, unknown to the First Sea Lord, Sir Roger Jackling, Head of DS11, Ministry of Defence, answered 'four or five pertinent questions' from the Prime Minister about what the chances of success were and what the casualties and cost might be. Jackling replied that the losses could be up to four or five escort ships and an aircraft carrier (200, p. 36).

There was no alternative for a Government thus circumstanced. The Conservative Party would have revolted if its front bench had baulked the issue. It may well be the case that, as President Reagan put it in colourful language, that no-one would go to war for an ice cold bunch of land in the South Atlantic; but Spain's recent strong reaction to a handful of Moroccan citizens landing on a barren and uninhabited rock off the Coast of North Africa suggests that sovereign territory is still today regarded as sacrosanct. On the other hand, the allegation that the British Foreign Office has been working to detach Northern Ireland from the United Kingdom, and has certainly engaged in serious discussions with Spain over a possible joint sovereignty of Gibraltar (secretly, and ultimately criticised by the House of Commons Foreign Affairs Committee) suggests that British Governments, or at any rate their diplomats, do not instinctively harbour an acquisitive attitude to British sovereign territory. But an open and unapologetic Argentine act of aggression, however justified by nationalist fervour and supported by a credible degree of legality in historical terms, was a challenge from which few governments could retreat. William Whitelaw (Lord Whitelaw) put it after his blunt fashion: the fact was that we had 'to do something, and if we didn't send a Task Force, what else should we do? Parliament was going to meet on Saturday. We were going to have a very hostile House of Commons, a hostile Press and many criticisms of what had happened'. And (he added significantly) 'if we hadn't reacted very strongly we probably couldn't have survived as a government'. [19, p. 295]

The decision to despatch the Task Force was taken on Thursday night, 1 April (subject to Cabinet confirmation the next day) before the special emergency debate in the House of Commons on Saturday 3 April, though it is safe to say that many, perhaps most, members of the Cabinet hoped that the crisis would not come to war. But the atmosphere in that debate was profoundly different from the carefully measured language of the previous day. This was an extraordinary event, in every sense of the word. The House seemed to see itself as standing at the bar of history. The Speaker, Labour's George Thomas, was circumspect in his description of his choice of members who sought to catch his eye in this, and subsequent debates on the crisis: 'I had to make sure that those who opposed the Government's action were given the right to be heard. I also had to bear in mind their number in relation to the rest of the House, which were in favour, and overall I think the balance was maintained'. He had no doubt about where his own sympathies lay: 'The first voice to be raised against the retaking of the Islands was the Scottish Labour M.P. George Foulkes, who wanted to let the Islands go, but I am convinced that if this view had prevailed, Belize would have gone, trouble in Gibraltar would have been inevitable and in a number of places across the world the bully-boys would have moved into action knowing that the democracies were afraid to respond'. 'We are still a tough little race', he concluded, 'and now the world knows it'. [204, pp. 208, 211]

The debate was not of course devoid of party political fencing. Mrs Thatcher reminded the Opposition that it had not reacted, when in government, to the Argentine presence on South Thule, and asserted that had she sent HMS *Invincible* to South Georgia when the Argentines landed there 'I should have been accused of war mongering and sabre rattling'. [114, cols. 634, 636] Her Defence Secretary, John Nott, was unequal to the feverish atmosphere in the House, and on his own admission, 'made a fantastic boob. Labour was yelling, Tory backbenchers were jeering, I lost concentration and blamed the invasion on Labour'. Nott later claimed that his speech 'actually reads very well', but admitted candidly Alan Clark's description of himself as 'rattled and blubbery'. [171]

But this was secondary to the character of the debate, which Mrs Thatcher focused on as deriving from 'a situation of great gravity'. MPs were in the House because 'for the first time for many years, British sovereign territory has been invaded by a foreign power'. [171]

Members' indignation at the Argentine seizure of the Islands outweighed, indeed overwhelmed, the party political dimension. Michael Foot rose to make a brilliant speech; as his biographer, Mervyn Jones, put it, 'What he saw was a clear case of unprovoked aggression, and he was vividly reminded of aggressions by Hitler and Mussolini in the 1930s: which were among the most emotionally powerful memories of his youth'. [129, pp. 484–5] Foot based his argument on moral grounds. He wanted to set on record what his party believed to be the international rights and wrongs of the crisis:

> There is no question in the Falkland Islands of being colonial dependence or anything of that sort. It is a question of people who wish to be associated with this country and who have built their whole lives on the basis of association with this country. We have a moral duty, a political duty and every other kind of duty to ensure that this is sustained.

The people of the Falklands had 'the absolute right to look to us at this moment in their desperate plight, just as they have looked to us over the past fifteen years. They are faced with an act of naked, unqualified aggression...The United Nations must declare that the Argentine invasion was "an act of aggression, for not to do so would injure not only the islanders, but the people of Britain" and "would enhance the dangers that similar, unprovoked aggression could occur in other parts of the world". This "foul and brutal aggression" must not be allowed to succeed, for it if were then there would be a danger to "people all over this dangerous planet"'. [114, cols. 638–9, 641]

Foot's biographer explained that some of his friends in the Labour Party held the view that an uncompromising demand for the restoration of the status quo might not be the only possible – or the wisest – policy, and pointed out that in the Callaghan Government, Foot had not objected to 'leaseback' suggestions: 'no one was actually afraid that the islanders would be made to wear yellow stars or be sent to gas chambers'. [129, p. 485] Tam Dalyell recollected that he had urged Foot not to support Mrs Thatcher: 'I know more about military technology than you do'. To which Foot replied 'Tam, I know more about Fascism than you do'. [57] The debate was not about the islanders only; and no-one suggested that the Argentines were intending to make the islanders wear yellow, or any kind of coloured stars. The debate was, in many, perhaps most, respects, about Britain, and the kind of country that she was, her history, her values. The Conservative

MP Edward du Cann agreed with Michael Foot that 'this nation has always been prompt to condemn dictatorship, to ally ourselves and fight against it and fight aggression'. [114, col. 642] Julian Amery took comfort in the fact that the British 'always win the last battle'. Patrick Cormack reminded the House that the eyes of people in Gibraltar would be upon Britain, as would the gaze of those in Hong King: this was 'one of the most critical moments in the history of our country since the war'. Peter Jay denounced the Foreign Office as 'saturated with the spirit of appeasement'. [114, cols. 648, 652, 658]

This was a claim of more than passing interest. The great trauma in recent British history was not the economic slump of the 1930s; not even Suez, bad though that was, for Suez was regarded by many in Britain, especially on the Left, as a foolish if not wicked neo-colonial adventure. It was the belief that appeasement, which at the time could be defended on both rational and emotional grounds, was the nadir of the role of morality in British foreign policy. Thus the Falkland Islands and their inhabitants were cast, not as colonists, but as something like a small nation that had, as Jay put it, the right to self-determination. Sir Bernard Braine fumed at the 'very thought that our people, 1,800 of British blood and bone, could be left in the hands of such criminals'; it was 'enough to make any normal Englishman's blood – and the blood of Scotsmen and Welshmen – boil too'. John Silkin referred to 'the bargain basement Mussolini, Galtieri'. Russell Johnson (Liberal MP for Inverness) criticised the *Guardian* newspaper for saying that the Falkland Islands had no 'strategic or commercial British interest worth fighting for (unless one believed reports of crude oil under their off-shore waters)'. It was 'shocking that in a great newspaper such as the *Guardian* the view should be put that the only things worth fighting over are commercial matters and not the rights and freedom of individual people'. [114, cols. 658, 659, 666, 655] The battle of appeasement was to be re-fought on the fields of the Falklands – and on the floor of the House of Commons.

This was not of course the only reason for fighting for the Falklands; and it must be emphasised that, with a few exceptions such as Sir Peter Emery, who urged that if Argentina did not withdraw within ten to 14 days, 'a state of war shall exist between Argentina and Britain', MPs and Government Ministers emphasised that diplomacy was still to be resorted to, though diplomacy backed by the possible use of military force. John Nott, in his reasoned but ineffectual statement, warned the House of the 'formidable difficulties with a crisis 8,000 miles away', though he affirmed that the United Kingdom had the ability to mount a major naval Task Force and to sustain it for a period at that distance. A force would be despatched in the next few days; but the Government would try to resolve the crisis by diplomatic means. If these failed, as they would 'probably' do so, then the Government would have no choice but to 'press forward with our plans, retaining secrecy where necessary and flexibility to act as circumstances demand'. [114, cols. 658, 661–8] But, as one historian points out, the debate of 3 April 'inflamed Parliamentary rhetoric', united the parties behind the Task Force and discouraged diplomatic compromise. [33, p. 7]

The decision to send the Task Force was now part of the dynamics of the crisis; for it was not merely a political or military act; not only ancillary to the diplomatic offensive that was now set in train. It was a highly emotional affair, as John Nott discovered when, seeking relief from a heated and bruising encounter with his party following the 2 April debate (when Lord Carrington was met by 'an element of cat-calling, derision and jeers' and subsequently felt he had to resign, and when Nott himself offered to resign, but was refused by the Prime Minister), he went to Portsmouth to visit the fleet. Unknown to the Press he had been 'besieged by rioting dockyard workers' on a visit less than a year earlier protesting about defence cuts and redundancies. Now these same people, several of whom had received their redundancy notices a few days before, rallied round: 'I sensed that these naval officers and dockyard workers did not see me as a visiting politician now, but acknowledged that I was there as the Defence Secretary; that the nation had a crisis; and that we just had to work together to put on a good show'. [172] Portsmouth, with its long tradition as a naval dockyard, was not the whole country; but this episode revealed that the Task Force would not only be a cold weapon of diplomacy, but a focus of loyalty in its own right: more, perhaps, of a focus of loyalty than any other actor in the unfolding crisis. As such, it could shed glory on the politicians; or, if mishandled by them, reflect disastrously on their reputations.

No subsequent debate in Parliament reached the same intensity and emotional pitch as that of Saturday 3 April. A few days later, on 7 April, some Conservative MPs began to reflect on the heat generated on the Saturday: Michael Mates spoke of his relief at the 'sense of perspective' that had returned to the debate. There was 'no escaping the logistical difficulties of mounting this operation'; 'People who wish that our imperial past will return are wishing for the impossible'. [114, 7 April 1982, cols. 1001, 1003] Maurice MacMillan asked for a 'minimum use of force' to achieve the British objective. [114, col. 1010] For the Opposition, Denis Healey continued to warn that if Britain turned her back on her responsibility to the Falklands, then Belize would be invaded by the brutal dictatorship in Guatemala; there was also Gibraltar and Hong King. It was only possible to negotiate with a dictator from strength. But he warned that the 'wrong use' of the Task Force 'could lead to unnecessary loss of life among our soldiers, sailors and marines'. There were two main dangers: a diplomatic solution that would 'sell the Falkland Islanders down the river', or a 'large-scale military conflict with Argentina in circumstances that will cost us the support of the United Nations and world opinion'. Too many people without experience of war saw the choice as between Armageddon and surrender. 'I hope that the principle of economy of force will always be the key to the British use of armed forces in a situation that requires a diplomatic initiative'. He suggested that perhaps the United Nations would provide an administrator for the Islands, and a peace-keeping force after Argentina withdrew. [114, cols. 965–8] David Steel urged the House and the Government to discuss openly the question of lease-back or condominion. [114, cols. 977–8] Michael Mates concluded with satisfaction that 'a sense of perspective' had returned to the debate, and called upon the British to make a 'graduated response with all the options that are available'. [114, col. 1002]

By this time the Government had reorganised itself for the conduct of 'Operation Corporate', as the task before it was called. The crisis so far had carried off Lord Carrington, Sir Humphrey Atkins and Richard Luce. It brought to the Foreign Office Francis Pym, Leader of the House of Commons, who replaced Lord Carrington, and who could command much support in the seething ranks of the Conservative Party. Mrs Thatcher disliked Pym intensely, and his performance as the new Foreign Secretary could decide not only the fate of the Government, but of himself, as potential leader of the Party should Mrs Thatcher fall as a result of the crisis. One of her favourites, William Whitelaw, Deputy Prime Minister and Home Secretary, did not press for the job, but was included in the small War Cabinet that would seek, in the words of Admiral Lewin (Chief of Defence Staff) 'To cause the withdrawal of the Argentinian forces, and to restore the British administration'. [90, p. 125] The other members of the War Cabinet were John Nott, who saw himself as obliged to help Pym and his determined efforts to reach a diplomatic solution; he would be a facilitator, not an uncritical Thatcher loyalist; [172] Whitelaw, who could use his good offices with the Party; and the Paymaster General and Chairman of the party, Cecil Parkinson, who was to deal with public relations. [90, pp. 125–6] A figure conspicuous by his absence was the Chancellor of the Exchequer, despite the fact that war was an expensive business.

The machinery of government that would coordinate military operations and diplomacy was the War Cabinet. The daily running of the war was done by the Ministry of Defence, under John Nott, assisted by two Ministers of State, one for the armed forces and one for defence procurement. The War Cabinet's principal military adviser was the Chief of the Defence Staff, who was Chair of the Chiefs of Staff Committee. The Chief of the Defence Staff had the right of direct access to the Prime Minister. The Services Chiefs of Staff (of the Naval, Air Force and general Staff) were the senior military advisers to the Government on their own services, with direct access to the Prime Minister. Sir Terence (later Lord) Lewin was Chief of the Defence Staff in the Falklands crisis. Admiral Sir Henry Leach was Chief of the Naval Staff, Field Marshal Sir Edwin Bramall led the general Staff, and Air Chief Marshal Beetham was Chief of the Air Staff. The principal adviser to the Defence Secretary on political, administrative and financial maters was Sir Frank Cooper, Principal Under-Secretary of State, a man noted for his shrewd yet combative style.

The structure of command was well thought out. Senior civil servants met after War Cabinet sessions to follow on the Cabinet decisions; military advice was channelled to the War Cabinet through the Chief of Defence Staff, Admiral Sir Terence Lewin. Other chiefs of Staff attended as appropriate. Admiral Sir John Fieldhouse, Commander-in-Chief of the Task Force, and based at Northwood, reported to Lewin, and was head of the operational commanders. [90, p. 127] But this well organised machinery was subject to the variables inherent in combining diplomacy and war; and subject also to the personalities and different views of its membership. Chief among those was the character and beliefs of the Prime Minister, and those of her new Foreign Secretary, Francis Pym.

The significance of the crisis for the Prime Minister is shown in her account of *The Downing Street Years*, in which she devoted two chapters to the Falklands War, the first called, in straightforward terms, 'Following the Flag'. For Mrs Thatcher, the issue was that of 'defending our honour as a nation, and principles of fundamental importance to the whole world – above all, that aggressors, should never succeed and that international law should prevail over the use of force'. [203, p. 173] She sought to assume the mantle of leader of the nation, and of a nation at war. She disliked the 'even-handedness' of journalists, with their 'chilling use of the third person' in their reports, their talk of 'the British' and 'the Argentinians' on 'our' news programmes. [203, p. 181] This was indeed not only the greatest challenge of her premiership, but the defining one, and she knew it. If she had not, then the unflinching eye and voice of Enoch Powell would have convinced her, when, on 3 April, he combined an attack on the Foreign Office for seeking to 'detach' Northern Ireland from the United Kingdom with an assertion that force was the only way to deal with aggression: the next few weeks, he insisted, would reveal of what metal the so-called 'iron lady', was made, to the House, the nation and to herself. [114, 3 April 1982, cols. 959–60]

John Nott in his personal history of the crisis claimed that 'Margaret Thatcher had, I believe, made up her mind from the outset that the only way we could regain our national honour and prestige was by inflicting a military defeat on Argentina'. This is a convincing assessment. But, as he noted, 'this did not prevent the painful and endless negotiations for a diplomatic settlement…'. [172] In his first speech as Foreign Secretary, Francis Pym set out to moderate the excitable mood of the House of Commons. He would approach the crisis in a spirit of realism and 'calm determination'. 'We intend to see that the Falkland Islands are freed from occupation and returned to British administration at the earliest possible moment. To do that, we must look forward in confidence, and not backwards in anger'. Argentina may now have a sizeable occupation force on the Islands. Britain had sent a large task-force. But 'there will be time before that task-force reaches the area to do everything possible to solve the problem without further fighting. We would much prefer a peaceful settlement… But if all our efforts fail, the Argentine regime will know what to expect. Britain does not appease dictators'. [114, cols. 959–60]

In the 1930s Britain did appease dictators; the failure of appeasement, not the effort, was what tarnished what was seen until 1938, perhaps until 1939, as a rational and indeed in many respects moral policy. Pym faced the difficulty that the effort itself could be regarded as not only futile, but immoral. Hence his carefully balanced statement, which juxtaposed words like 'strength', 'strength of will', 'spare no effort to reach a peaceful solution'. [114, col. 962] His disappointingly opaque memoir was different, in a small but significant way: 'We resolved that, while we would pursue every available avenue for peace, we would not concede the sovereignty of the Islands under duress and without the consent of the islanders, and we would insist on the withdrawal of the occupying force. Those principles we held sacrosanct; on others we would compromise'. [183, p. 99] The use of the word 'sovereignty' instead of his House of Commons expression 'administration' was picked up by some of his listeners. David Steel, while agreeing that the Argentine forces must leave the Islands, urged that Britain must then discuss openly the question of lease back or condominion; that was why the word 'administration' rather than 'sovereignty' was being used in ministerial speeches. [114, col. 978] Tony Benn noted the distinction between sovereignty and administration: administration could be worked under someone else's sovereignty. Eric Ogden was more forthright: 'I smell the smell of appeasement. I smell a sell-out. These are words that have to be used'. He went on to point out that

> Part of the difficulty may be that two different sets of advice are being given to Ministers. The Prime Minister says that we should keep our word, restore faith and regain our sovereignty over the Falkland Islands. However, someone else says that the Falkland Islanders might not be as anxious to insist on something they insisted on before they were invaded and that the fleet is going there only to restore British administration. If that is so, by the time the fleet has reached the Falkland Islands, the Argentine Government will have offered a 25-year package deal of administration and of a lease-back in return for sovereignty.

Ogden claimed that he sensed a pact between Pym and the American mediator, General Alexander Haig (who had been offered by President Reagan as part of the British diplomatic offensive) 'that will have much in common with that of Hoare and Laval'. [114, col. 1033]

This was a wounding criticism, harking back to what was seen as one of the most disreputable episodes in the appeasement diplomacy of the 1930s, when in December 1935 London and Paris agreed to acquiesce in the Italian attack on Abyssinia: a policy that was disowned by both countries and led to the downfall of its inventors, Samuel Hoare and Pierre Laval. Alan Clark alleged that for the last 35 years British Governments had betrayed minorities, 'allegedly for reasons of State and expediency' such as Sudeten Czechs. What was the Government seeking: Sovereignty; or administration? Was leasehold (sic) a possibility? On what terms? [114, col. 1037]

John Nott was obliged to shore up the Government's position. Sovereignty remained; it was therefore the administration of the Islands that the Government was seeking to restore. British people must be protected wherever they chose to live, even if 8,000 miles away from the Houses of Parliament, and if Britain had to fight to restore to the people of the Falkland Islands their right to self determination, she would do so. [114, cols. 1045, 1050]

This exchange suggested that there was substance in General Haig's claim that 'In these early days of the crisis it was evident that Mrs Thatcher, though she was strongly backed by Nott and also by Admiral Lewin, did not enjoy the full support of other members of her Government'. [63, p. 102] Mrs Thatcher, for her part, was suspicious of what she called Foreign Office 'flexibility'; [203, p. 181] a suspicion which she shared with the Governor of the Islands, Rex Hunt, who claimed that he was deliberately excluded from the War Cabinet because he had, as he put it, 'gone native', [120] which suggested that the War Cabinet was by no means wholly unequivocal in its determination to restore the Islands to the status quo ante bellum. She wrote in her memoirs that she was determined that, whatever role the United States of America, the United Nations, or anybody else would play, the management and resolution of the crisis would not be removed from the War Cabinet's hands. Nor from her own hands: from the beginning she was suspicious of Francis Pym's role in searching for a settlement. She claimed that she regarded him as the right person for the crisis, because he was the 'enemy of ideology'; she preferred to question his 'judgement'. [203, p. 187] John Nott agreed that Pym was anxious to attain a diplomatic solution and that his first speech as Foreign Secretary in the House was 'a good speech'. But, he went on, 'by emphasizing our desire for a peaceful settlement with almost every other word, he gave the impression that he could see one in sight – that it was only a question of one final heave and we would be home and dry'. [172] Pym was reflecting the Foreign Office view of the crisis, one that Mrs Thatcher described as derived from the fear of a backlash against British ex-patriots in Argentine, problems with getting support in the United Nations Security Council, the lack of reliance that Britain could place on the European Community or the United States of America, the risk of Soviet Union becoming involved and the disadvantage of being looked at as a colonial power, all of which Nott summed up as the 'never ending feebleness' of the Foreign office. [172]

Mrs Thatcher described the Saturday 3 April debate as the House giving her 'unanimous but grudging' support. [203, p. 184] This was hardly fair: indeed, the left wing Labour MP, Eric Heffer, wrote in the

Listener in April 1984 that 'Labour's initial response…bordered on the jingoistic and only later did it become more balanced'. [107] But Mrs Thatcher believed that this initial response did not mean that everybody was thinking the same thing. 'Some saw the Task Force as a purely diplomatic armada that would get the Argentines back to the negotiating table. They never intended that it should actually fight'. She admitted that she 'needed their support as long as possible, for we needed to demonstrate a united national will both to the enemy and to our allies'. [203, pp. 183–4]

The Prime Minister's Falkland chapters are littered with words such as 'quite unacceptable', the need to 'stop this', her determination not to 'hold up military progress'. [203, pp. 204, 208, 217] Labour was picking its words carefully: Denis Healey, while supporting the principles at stake, warned that 'too many people without experience of war see the choice as between Armageddon or surrender. I hope that the principle of economy of force will always be the key to the British use of armed forces in a situation that requires a diplomatic settlement'. [114, col. 967] This not only reflected Healey's own instincts: on 6 April some members of Labour's National Executive Committee only narrowly failed to disassociate the party completely from the Government's handling of the crisis. [63, p. 121]

Despite Mrs Thatcher's firm language, and while acknowledging John Nott's opinion that she always thought that a war was the only means of restoring British honour and prestige, her Government must pursue a diplomatic as well as a military response. This reflected the character of international politics since 1945: states could no longer go to war, until the second Gulf war, as their fancy took them, at least not without risking their being branded as pariahs. The United Nations could not be ignored. Moreover the United States of America, as the dominant power in the Latin American region, could not be ignored. Argentina had launched her invasion of the Falklands in the belief that the United States would be reluctant to oppose it. 'Mediation' – the insertion of a third, neutral party into an international dispute – was to be expected; this was a development that had, since the 1960s, gained considerable momentum as a means of breaking the stalemate in world conflicts. [109, p. 263] But the role of mediator was a difficult one, especially when both parties to the dispute, as in the Falkland Islands case, believed they had a particular claim on the mediator's loyalty, and sought to make it good. Moreover, neither Argentina nor the United Kingdom would wish to hand over their case to binding international arbitration. This was effective only in matters of legal dispute;

but the Argentine-British dispute, though it had a legal aspect, was by now assuming the character of a political one. The best that could be hoped for in this crisis was a mediation that reduced the intensity of the confrontation and facilitated the making of concessions; this meant identifying a 'zone of potential agreement' between the contestants. The mediating party could then try to move the disputants towards an outcome within this range. In endeavouring to do so, saving face would be an important consideration. The mediation process was thus 'an exercise in power and influence'. [109, pp. 264, 266] But the mediator in the Falklands dispute, the United States, had its own interests to consult; nor was its administration unanimous in deciding how the balance between mediation, its perceived obligations to the two states involved in the crisis, and its own self-interest might be struck.

The United Nations' role might at first sight seem to be more clear cut: aggression had clearly taken place; Argentina was the aggressor; and the United Nations stood for opposing aggression anywhere in the world: providing, that is, that its member states could be persuaded of the rights and wrongs of the particular act of aggression.

The British Government worked quickly to put pressure on Argentina, securing from the United Nations on 3 April Resolution 502, which stated that there had been a 'breach of the peace in the region', demanding an 'immediate cessation of hostilities' and 'an immediate withdrawal of the Argentine forces from the Falkland Islands (Islas Malvinas)'. The Resolution also called on both sides to seek a diplomatic solution. [89, p. 40] This gave the British much; but it also withheld much of what they wanted. It did not condemn Argentina as an aggressor; nor did it insist upon a return to the status quo ante. It called for a cessation of hostilities; but Argentina had in a sense already 'ceased' hostilities, and Britain was now asked to do the same. No mention of a deadline for the withdrawal of Argentine forces was made. There was no mention of the sovereignty issue. The emphasis was on negotiations, which suited Argentina best. [158, p. 46] Nor was the expression 'act of aggression' used, which the Resolution could have included under Article 39 of the United Nations Charter. There was no explicit statement of which party to the dispute was responsible for the 'breach of the peace'. [113, p. 394] Nonetheless, as Rueben Moro pointed out, Britain had already won its first major battle, 'one whose military and political implications were perceived by few at that juncture'. [159, p. 41] Francis Pym was not justified in claiming that the United Nations Security Council had 'endorsed' Britain's view of the crisis [90, p. 40] (certainly not the Prime Minister's view); but

Sir Anthony Parsons, Britain's representative to the United Nations, believed that the Argentines had miscalculated the mood of the General Assembly, and that its Foreign Minister, Costa Mendez, seemed to have brushed it aside: 'so we did have a lot of luck'. Argentina believed that Britain was unlikely to do anything more than 'jump up and down at the United Nations and accept the status quo'. [19, pp. 32–4] But she had assembled her Task Force eight hours before the Security Council Resolution, without forfeiting the advantage which the Resolution gave her. [94, p. 48] In the Security Council, of its 15 members only Panama voted against Resolution 502; the USSR abstained, as did China, Poland and Spain. [90, pp. 136–40]

Britain could also work out from Resolution 502, referring to Article 51 of the United Nations Charter which allowed the 'inherent right of individual or collective self-defence if an armed attack occurs against a member of the United Nations'. However, this was by no means an unqualified right. While the right to collective self-defence was a sound basis for a British military response, it must not be disproportionate. [96, p. 86]

The second part of the British response was announced by Mrs Thatcher on 3 April, when she told the House of Commons that she had contacted President Reagan and asked him to intervene with the Argentine President directly, offering in return a promise that 'in the meantime, to take no action to escalate the dispute for fear of precipitating (interruption) the very event our actions were directed to avoid'. [114, col. 636] This, rather tentative, claim on the United States' good offices contrasted with General Galtieri's conviction that 'The Americans and I understand each other very well'. [187, p. 378] Argentina had some powerful friends in the United States administration. Mrs Jeane Kirkpatrick, United States Ambassador to the United Nations, angered British MPs by showing what they regarded as an unwarranted even-handedness (to say the least) between the aggressor and the victim. Denis Healey, who always stressed the need for a diplomatic settlement, criticised Mrs Kirkpatrick for saying that a Government which used force to pursue a territorial claim that it believed to be justified on historical grounds was not committing aggression. [114, col. 1200] The Argentine Press agreed, arguing that colonialism was dead and that 'Great Britain has accepted the fact, except in the case of Argentina's southern Atlantic islands'. The Press expressed no hatred of the British, but simply a determination to 'recuperate' something that belonged to Argentina. Mrs Thatcher personified the England of 'Captain Morgan' not Shakespeare. [7, pp. 51–2]

Mrs Kirkpatrick explained that her position on the dispute was based on two perceptions: that the United States had a long-standing commitment to the United Kingdom, which would involve her 'on Britain's side'; but that the United States shared a heritage with the Latin American countries, and all Latin America (with the exception of Chile) supported Argentina. [19, pp. 26–7] David Gompert, Deputy Under-Secretary of State for Political Affairs, spoke in similar terms: the United States was trying to reverse the tide of Communism in Central America and to build 'strong relationships with sympathetic regimes', including Argentina. The United States also recognised its need to exert leadership within NATO, 'energising' the Alliance around American leadership: 'These two external challenges constituted our approach'. To provide open and material support for the United Kingdom would do serious damage throughout Latin America, setting back United States' policy for years. Yet the memory of Suez haunted the United States as much as it did the United Kingdom, and made the United States anxious to avoid the 'worst possible outcome': which was for Britain to try and fail to recover the Falkland Islands, and to fail because the United States had withheld or withdrawn support. [19, pp. 18–19]

American policy was rendered harder to define by the fear of the Soviet Union taking the opportunity to make mischief in the region. Argentina had since 1946 constructed good relations with the USSR. Peron established formal diplomatic relations in 1946 and in 1953 the first trade treaty was signed. Economic ties were strengthened and by the mid 1970s the two countries were moving closer together. Despite the anti-Communist views of the military junta after 1976, relations continued to develop: the Soviet Union and Cuba blocked all discussions of Argentina's human rights record in the United Nations' Commission on Human Rights. In 1980 Argentina ignored the United States' embargo imposed after the Soviet invasion of Afghanistan. In April 1981 the Argentine Foreign Minister, Oscar Camilion, reaffirmed Argentina's independence of American foreign policy and declared his country's intention to continue trade with the USSR. [121, pp. 183–4, 189–91] It was not, therefore, in the United States' interest to offend Argentina, and risk her falling more deeply under Soviet influence.

The best course for the United States was to act as mediator, and the choice of Alexander Haig to play this part suggested that the balance of mediation, so to say, would fall on Britain's side. Haig was sympathetic to the British predicament, and no admirer of Argentina. But he believed that the best way in which he could express his mind was to act as a neutral honest broker; [19, pp. 18–19] but at the same time the British Ambassador in Washington claimed that Haig assured him that the United States was not at heart impartial. [108, p. 50] This was perhaps unfortunate for his mission: for America to declare herself impartial might arouse British concern, and even resentment at America's unwillingness to stand up to aggression; but for him to admit that he was not at heart impartial was to undermine his authority as an honest broker. And the Latin American group in the United States' administration was not prepared to allow its views to be eclipsed. Thomas Enders, Assistant Secretary of State for Latin American affairs at the State Department took a pessimistic view: the British 'did not actively seek to reach a negotiated conclusion'; 'we found ourselves pursuing them'. [45, pp. 171–2] But they would be pursued; though the American desire to discern 'pragmatism' in London and Buenos Aires, and to see 'hope' was, in retrospect at least, ill-founded.

The final arm of the British diplomatic response was to seek support from the European Community. It was not usually regarded as a dynamic force in international affairs; and indeed much of the conduct of its member states was governed by enlightened self-interest. The United Kingdom was engaged in a dispute with other members of the Community over agricultural prices and the British budgetary contribution: as one French Member of the European Parliament put it, 'we support Britain in this issue but European solidarity ought not to be one way. When we are in need of your solidarity (on agricultural prices) we hope it will be there and we hope you will not show excessive nationalism'. [73, p. 49] But the European support for the United Kingdom was significant. Argentina's action was condemned by the ten member states, many of whose Political Directors happened to be meeting in Brussels on 2 April. Four days later the British Government asked the European Community to ban Argentine imports and this was agreed on 14 April, and put into effect ten days later: 'Rarely had the Community moved with such speed'. [211, p. 8]

All this, however, was not an unmixed blessing for the British Government. Although the United Nations' Resolution 502, American mediation, the European Community support were all helpful (and by no means guaranteed before the crisis broke), yet there was a price to be paid. Britain must be careful to show herself willing to be reasonable, and not to resort to the use of force until all diplomatic options were exhausted, or at least attempted. Support might dissolve if Britain were to take any action, military or diplomatic, that seemed to brand her as not serious about seeking a peaceful settlement. The character of any such settlement was as yet undefined, but could hardly be one that left British sovereignty over the Falklands clear and undiminished. On 6 April Alexander Haig told Costa Mendez that the British would not compromise on sovereignty, but 'perhaps there would be some sort of joint administration for a time until the transfer is effected, but I somehow do not believe such a solution would sit well with Mrs Thatcher'. [158, p. 45] He was not far wrong. All this would be anathema to Mrs Thatcher, or at least was not likely to appeal to her temperament. It might divide her War Cabinet, her party, parliament and British media and public opinion. More appealing to her – and she must have hoped to all the elements that constituted the judge and jury of public and political opinion – were the words of *The Times'* leader of 5 April: 'We are all Falklanders now'.

That the leading newspaper in the United Kingdom could use these words about a remote pair of islands is significant. On the map of the South Atlantic (let alone the world) the Falklands looked far away and tiny. But maps express things deeper than simple geographical facts. In Argentina the islands were shown as an integral part of Argentine territory, exhibited in school textbooks and postage stamps. An Argentine football world cup cartoon showed the team's mascot holding a map of the islands. [7, pp. 8–9] In Britain, there was no long-standing practice of using maps to confirm the legitimacy of the British claim. This deficiency had to be made good. Newspapers and television provided more and greater detail of the islands, showing for example details of the Exclusion Zone declared by the British. For the British public, coming to terms with the possibility of a war, this was particularly vital. Maps ensured that the islands were no longer an unknown place, but real territory with settlements and a 'capital' Stanley. Their very remoteness, which might be expected to work against fighting a war for their possession, emphasised the importance of the Royal Navy in projecting British military power, as it had done since the eighteenth century. Now *The Times* turned to William Shakespeare for inspiration. No man was an island. These words were appropriate 'for every Briton, for every islander, for every man and woman anywhere in the world menaced by the forces of tyranny'.

This stirring appeal did not meet with universal approval, not even amongst the readers of *The Times*: on 8 April a reader described it as 'jingoistic claptrap' and as viewing with equanimity the death of British, Argentines and Falkland Islanders. It was yet to be demonstrated that *The Times* spoke for England – let alone the whole United Kingdom. Many – perhaps most – people in Britain did not even know where the Falkland Islands were: random interviews in the street produced uncertain responses, such as that the Islands were somewhere in the 'North'; 'off the coast of Scotland'; 'near France'; and 'something to do with Denmark'. [44] When the Task Force set out for its far away destination, there were many diplomatic obstacles as well as opportunities with which the War Cabinet must cope. For as Michael Mates put it, almost prophetically, on 7 April: 'On Friday morning had we, in the fog of war, caused the first casualties, if 1,000 Argentines had been killed and if their aircraft carrier had been sunk, I wonder what our friends' attitude to us would have been and what the international voices would have said. Some people may say that they do not care. That is the sort of remark that we would have lived to regret through the difficult days and weeks ahead'. [114, 7 April 1982, col. 1002]

3
The Armed Forces

The British and Argentine army, navy and air force which would be the instrument of diplomacy and, if need be, of war, reflected the different characters of their societies and functioned in different ways. As Professor Jeremy Black has said, war is inevitably concerned with other sets of attitudes: above all with confronting and justifying (or criticising) loss, suffering, the risk of pain and death. And with attitudes towards hierarchy, obedience, and discipline and towards the readiness to serve 'all of which are crucial to military capability'. [21, p. 1] The justification of war with Argentine over the Falklands had got off to a good start with the debate in the House of Commons on 3 April; and, despite claims about the decline of parliament, the role of the Commons in defining the British case, and the pleasing, if not complete, degree of success for British diplomacy at the United Nations, gave the British Government much cause for satisfaction. Nonetheless, the Government could not take this for granted; nor could it neglect the vital need to try to shape and mould the public at large. Thus it was not the British armed forces alone that would be engaged in the crisis, and perhaps in fighting; the Ministry of Defence must play its part also. But, whatever the undoubted importance of the propaganda war, and despite the fact that it was politics that constituted the shaft of the spear, the tip must be sufficiently sharp to fulfil the military function.

For both Argentina and the United Kingdom, the armed forces were an essential part of their history and identity. The two world wars in the twentieth century had transformed the British Army, in particular, from a small, professional force, regarded with some suspicion by the public because of the tendency of the common soldier to misbehave, especially in public, to a citizen army, one that drew its strength and inspiration from its roots in the nation. The end of universal military conscription in 1958 resulted in the army reverting to its smaller size and professional character; but it still retained its role as a central and enduring part of the British national tradition. It rarely exercised any function in domestic politics, except if it were deployed in maintaining essential services during industrial disputes; but since 1969 it had been playing a key, and at times controversial role in counter-terrorist operations in Northern Ireland. Despite the fact that this role, and other engagements in complex and at time ambiguous conflicts might be said to reflect the 'new wars' in which it might be involved, the army still held to its belief that this was not 'real' soldiering. Colour Sergeant Ian Bailey of the third battalion Parachute Regiment, recalled that, on hearing about the preparations being made to create the Task Force,

> People on leave, people who didn't really have a job, who were in limbo, between jobs, were turning up and saying, 'now do you need anybody to do this'. And, officers, senior officers, willing to be platoon commanders. Nobody wanted to miss this, if something did happen. This was perhaps the only time in your whole career you might do something that you've actually trained for.

Julian Thompson wrote that 'among one and all was the feeling of intense satisfaction that there was a job to do and pride that they had been chosen to do it. The members of this close-knit family, with their different cap badges in their green berets, their expertise well tried on many an exercise, got down to apply those skills in getting the Brigade off to fight'. [22, p. 50]

The fact that the British Army (including the Parachute Regiment) had done many things in Northern Ireland that, arguably, they had trained for, seemed to pale when set beside the chance of fighting a regular army in a 'real' war. Patrick Bishop observed a paradoxical side to the British soldier: he and his commanders 'wanted to be tested'. They had no particular animosity towards the Argentines, and did not seem to feel particularly strongly about the Falklands dispute. Everyone agreed that a peaceful outcome would be for the best; but 'every time it appeared that diplomacy might be working, the initial relief was quickly replaced by a sense of disappointment and frustration that the force might be turning for home without seeing the action they had trained so hard for'. [57]

The units deployed in the Falklands were from some of the elite regiments of the army: the Royal Marines of 40 and 42 Commando (to which another Commando unit was later added); the 3rd Battalion of the Parachute Regiment; and men of the Royal Artillery, Royal Engineers and Horse and Life Guards, the latter with Scimitar and

Scorpion light tanks. They were later reinforced by men of the 5th Infantry Brigade: the 2nd Battalion Scots Guards, 1st Battalion Welsh Guards, 1st Battalion 7th Gurkha Rifles and their supporting units. The SAS played a vital role in probing the enemy's defences and conveying intelligence to the Task Force. One bold enterprise was the landing of a Sea King helicopter in Argentina on 17 April, with eight SAS soldiers, who relayed information until the Argentine surrender. They were then taken off by submarine. The Sea King was unable to return to HMS *Invincible* because of bad weather and landed in Chile, where it was destroyed by its crew (31, p. 169). Both the official explanation, that it had lost its way, and the tantalising rumour that the SAS has decided to make for Chile without carrying out their mission (184, pp. 171–3) were wrong.

The Argentine Army occupied a strange position in Argentine politics and society. It had been the instrument of Government repression of political opposition, and had been responsible for some of the most illegal and cruel acts of violence against Argentine citizens. But this made it believe all the more that it was the saviour of the nation. In their own minds, the soldiers identified themselves with national freedom and national identity; and this was no spurious claim, for the bulk of public opinion in Argentine likewise saw the army in this light. When the military invaded the Falklands to claim Argentina's 'little sisters', any doubts about its recent activities in suppressing political dissent were quickly forgotten. [32, pp. 178–9] Moreover, this was an army that still drew the bulk of its recruits from military conscription. It had much glory to gain, but also much face to lose, if it performed well or badly. Its performance would resonate deeply into the public mind; and if it failed, then not only the army, but the military junta that governed Argentine would be deeply, perhaps fatally, compromised.

The use by Argentina of her conscript soldiers has deeply influenced the British image of their enemy. Lieutenant Clive Dytor, of 45 Commando, described how the Argentine Marines (generally considered her best troops) had stationed themselves behind the conscripts to make sure that they did not run away from the front. And while the Argentine Marines were 'professional, and fought to the death', the conscripts were 'frightened and tired and wanted to go home'. [57] John Nott declared that the British were lucky with their enemy: 'The truth is that the Argentinian generals were dreadful. The conscripts were appallingly fed, the officers lounged around while the men froze in the trenches. Morale was non-existent'. [171] Thus the criticism of the Argentine Army was expanded to give a picture of what might be called the Northern European image of a Southern European army (worse still, of a South American one): lacking in the essentials of dedicated and efficient command, disorganised, almost a rabble.

This might be seen as helpful to the Argentine Army's British opponents, steeped in their regimental traditions, proud of their professionalism. The danger was that this might lead the British to underestimate their foe: a fault as dangerous as exaggerating their enemy's capacity. The assessment of the Argentine Army offered by the one British journalist who remained in Argentina during the whole of the Falklands crisis provides a deeper analysis. Jimmy Burns noted that Argentina's military effort was given an uncertain start by her desire not to land too powerful a military force on the Islands. The Junta's original plan was to deploy only a token military presence; this was abandoned in favour of a build-up of over 12,000 troops. [32, pp. 343–4] But the military command structure was flawed. General Mario Benjamino Menendez had agreed to go to the Falklands as military governor, but within days of his arrival he was also fulfilling the role of commander-in-chief of the Argentine forces. His military experience was limited to counter-subversion within Argentina, and then as a staff officer teaching in a military academy. He felt that he should depend on instructions from Buenos Aires, and, in default of any such instructions, he was influenced by one of his brigade commanders (General Oscar Joffre, who was older than Menendez) and who recommended that the military concentrate its defence on Stanley. Thus the Argentine Army would forfeit its great advantage, that of a mobile, flexible defence. Menendez was also troubled by rivalry between the three arms, the army, navy and air force: [32, pp. 343–6] but this was a phenomenon not unfamiliar to the British Army and its commanders, and was to resurface in their Falklands campaign too.

The quality of the Argentine Army was, according to most authorities, compromised by its conscripted element. Conscripts served a tour of duty of only one year; they lacked the effect of thorough training, discipline and (in that ever-present phrase) professionalism. There did appear also to be a considerable gap between the officers and their men; officers did not look to their troops' welfare in the way that the British Army insisted they do. [179, pp. 110–11] The conscripts were young – between 19 and 20 years of age – but were not significantly different in their age from the British soldiers. One of the myths that arose from the war was that the Argentine Army contained 15 year-old soldiers; but the most recent call-up category was one consisting of

19 year-olds of the 1962 register. [84, pp. 12–13] They were ill-equipped to encounter the climate on the Falklands; and certainly elements of the British forces, notably the Royal Marines, conducted frequent exercises in extreme weather as part of their NATO training. Some Argentine conscripts appear not to have known quite where they were. 'I had a rough idea that my position was four or five kilometres from Puerto Argentina (Stanley), but beyond that I wouldn't even guess…'. The command system, from the top down, was not calculated to raise the morale of the Argentine soldier. Punishment for dereliction of duty, or other misdeeds, was severe and even brutal. [32, pp. 347–50] Moreover, the character of the Army was not merely compromised by its conscript elements; as Burns pointed out, the Argentine armed forces were deeply influenced and corrupted by their involvement in Argentine politics. Internal political duties (to use a neutral phase) in the 1970s helped politicise the Army in particular, and affected its promotion system. [32, p. 346]

But these observations and criticisms, (though well-founded) were made after the Argentine defeat in the Falklands War; victory – or at any rate a few serious defeats inflicted on the British – would no doubt have elicited a different assessment. One authority has noted that there was no stark difference between conscript and 'regular' units of the Argentine Army; and that all units, apart from certain small elites, were of mixed composition, which is normally the case in any army based on national service. The same criticism would have applied to the British Army in the period 1939–57. Conscript units posted to the Falklands were brought up to strength by hasty cross-posting from other regiments, and some had a higher proportion of men with very little time in uniform than the 'normal average of roughly 25 per cent'. [84, pp. 12–13] This cross-posting reduced the cohesion and even the morale of the Argentine forces; and this helps explain why some officers did not seem to know who they had under their command, let alone who had survived any battle. [84, p. 24] The composition of the initial landing force was changed, because the Junta had not envisaged that the British would do other than accept the fait accompli. The landing force consisted of the 2nd Fleet Marine Force, spearheaded by special forces of Marine Commando Company 601. The British response meant that Argentina had to reinforce its garrison on the Falklands, and General Galtieri, concerned that there were not enough troops to defend the whole territory, sent on his own initiative a full brigade, substituting numbers for quality, and increasing his own logistical difficulties, especially in keeping his troops sufficiently fed. [90, pp. 145–6] General Menendez was uncertain about how many men he had under his command at the time of the Argentine surrender, which reflected this hurried reinforcement of his garrison. [84, p. 24]

The Argentine Army has also suffered in its reputation from the pictorial record of its appearance. Denis Blakeway's authoritative account of the crisis carries a picture of surrendered Argentine troops, huddled together in their ungainly winter outfits, as does Martin Middlebrook's excellent study of the Argentine forces in the war. Another expert compilation work, *Battle for the Falklands*, shows 'some of the 1,200 Argentine prisoners taken at Goose Green in their inferior 'winter parkas, made in Israel'. [84, p. 14] Such photographs contrasted with the magnificently uniformed military Junta, emphasising the discrepancy between Argentine military ambitions and illusions, and the reality of the miserable and defeated 'conscript' army. They also contrasted with the tough, battle-hardened British commandos and paratroops whose character was formed by two formidable elements in their training and attitude to war: ferocity and discipline. It was these, as much as tactical skills, that enabled them to win the harsh and brutal close quarter fights at Goose Green, Mount Longdon and the other Falkland battlefields. One of 2 Para's company commanders caught the mood: 'It's not going to be easy and that's why we were chosen…because we're Paras and they know we're going to get stuck in. If we hit these bastards hard enough, make no mistake, they'll fold'. [54, p. 111]

A professional and voluntary army had the advantage over this mixture of conscripts and professionals. But the Argentine Army on the Falklands was by no means destined to fail in this its first taste of regular warfare. British soldiers made much of their disgust at the Argentine officers' attitude to their men. Two Argentine critics noted the 'highly bureaucratic nature of the Argentine military apparatus' that 'led a generation of officers with an inflexible command structure, slaves to routine and parade ground discipline and lovers of needless paperwork'. They argued that this was significant for 'the lack of cohesion, initiative and fighting morale of their subordinates'. [55, pp. 102–3] On Mount Harriet one authority claimed that the officers and NCOs 'tried to shoot those among their soldiers who tried to escape or surrender'. [32, p. 387] But such drastic action was not absent from the British Army's experience, certainly in the Great War. [110, p. 199]

Then there was the contrast between the over-blown military rhetoric of the Argentine Commander, General Menendez, and the reality of war. Menendez on 1 June issued a proclamation to his troops in which he declared that the hour of the 'definitive battle' had arrived. Each man must understand his duty and 'fight with the courage and heroism that has always characterised him'. 'We have taken on the sacred duty of converting the personal sacrifice of our fallen comrades into a page of Argentine glory, and we will not allow their heroism to be in vain...To Arms! To Arms! To the Battle!' [32, p. 380] This language was bombastic; but it was not so far from the call made by Field Marshal Haig in April 1918 when he urged his soldiers to 'fight it out!' 'Every position must be held to the last man: there must be no retirement. With our backs to the wall, and believing in the justice of our cause, each one of us must fight to the end. The safety of our homes and the freedom of mankind alike depend on the conduct of each one of us at this critical moment'. [110, p. 201] An army that had engaged almost continuously in fighting since 1919 was more likely to have abandoned such florid and heroic language in the light of experience. Another incident, when the Argentine commander at Goose Green, Air Vice-Commodore Wilson Pedrozo asked as a condition of surrendering that he should have the opportunity to parade and address his men seemed at odds with British military practice; [84, p. 22] but it was a not unreasonable response of a military commander to reassure his defeated forces that they had fought well, and should feel no sense of disgrace.

The Argentine strategic position on the Falklands compounded any weaknesses in General Menendez's forces. When it seemed possible (though not yet likely) that Argentina would have to fight to retain the Falklands, the Junta had to rethink its original plan of a bloodless coup and a withdrawal of the bulk of its armed forces. Now Menendez and Joffre met to draw up a response. They had to work out, in so far as they could, their enemy's strengths and weaknesses. They believed that the British possessed enough helicopters to give them 'all the options'. The main British landing was anticipated to be on the beaches south and south-east of Stanley; but there could be diversionary landings, or even a main landing, at Uranie Beach on Berkeley Sound 12 miles north-west of Stanley. [152, pp. 54–5] Menendez had to defend everything, and might end up defending nothing. Moreover, he might not have to defend anything, if (as the Junta anticipated) the British and Argentina would end the crisis by a negotiated settlement favourable to Argentina. The decision, to retain the main Argentine forces around Stanley, was in a sense forced on him by his belief that he could not possibly anticipate all the landing places that the British might choose;

and by the fact that they might not land at all. General Galtieri's decision to reinforce Menendez with a full brigade was welcome, but it was, Menendez claimed, 'the start of a lot of new problems, fundamentally logistic problems. One regiment (about 600 men) would have been a useful reserve. It would have given us a good helicopter-borne force to control the outer sectors'. [152, p. 56] Still, in a defensive strategy, weight of numbers could not be discounted. The Argentine forces on the Falklands comprised some 13,000 troops, three quarters of which were in the Stanley area, a force almost twice as large as the landing units of the British Task Force, though its 7,300 men were soon to be reinforced by another 3,200 troops. [152, p. 63]

Argentine preparations were influenced by some wishful, but understandable, thinking. Menendez and Joffre concluded that a direct assault by the British would be too costly in lives; and that an indirect approach would be too slow, as the United States and the USSR would seek to prevent or stop the fighting through the use of political pressure. But their assessment of the enemy's pre-landing operations was not far off the mark:

> Amphibious reconnaissance by the SBS landed from one or more submarines ahead of the main Task Force. Isolation of the zone selected for the amphibious assault by the Task Force, and establishment of air superiority over the zone.
> Clearing of any minefield laid on the stretch of coast selected for the landing.
> Final reconnaissance by the SBS and eventually by the SAS.
> Special operations by members of the SBS and SAS, especially in the night before the principal amphibious landing. [84, p. 14]

Menendez placed his troops in intelligent positions: Pebble Island and Fox Bay in West Falkland (self-contained garrisons); the spine of high ground running from San Carlos through Mount Usborne, Wickham Heights, and eastwards to Mount Challenger and Mount Kent (picketed with observations posts and good radio communications with Stanley). When they saw major movements by the enemy, or landings, they would call in, and the middle reserve would be lifted by helicopter to seal off a landing or to launch a counter-attack. [84, p. 14] But here a good plan would be undermined by insufficient resources: Menendez had only 26 helicopters (four of which he lost in an SAS guided air-strike on 20 May) a serious deficiency if the idea of mobile action or of 'harassing' the enemy was to be realised. [152, p. 64] Thus he ran the risk of losing the initiative and allowing the enemy to dictate the general course of operations; and his overall numerical superiority might be lost, or at least reduced, in particular encounters with the British forces. Moreover, the long delay between the British landings at San Carlos and their break-out from the beachhead (which irritated the War Cabinet) worked against the Argentine strategy of concentrating their defences around Stanley. The Argentine soldiers spent a long time waiting in tents, trenches or shelters made of stone and turf. 'Many of these units will never forget the cold, the wet, waterlogged trenches and their hunger and fatigue during the long wait'. [152, p. 220]

The British Army was, rightly, commended for its professionalism, which meant that the men were well led, that the other ranks understood what they had to do, and that they could sustain their morale and their determination in the face of the violence and shock of battle. Not all of them were sufficiently battle-ready, however; Max Hastings, no critic of the British Army, was reluctant to be drawn by his interrogators during the Franks Commission's gathering of evidence on his comment that the Scots Guards were less than ready for the campaign [115, paras. 695–9] (though this was attributed by other commentators to their over-hasty assignment from ceremonial to full military duties). The two Guards battalions were hastily despatched to Sennybridge in South Wales to bring them up to 'peak efficiency', using live ammunition and training in live air attacks. [22, pp. 171–3] Even the best prepared soldiers could fail. This was shown in the British recapture of South Georgia, which had to be temporarily abandoned because of severe weather, and which cost two helicopters which crashed in their attempt to lift SAS soldiers who were suffering from exposure. [184, pp. 155–7] The disaster that befell the Welsh Guards at Bluff Cove, when Argentine jets bombed the LSL *Sir Galahad*, killing 50 men and injuring 46, many of them with severe burns, was attributed to the refusal of their commander to accept the advice of the Royal Navy Officer and disembark his men; a refusal based on the convention that troops must not be separated from their kit, but one that, in this case, proved disastrous. [22, pp. 145–6]

These, and other incidents, were part of the confusion and chance of war; they did not reflect on the character or performance of the British Army in the Falklands. But they revealed that those officers who believed that this would be a 'hazardous enterprise', that their men would 'experience danger, physical adversity, disappointment and loneliness', [216, p. 19] and that, in the words of Brigadier Julian Thompson, 'this will be no picnic', [215, p. 97] were right not to underestimate their enemy, and equally important, the physical conditions that would determine the shape and to a large degree the outcome of this campaign, as they did all military enterprises.

The Falklands campaign was a combined operation; and it revealed that, while individual bravery and resolution counted for much, yet the failure of one or more of the three arms of the service could mean the failure of the whole campaign. As David Brown observed, the main defences of the Islands against a British attempt at repossession were the Argentine Navy and Air Force; in combination, they alone could inflict such attrition on the Royal Navy that landings would have to be abandoned, before or after they had been attempted. [31, p. 113] The Royal Navy was regarded by its admirers as more than a simple branch of service; in the words of one of its historians, the Navy was 'one of Britain's prime assets…besides its intrinsic worth, the Navy is a hardy and vivid fibre in the cloth of the history and traditions of the nation.' [173, p. 207] The Commander-in-Chief of the Task Force echoed this belief. The Royal Naval College was built 'not only as a place of learning and training, but also as a symbol of British sea power'. Its position, looming over the river Dart, beyond which were the waters of the English Channel ('the waters of Jervis and Hood, of Hawke and Rodney, of Hood and Nelson, of Fisher and Jellicoe…') was carefully chosen. 'Those are the kinds of men who have always commanded the Fleets of the Royal Navy, and the kind of men you should try to emulate'. [236, p. 26]

This was a stirring account; and the self-belief of the Royal Navy was not to be underestimated in assessing its character and readiness for war. As one naval officer put it, the British naval tradition was based 'not upon administrative machinery but upon humanity'. When on 21 May, after some determined Argentine air attacks, he called his ship's company together to remind them of the words of Admiral Cunningham after the Navy had suffered very heavy losses in the Mediterranean in the Second World War: 'It takes three hundred years to build a tradition but only three to build a ship'. He told his ship's company that they were 'now part of that tradition'. [234, pp. 211, 215]

This was not a view universally accepted. Chief Petty Officer Arthur Gould, on HMS *Arrow*, wrote to his wife on 29 May that

> This little escapade in the South Atlantic is costing us dearly and the morale of the young lads has taken some blows, not only the young

lads come to that, a lot of the senior ratings are beginning to question things. Our Admiral, safe out of the line of fire on the *Hermes*, seems to be trying to get all of the existing frigates and destroyers sunk or damaged, and he is succeeding. [234, p. 181]

Chief Petty Officer Gould had other uncomplimentary remarks to make about his superior officers; [234, p. 184] but this view is contradicted by that of a sailor on *Hermes*, who said that 'there is no privilege or place for standing back and observing others. Everyone is, literally, in the "same boat". What affects one affects all'. There was a 'band of colleagueship that has been forged out of the heat of our corporate experience together in this floating metal community'. There was a 'common sense of purpose and direction'. [234, p. 186] But Mike Till, who was killed when HMS *Sheffield* was struck by an Exocet missile, wrote to his wife on 7 April that his morale was 'at rock bottom'. [128]

No firm generalisation can be made about the Navy's morale when tested in battle on the basis of a few examples. It is safe to conclude that it remained high, though the loss of HMS *Sheffield* on 4 May shocked Admiral Woodward, because it was the 'first Royal Navy ship to be hit by an enemy missile since the Second World War. Almost forty years on'. [236, p. 14] There were two other main considerations about which the Navy felt uneasy. One was put bluntly by an Admiral: 'The Royal Navy, continually run down since 1945, was but a shadow of its former glory, when it had equalled the combat fleets of the rest of the world combined'. [74, p. 7] This was of course a longing for a happier age, when Britannia did indeed rule the waves. But it expressed, albeit extravagantly, certain shortcomings in the Navy. One of the most serious was technological. The Navy attempted to maintain a radar picket screen about 220 kilometres from the main Task Force, but no ship had been designed for duty as a radar picket or 'for survivability against multiple air and/or air-to-surface missile attacks in such a role'. Ships sometimes failed to detect either Argentine radar scanning or Exocet lock-ons. The radar range of ships was confined to 30–35 nautical miles of coverage at low altitudes under any conditions because of the earth's curvature; but they also had to combine air surveillance and warning with air and missile defence. Their radar gave them inadequate time in which to react. 'Ships lacked fully automatic and integrated fire control'. [52, pp. 275–6]

The second main concern was that the 1981 Defence Review was specifically designed to reduce the Navy to an anti-submarine force operating on the eastern half of the North Atlantic sea route. It had two anti-submarine aircraft carriers, 16 destroyers, 44 frigates, and 31 submarines, of which about 12 frigates and a similar number of submarines were either undergoing extensive refits or were 'moth-balled' in reserve, requiring several months work for re-activation. [74, p. 7] Now the Navy had to undertake a task for which the 1981 Review had not intended. Fortunately, the cuts proposed in that review had not yet been implemented, for they included the disposal of the Navy's two amphibious assault ships. As it was, the Navy could put together an impressive Task Force, especially the two aircraft carriers, *Hermes* and *Invincible*, though in so doing she was obliged to strip 'her naval commitment to NATO to the bone in the process'. [74, p. 32] The insufficient numbers of 'troop and military transport lift capacity' required the Navy to take up ships from trade (STUFT), the first of which was the P & O flagship *Canberra*. The Falklands crisis was in another sense a great opportunity for the Royal Navy to demonstrate its versatility as well as its indispensability; but its technological defects were real. An if one of the aircraft carriers were seriously damaged or sunk, then the whole enterprise would be, to say the least, in jeopardy. It was for this reason that Admiral Woodward, commander-in-chief of the Task Force, must endure criticism that he had placed his carriers at a safe distance from the immediate combat zone.

The Argentine Navy has not come under the same critical scrutiny as the Army. Yet its political role in the Junta that took power in March 1976 was significant: of the six military posts in the eight-man Cabinet the Navy occupied the Ministries of Foreign Affairs and Social Affairs (the Army took the Ministries of the Interior and Labour; the Air Force got Justice and Defence). In Buenos Aires the Navy controlled the port and Customs. [32, p. 84] It was a naval man, Rear Admiral Oscar Montes who, as Minister for Foreign Affairs, inaugurated in 1978 a period of increasingly tense diplomatic brinkmanship. [32, p. 114] The confrontation with Chile, which nearly brought the two nations to war at Christmas, 1978, led to the Navy ordering six submarines and four destroyers from West Germany and two coastal patrol boats from Israel. [32, p. 90] In June 1982 it was due to receive a delivery of 14 Super Entendards and their accompanying Exocet missiles. [32, p. 144] The Argentine Navy had been the 'premier navy in Latin America since it had won a naval arms race with Chile at the turn of the century', but had been 'nudged into second place' by Brazil during the late 1960s. But it remained formidable, and had 'actually narrowed the gap between itself and the Royal Navy due to the latter's decline'. In April 1981 it included one aircraft carrier, one cruiser, eight destroyers, five frigates and four submarines, with a further four destroyers, six frigates and six submarines under construction. [74, pp. 7–8]

The Navy played its part in domestic political repression. Its Mechanical School became a secret detention camp after the 1976 coup: two young naval officers who later served in the Falklands War were among those who formed a special Task Force to help gather intelligence, arrest suspects and participate in their torture and execution. The Navy head, Admiral Massera, was a significant influence in organising the Navy's political/military counter-subversion campaign. As it happened, relations between the British and Argentine navies were cordial, with junior officers enjoying the benefit of renewed military training facilities under the Thatcher Government. [32, p. 105]

The politicisation of the senior Naval commanders seems to have less imprint on the character of that branch of the service than it did on the Army. But its brief Falklands War began with an ill-directed foray which ended with the sinking of the *General Belgrano*, built in 1936 and now having the distinction of being the last survivor of the Japanese attack on Pearl Harbour. It was acquired by Argentina in 1951, and was one of the few armoured ships still afloat. [74, p. 12] Described as 'an ancient ship of very limited military potential in conditions of modern warfare', [74, pp. 21–2] it was despatched to threaten the British Task Force; but its loss seems to have blunted the entire Argentine naval effort. The Argentine Navy's failure to devise and display a more enterprising spirit is hard to understand; but it was a relief to Admiral Woodward, whose main threat, the Argentine Air Force, was not so readily deterred.

The Argentine Air Force gained the admiration even – or perhaps especially – of its enemies. Its pilots were brave, and enterprising, if not always capable of making the best use of their weapons. Luckily for the British, the Argentine Air Force was not as well equipped as it might have been. It had benefited from the free spending policy of the late 1970s, when Argentina anticipated a war with Chile over the Beagle Channel dispute; and it was one of the strongest in Latin America, capable of mobilising 120–180 combat aircraft and plentiful supplies of ammunition, bombs and rockets. Argentina's Navy also had an air arm, which (had the British effort to market its products succeeded) would have been equipped with Sea Harriers. Instead, Argentina purchased some 14 Dassault-Breguet Super Etendard attack aircraft, to be armed with AM-34 Exocet anti-shipping missiles. Only five of these had been delivered by the start of hostilities with Britain. [74, pp. 5–6]

These figures must be scaled down. The number of usable combat aircraft was less than the roll call suggested: for example, the Argentine Air Force had only 11, not 16, Mirage single-seat fighters. The total of attack aircraft that were combat ready was about 97; Argentine sources put the number at 82, but to these were added the Naval Air arm's 11 Skyhawks and five Super Etendards. [75, p. 26] This still left the main British combat airplane, the Sea Harrier, outnumbered by more than 6:1, but of the aircraft able to reach the Falklands, only a small number were crewed by men fully trained to attack ships. The Air Force fighter-bomber and bomber units were trained mainly to support a land battle against a neighbour. The pilots of the small Naval air arm were trained in the specialised task of attacking warships in the open seas. The Super Etendards with their Exocet missiles were formidable, but other aircraft had only old fashioned bombs and unguided rockets. The Super Etendard pilots had only about 45 hours basic training: 'We did no night flying training and we flew no tactical training missions'. Nonetheless, it was fortunate for the British that the French President Mitterand declared his country's support for the United Kingdom and placed a rigid embargo on the delivery of military supplies or expertise to Argentina. This greatly angered the Argentine Commander Jurge Colombo, who complained that one of the terms of the contract with France was that she should supply technical assistance to set up the computer systems to ensure the correct functioning of the aircraft and Missile system. [75, pp. 26–7] Two analysts of the Argentine forces identified her weaknesses as follows: a high-level politico-military system that operated with a highly politicised view of reality; an army system in the Falklands with poor leadership and organisation and weak tactical and theatre communications; a navy system 'unsuited in scale and sophistication for fleet operations'; and an air force that was 'highly professional but lacked the assets and technology to provide sensor and communications coverage for the Falklands'. [52, pp. 281–2] This seems a fair summary; but it must not obscure the fact that the British never gained what they most needed to guarantee the success of their enterprise: control and mastery of the air.

The air war was not a single, decisive battle; it was more demanding than that. The Argentine Air Force had to attack surface vessels, and, after the British landed, provide their own forces with protection against the enemy, and attack that enemy as the opportunity offered. For the British, the task was similar, but they also had the difficult task of assisting and defending the surface fleet, hindering the enemy as they attacked that fleet, and supporting the ground troops. They must also try to disrupt the Argentine use of the Stanley airstrip by bombing. In this sense the air war was one of attrition; skilful pilots must be ready to suffer not only the danger of combat, but the exhausting experience of flying numerous sorties. This did not appeal to the temperament of Commander Nigel 'Sharky' Ward, 'leader of the swashbuckling crew of Harrier pilots', who 'exudes confidence', as *The Times* report put it. 'All of us knew we were going to fight, or we hoped we were going to fight'. Commander Ward 'issued a challenge to the Argentine pilots to meet (his team) anywhere in the skies'. [207, 12 April 1982] This picture of skilful and brave gladiators engaged in a decisive battle, almost in single combat, was always part of the tradition of war in the air; but it missed the point of the main purpose of the British air contribution, which must be to gain mastery of the skies so that the surface vessels and the ground troops would be protected from the enemy. The fate of the entire Operation Corporate lay with the fleet, and especially with the aircraft carriers.

British air cover was hampered by several shortcomings. The Sea Harrier's AIM-9L missile was able to home in on the target aircraft from almost any aspect 'and even had a limited head-on capacity'; [75, p. 22] but it had not performed as well in action as its manufacturers claimed. The Task Force had no early warning aircraft to alert it to the approach of low flying raiders. There would, initially, be no long range reconnaissance cover once the ships had passed beyond the operational radius of the Royal Air Force Nimrod patrol aircraft based on Ascension Island. The Sea Harrier squadrons were not fully trained for ground attack missions, and had only unguided rockets with which to attack enemy warships. Initially, none of these aircraft had the chaff or infra-red decoy defences necessary for operations against modern gun and missile systems. The transport helicopter force had only sufficient lifting capacity to support landings on the Falklands by small raiding parties. [75, p. 22] though this deficit was remedied by reinforcing the helicopter fleet with three new squadrons (No. 825 with Sea Kings, and Nos. 847 and 848 with Wessex helicopters); though this augmentation was lost with the sinking of the Atlantic Conveyor at a crucial stage of the campaign.

Steps were taken to remedy at least some of these defects. The Royal Air Force GR3's operational capacity was enhanced by altering the aircraft to enable it to carry and launch Sidewinder air-to-air missiles. This required a few weeks of intensive work, and the retraining of pilots for their role in air-to-air combat. [75, pp. 23–4]

Once again improvisation was to compensate for lack of readiness. The Sea Harrier squadrons began to arrive on 2 April, with eight aircraft flown in on to the carrier *Hermes* in the Portsmouth dockyard. Three more arrived on 4 April, and eight went to *Invincible* the same day. Originally, these squadrons had only five aircraft each, but by absorbing the headquarters training squadron, calling forward reserve aircraft, and adding a trial aircraft from the experimental establishment at Boscombe Down, a total of 20 fighters was assembled. Maintenance crews were gathered together, but such was the shortage of pilots that, 'in spite of the attachment of seven fully-mobilised Royal Air Force pilots, two pilots who were still undergoing operational flying were also taken along, to complete the course en route'. [31, p. 69]

But the British possessed one important advantage over the Argentine Air Force. Admiral Woodward placed his aircraft carrier group within easy flying range of the Falklands, but at the outer limit of Argentine fuel endurance. Thus, while Argentina never conceded command of the air, British planes were able to operate continuously over and around the Islands, while the Argentine first-line jets were only able to operate for limited periods, because the only hard runway on the Islands (at Stanley) was too short for the Mirages and Skyhawks to use, and so they had to operate from mainland airfields over 400 miles away: which placed the Falklands within operational range 'but only just'. This meant that the Argentine aircraft could spend only minutes over their target zone before fuel shortage compelled them to return to their base on the mainland. [179, pp. 8–9]

There was much to admire in the improvisation that enabled a large Task Force to be sent to the South Atlantic at very short notice. This continued down to the smallest scale. The Army discovered that its boots were unable to withstand the rigours of the wet and cold Falklands weather, and that their enemy had better night-fighting aids, and in some cases better weapons and superior electronic equipment. [84, p. 11] Some Marines wore civilian fell boots and waterproof legging; civilian rucksacks, 'which seem to have been bought up from a well-known chain of sports and working clothes suppliers at short notice' [84, p. 33] were also preferred to official army issue. The Scots Guards used the .50 calibre Browning M2 anti-aircraft machine gun, large quantities of which were bought from the United States in the early 1950s. [84. p. 35]

The Task Force set off from Southampton with that curious mixture of sentimentality, pride, sense of duty and vulgarity that seems to be inseparable from the British armed forces. Lieutenant Colonel Nick

Vaux of 42 Commando marched his men off to war under the final order: 'to the South Atlantic – Quick March', an arcane command that earned 'an astonishing wave of publicity'. [216, pp. 16–17] The popular song 'Sailing' (made into a hit by Rod Stewart) and Tim Rice and Andrew Lloyd Webber's 'Don't cry for me Argentina' accompanied the departure of the Task Force. [84, p. 10] One serviceman's wife's bra was removed by its owner and swung aboard the *Q.E.II* liner which was serving as a troopship. [84, p. 11] This might be taken as signifying 'separate gender roles', [167, p. 167] but it was perhaps an inevitable accompaniment to a British military expedition.

There were several factors influencing or even governing the performance of the Task Force, some common to most if not all military enterprises, some unique to the British armed forces as they were in 1982. The servicemen, their families and the British public and Government must be prepared to accept casualties, possibly significant ones. The Army, for its part, had suffered a steady, if gradual, series of losses in their counter-terrorist campaign in Northern Ireland. But, as Lieutenant Nick Vaux put it, in issuing his final orders to 42 Commando before the Mount Harriet battle, 'unlike in Northern Ireland where normally casualties take precedence over operations, for obvious reasons that cannot be so here'. [216, p. 165] In the Falklands, victory must be achieved, and as quickly as possible, given the long logistical trail, not to mention the political pressures to bring this war to a speedy conclusion. The Royal Navy was confident because, as Petty Officer Sam Bishop, serving on HMS *Antelope* put it, it 'was never beaten before, and when they hear us arriving they'll get out and I'll be home'. [19, p. 70] But it had not lost any ships since the Second World War, and would find itself having to adjust to this, for its officers and crews, unique experience.

Above all, there was what the great Prussian military thinker, Carl von Clausewitz, in his *On War* (drafted between 1818 and 1827) called 'friction'. Clausewitz compiled his classic work long before the coming of the technological revolution that changed the nature of war, but his words resonate. 'In war', he explained, 'everything is uncertain, and calculations have to be made with variable quantities'. There was the problem of gauging the enemy's intentions and reactions. There was the incalculable moral factor, 'with uncertainty in one scale, courage and self-sacrifice must be thrown into the other to correct the balance'. War was dangerous: so much so that no one who had not experienced it could conceive of what it was like. It was the realm of uncertainty and chance, but also suffering, confusion, exhaustion and fear, and all these elements combined to create what von Clausewitz called 'friction', which was the environment in which all military activity took place; 'everything in war is very simple, but the simplest thing is very difficult...Countless minor incidents – the kind you can never really foresee combine to lower the general level of performance, so that one always falls short of the intended goal...' The tendency for things to go wrong was compounded by other variables, such as the weather. It was 'friction' that distinguished real war from war on paper. [48, pp. 24, 25, 26]

The Falklands War would be one in which friction would insert itself into every operation, as the Task Force set off, guided by 'hastily photocopied pages taken from *Jane's Fighting Ships* and copies of private air-spotters' collections as the only current source of decent photographs of military aircraft taking off from obscure Argentine airfields' [118, p. 305] and with, as its Commander Amphibious Warfare put it, 'little idea of what lay ahead and even for what we should plan'. [46, p. 61]

4
Diplomacy and War

The echoes of a peaceful diplomatic settlement of the Falkland Islands crisis always rang in the ears of the British Government, however strong its resolution to restore British sovereignty; and that resolution was less strong in at least one member of the War Cabinet, Francis Pym, who had replaced Lord Carrington as Foreign Secretary. There was also the nagging question of proportionality; the question of what losses the British could sustain before the task of freeing some 1,800 islanders was accomplished (the War Cabinet had in mind the figure of 1,000 lives). As Professor Charles Townshend remarks in his history of the Anglo-Irish war of 1919–21, 'The Army is only the spear point; it is the shaft of the spear and the force behind it that drives the blow home'. [210, p. 206] Yet the spear point had, to some degree, a life, or at least a momentum of its own. This would be no 'war by timetable', yet the Task Force's own needs and priorities could play a significant role in the outcome of the crisis. The power of decision must lie with the Government; yet the decisions taken could hardly be divorced from the requirements of the Task Force. The Chief of the Defence Staff, was determined 'that we should not make the mistakes of Suez. The military must have a clear operational directive from ministers as to what they expected us to do, and we would carry it out'. Before he arrived at the first War Cabinet meeting he had a 'clear and concise objective typed out. It read in part, "to cause withdrawal of the Argentine forces and to restore British administration"', which he described as an 'execution of United Nations Resolution 502'. [96, pp. 163–4]

This would prevent the Task Force being placed in a false position; its objective was clear. But there were complications, which Mrs Thatcher touched on in her admission, made on Saturday 3 April, that 'I stress that I cannot foretell what orders the task force will receive as it proceeds. That will depend on the situation at the time'. She still had hopes that diplomatic efforts would succeed. [116, 3 April 1982, col. 637] There were four main difficulties confronting the commander of the Task Force: he had to 'wrest control of the sea from a fleet which, although admittedly smaller than his own, possessed equally powerful weapons and which, if handled with aggression and skill, had the capacity to inflict very serious loss'. He would have to establish air superiority in circumstances in which his first wave of 20 Harriers was outnumbered by ten to one. He would have to make an amphibious landing 'which might or might not be opposed'. He would have to maintain support for his ground troops until the invaders had been ejected. This would be a small-scale war; but it could nonetheless be a disastrous one. [179, pp. 10–11] Christopher Wain, the BBC's defence correspondent, wrote that a 'senior officer' who was 'in a position to know' had calculated that British casualties would be 25 per cent. [217] The historical precedents (had the Task Force Commander known about them) were discouraging. Expeditions to the Low Countries (1809), Buenos Aires (1806–7) and Gallipoli (1915) all revealed the pitfalls of combined operations, from poor co-operation between the different branches of the armed forces, to troublesome logistics, and bad weather. [25, pp. 9, 13–20, 91, 121–3; 100] These frictions of war would persist down to the most minute detail. Brigadier Thompson offers an example of the complex nature of just one episode: the initial landing of 40 Commando, which is the equivalent of an army infantry battalion, with 650 men organised in three rifle companies, a support company (with machine gun, mortars, assault engineers, snipers and Milan anti-tank missiles, and an HQ company:

> 8 Battery in Direct Support (including BC (Battery Commander) and FOO (Forward Observation Officers) parties.
> 3 Troop B Squadron Blues and Royals in Direct Support.
> 2 Scouts (Anti-Tank Guided Weapon/Reconnaissance Helicopters) in Direct support from first light.
> 2 Troop 59 Independent Commando Squadron Royal Engineers in support and under command for movement… [205, pp. 47–8]

Above all there was the simple fact that Argentina had, in her view, 'repossessed' the Falklands. She could afford to make many mistakes before their impact would be felt. But the British Task Force, on the end of a long logistical tail, could afford few, if any, errors. As one commander of the Parliamentary Army in the civil wars of the 1640s put it, if they beat the King 99 times, yet he would still be King; but if the King beat them once, they would all be hanged. One serious reverse, the loss of an aircraft carrier, the loss of a troopship, the repulse of a landing, would jeopardise the whole British enterprise.

The Argentine fait accompli also afforded them a diplomatic advantage. Resolution 502 was a setback. But the United States of America, the European Union, the United Nations itself would undoubtedly prefer a peaceful resolution of the crisis; and this might, in the eyes of these states and institutions, and the world, fall short of the complete restoration of British sovereignty. But if Britain declined such a settlement, falling short of her original objective, then she might be cast as the more intransigent party in the dispute.

The British War Cabinet must therefore walk a careful line between preparations for war and the search for peace. This is hardly a unique predicament in military and diplomatic history. But the distance that would be travelled by the Task Force, and its limited time available if force were to be used, put an unusual degree of pressure on the British. The first question facing the Task Force was how to beat the enemy; the first answer was to beat them by blockade, but this must not be called a blockade as it 'created problems under international law' and so the 'more neutral terminology' of an 'Exclusion Zone' was adopted. This Exclusion Zone around the Islands (a circle of 200 nautical miles from latitude 51+ 41' south and longitude 59 + 39' west) was declared on 7 April to come into force on 12 April. From its inception any Argentine warships found within the Zone would be treated as hostile, and were 'liable to be attacked by British forces'. [90, p. 248] When the British implementation of the Zone was met with an Argentine declaration of her own Exclusion Zone, Admiral Woodward reflected that it was 'impossible now to miss the confrontational nature of the lethal game the two sets of politicians were playing'. The belief that a landing on the Islands would be necessary quickly supplanted the original plan of 'planting' the Task Force as far south as possible ('just in case the diplomats negotiated a "freeze" on any further movements pending some other, larger settlement of the dispute'). [236, p. 82]

That a 'larger settlement' was possible concerned Admiral Woodward, who watched with anxiety the United States' representative, General Alexander Haig, as he set about the business of using shuttle diplomacy to resolve the crisis ('not much short of a disaster in the making…every day he kept everyone chatting was another day's delay to us, so far from the base support…'). [236, p. 83] Woodward's use of the word 'chatting' indicated his concern about shuttle diplomacy undermining the British military position; but it was one of the essences of modern diplomacy that states could not go to war as and when they pleased; and that 'chatting' was a way of breaking stalemates in international conflicts. Mediation was seen as in some cases the only way to take the bitter edge of crisis or war, and it was used (to the general approval of most) in attempting to resolve the Northern Ireland crisis in the 1990s. The central idea was to reduce the intensity of conflict by a mediator who would facilitate the making of concessions; this meant identifying a 'zone of potential agreement' between the contestants. The mediator could then try to move the disputants towards an outcome within that range. In this, saving face would be an important consideration. [109, pp. 266, 268]

The mediator would not necessarily be a completely neutral party; there might be significant interests of his own to pursue. The mediator might also have a particular relationship with one of the contending parties. This would cast the mediator in a role different in important respects from that of a facilitator. The facilitation approach would rule out this more involved dimension, and instead involve the facilitator in analysing the causes of conflict, acting inclusively and avoiding advocating specific solutions. The 'solution' would be derived from the contending parties themselves. [109, pp. 270–3]

The chief mediator in the Falkland Islands in the first three weeks of the dispute was General Haig. He was perhaps less than adroit in his methods, lacking the sure touch that is needed to reconcile antagonists; but he had, as he admitted, an agenda that was to a significant extent shaped by American interests; and these were to avoid war, avoid Britain fighting a war and losing, avoid a solution that would suggest that the use of unlawful force paid dividends, avoid a repetition of the crisis, and avoid the United States having to come down on one side or the other. Out of all these negatives must emerge a positive.

Haig's first proposals, made on 6 April, were that the British fleet should be diverted, that the Argentines should withdraw from the islands, and that a neutral peacekeeping force, drawn from Canada, the United States and two Latin American countries should be substituted. Negotiations could then take place. The British response was that negotiations could not begin until Argentine forces withdrew from the Islands and British administration was resumed. [90, pp. 166–7] There was another problem. And in many ways an equally serious one. Britain had from the first regarded and presented the question as a moral one; the House of Commons debate, the bulk of the Press, and above all the Prime Minister's own statements cast it in that mould. It would be hard to break the mould. But if Haig used moral, instead of studiously neutral diplomatic language, then he might jeopardise his whole mission. Yet if he did not use moral language, condemning the Argentine invasion, he would seem to be leaning towards the Argentine view of its actions: that they were not some kind of smash and grab raid, but a necessary (and indeed moral) act, one taken to end British perfidy. In the early days of his mission, Haig found Argentina prepared to accept joint administration; [90, pp. 168–9] but then, as later, the question was what the eventual outcome of that would be: British or Argentine sovereignty over the Falklands. Thus it was not only the immediate settlement that mattered to both sides, but the direction and above all destination of any such 'peace process'.

By 12 April Haig came up with specific proposals. These were that there should be a withdrawal of Argentine forces from the Islands, and that the British fleet should halt some 1,000 miles from the Falklands. Economic sanctions imposed on Argentina should end. The United Nations, the United States, Argentina and the United Kingdom should constitute an interim authority to maintain an agreement. There should be a continuation of traditional local administration with Argentine participation. There should be co-operation in development of the Islands. [36, p. 286] And that there should be a framework for negotiation of a final settlement, taking into account the wishes of both sides in the conflict and of the inhabitants of the Islands. Mrs Thatcher in her memoirs described these proposals as 'full of holes', but admitted that they also had 'some attractions'. [203, pp. 194–5] But these attractions were the kind that she identified as most helpful to the fundamental British desire to restore their control of the Islands: if Argentine forces could be got off the Falklands, by conceding what 'seemed a fairly powerless commission, very limited Argentine representation on each council (the executive and legislative councils) drawn from local residents and not nominated by the Junta – and an Argentine flag flown alongside others at Headquarters there would be something to be said for these ideas'. But on 'closer inspection' there were difficulties: what security could be given for the Islanders after the interim period? Argentina would remain close to the Islands, but a British withdrawal to 'normal areas' could be damaging to Britain's position. Where would the British forces be? There was nothing to make it clear that the Islanders' wishes were 'paramount' in the final negotiations. [203, pp. 194–5]

These were significant doubts; equally significant was the question of who would make the first move. General Haig told Mrs Thatcher that 'President Galtieri would not survive if after the Argentinians had committed themselves to withdrawing from the Falkland Islands in two weeks the British newspapers continued to report that the Task Force was proceeding south'. Mrs Thatcher was justified in replying that 'I would not survive in the House of Commons if I stopped the Task Force before Argentine withdrawal had been completed...I was ready to let the troop ships proceed more slowly once an agreement had been signed. But the main Task Force must maintain its progress towards the Falkland Islands'. [203, pp. 197]

This consideration was not unusual in diplomatic negotiations, and it was in essence a simple, but compelling one. If two governments were to make a mutual exchange, there must come a point where one of them possessed the advantage, unless a third party existed who could compel an even and equal arrangement. The simple analogy of two small boys, one with a packet of sweets, the other with ten pence, who wish to swap, but know that at some stage one of them will hold in his hand both sweets and money, is not inappropriate: some guarantor would be required to ensure that the exchange is completed fairly. Neither the Argentine nor the British Governments trusted each other; but neither were they sure that the United States was willing to play the part of the completely honest broker, for each Government knew that the United States had a significant self-interest in the outcome, and Britain was as worried about the 'Latino' influence in the American administration as Argentina was encouraged by it.

And then there was the military dimension. Force, or the threat of force, must surely be useful in weakening the resolve of the enemy. As Mrs Thatcher put it in the House of Commons on 14 April, diplomatic efforts were more likely to succeed if backed by military strength. [114, 14 April 1982, col. 1147] This worked both ways. Argentina was in possession of the Islands; this gave her the upper hand, for the moment. Britain had assembled and despatched a powerful Task Force: this must give her leverage, especially as General Haig assured the Argentine Government that Mrs Thatcher would fight if need be. As he put it, in vivid and indeed accurate language, '"that woman" has let a number of hunger strikers of her own basic ethnic origin starve themselves to death, without flickering an eyelash'. [90, p. 176] General Galtieri assured Haig on 10 April that 'only soldiers could understand how critically important it was to avoid conflict', [90, p. 179] which Haig took as implying that he might be flexible; but the only conflict that General Galtieri had experienced was one against his own, subversive (in his eyes) civilian population. He knew that he could not survive if he withdrew his soldiers from the Falklands.

On 14 April Mrs Thatcher told the Commons that one of the problems of the present negotiations was that the Argentines would not admit that the wishes of the Islanders must come first. [114, col. 1146] But she showed some flexibility: these wishes might have changed as a result of 'their recent experiences'. [114, col. 1150] This phrase reflected the influence of Francis Pym. General Haig described how at a working dinner on his first visit to London after the Argentine invasion, Mrs Thatcher pointed out portraits of the Duke of Wellington and Lord Nelson. At one point during a discussion of the capabilities of the Task Force, Pym mused, 'Maybe we should ask the Falkland Islanders how they feel about a war', upon which Mrs Thatcher 'heatedly challenged him'. Pym declared in retrospect that this was a 'nonsensical passage' in Haig's account of the exchange, but added that if Haig said this then 'no doubt it is quite true'. [45, pp. 191–2] But he insisted that the War Cabinet and the main Cabinet were in full agreement about all peace proposals: a claim refuted by Mrs Thatcher in her memoirs. [203, p. 205] The Thatcher account is the more reliable; but in any event, even if Mrs Thatcher had been prepared to develop the theme that the Islanders themselves might have changed their minds about exchanging British for Argentine sovereignty, she would have found it hard to maintain this, not only in the face of opposition from her own Party, but from other influential voices. David Owen urged that the right to self-determination was one of the 'sacred principles' of the United Nations. Britain was not defending 'some minor issue 7,000 miles away from our shores, but a fundamental issue'. [114, cols. 1155–6]

The War Cabinet became more, not less, anxious about the Haig mission as time went on. It knew that time was not on the side of the Task Force. There were only two to three weeks in May during which British forces might land on the Falklands without encountering 'terrible conditions'. [203, p. 201] Admiral Woodward calculated that 25 May was the latest date by which the troops could be 'given reasonable time to do their stuff'. He 'duly pinned' his cardboard dates into place on the overall calendar: 'we must be here by X, there by Y, have established an airstrip by Z'. [236, pp. 92–3] Mrs Thatcher was for her part encountering one of the most fundamental of military facts: the logistics of campaigning. The War Cabinet must decide how many more troops and aircraft should be despatched to the region to support the Task Force's present complement. This, she noted, was 'a lot for them to take in'. [203, p. 201] On 16 April the War Cabinet discussed rules of engagement, which would be necessary and indeed vital in a crisis that might end in an undeclared war. Mrs Thatcher was particularly concerned lest a motion tabled in the United Nations Security Council might further stall military moves. [203, pp. 202–3]

Mrs Thatcher was alert to the importance of obtaining the right combination of the diplomatic and the military, and was critical of Pym, whose position was that 'force would not be used as long as negotiations were continuing'. [203, p. 204] Her perception of the difficulty was that Argentine proposals invariably led in one direction: Argentine sovereignty over the Islands. The Argentine policy of 19 April contained four main points: that troops should be withdrawn on both sides to their normal places of occupation, that is, to Argentina and the United Kingdom respectively; that there should be an interim administration by a Council of equal composition of Argentines and Falkland Islanders; that the United Nations should supervise the transition which would end on 31 December; and that, meanwhile, Argentines should have the right to buy land and settle on the islands: terms which Mrs Thatcher on 20 April declared fell 'far short' of a settlement. [36, pp. 97–8] Her suspicions were not unjustified, for on 21 April the Argentine Government issued a communiqué stating that the 'ultimate result can be nothing less than the speedy exercise of our sovereignty over the Malvinas Islands'. [36, p. 99] She was equally suspicious of what she regarded as the pliant attitude of her Foreign Secretary, Francis Pym, and his 'lobbying' for support in the War Cabinet. [203, p. 207] When Pym left for Washington on 21 April, he did so in the context of the Prime Minister's warning to the House of Commons on 20 April that 'Argentine proposals at present before us fall far short in some important aspects'. [90, p. 215]

Pym claimed that he would not exclude the use of military force, but that he would exclude it 'so long as negotiations are in play' – words which he later modified to explain that the use of force 'could not at any stage be ruled out'. [90, p. 217] But the Task Force had been given an agenda which military logic obliged it to follow. This was set out in orders given to the Commander of the Task Force on 11 April.

(a) Enforce Falkland Islands Exclusion Zone
(b) Establish sea and air superiority in Falkland Islands exclusion zone as soon as possible.
(c) Repossess South Georgia
(d) Repossess Falkland Islands.

The Task Force was told that 'priority and urgency attached to (b) will heavily influence (d) which may now be later than planned heretofore. Hence rethink is underway and assessments of practicable loiter policy for amphibious group in hand'. [46, pp. 68–9] 'Possessing' was not a 'pleasing prospect', the Commander Amphibious Force noted. But his explanation was that the Ministry of Defence was cautious and sceptical about the whole operation, and the repossession of the Falkland Islands would be attempted only when sea control was firmly established and South Georgia recaptured. [46, pp. 69]

The recapture of South Georgia was always part of the overall plan. The decision to order its implementation was made by the War Cabinet, and was characteristic of the kind of military action that the state of undeclared war required. It would offer a victory and raise morale; it would show the Argentines that the British were prepared to use force to reassert their rights; but it must be minimum loss of life and the minimum damage to property. [90, pp. 218–20] Admiral Woodward seems to have regarded the creation of the 'Operation Parquet' group (a fuel tanker, and HMS *Antrim* and *Plymouth*) as 'adding difficulty to my task of bringing my ships together for work-up as a coherent group'. [236, p. 81] His misgivings were better founded than he thought; what was supposed to be a relatively easy task, one that would satisfy public opinion and raise the Task Force's morale, turned out to be a near-disaster for British arms.

South Georgia is a crescent-shaped island, 105 miles long and 18 miles across at its widest point, 800 miles to the south-east of the Falklands. It is snow-covered for most of the year and susceptible to violent and unpredictable winds. The Argentine garrison was estimated at about 60 marines; the island was beyond Argentine land-based air-cover. It was believed that the Argentine garrison would be at Grytviken or Leith. The task of overcoming it was allocated to 42 Commando, which had experience in winter training in Norway in 1982; with support, including D Squadron of the SAS, the attacking force comprised some 230 men. The encounter that followed was, in the diplomatic language of Field Marshal the Lord Bramall, one that was 'not without incident'. [26, p. 10]

Major Guy Sheridan of 42 Commando was told by Major General Jeremy Moore that although a political solution might be found that would preclude a landing, he, Sheridan, had been appointed military commander for the recapture of South Georgia. [215, p. 65] The force set out on 7 April, and nuclear submarines were also deployed to prevent the Argentine aircraft carrier or any other surface vessel from providing support to the Argentine garrison. The plan was that the garrison should be contained and brought to surrender, but the SAS and the SBS began to emerge as the leading operational troops, who would reconnoitre at Leith and Grytviken and, if they encountered resistance, would be supported by the Commando unit. The SAS insisted on being landed on Fortuna Glacier, ten miles to the west of Leith. The 'friction of war' now made itself felt. Within 12 hours the small SAS party were suffering so much from severe weather that they requested immediate evacuation. Two Wessex helicopters sent to evacuate them crashed. A third succeeded thanks to the skill and resolve of the pilot, who was loaded well over the maximum permitted weight. The SBS group also became stranded on the Island. Further disaster nearly occurred when an Argentine submarine met *Endurance*, which had been co-opted into the British Naval force, but did not fire on it because the Argentine captain felt he could not torpedo a defenceless ship. [215, pp. 67–73]

The Argentine garrison was now alerted to the presence of the British, who were now reinforced by the frigate *Brilliant*. Sheridan now went ahead with the attack on the island, and an ad-hoc team was scraped together, and landed by helicopter, with naval gunfire support, but the confusion that ensued was summed up in Sheridan's orders that 'everyone must sort themselves out and get on with it'. There was a nice, if alarming, touch of SAS bravado when Major Delves strolled into Grytviken wishing an Argentine machine-gun detachment 'good afternoon'. The enemy at Grytviken surrendered, as did the garrison at Leith, on 26 April. [215, pp. 73–7]

This was an inauspicious beginning, or, as Nicholas Barker, a naval officer put it: 'In military terms the whole operation had become a monumental cock-up'. 'Our troops were fortunate', he concluded. 'Any serious resistance could have caused heavy casualties'. [8, pp. 183, 193] Tension between the SAS and Sheridan; the SAS underestimation of the environment; the way in which the character of the operation changed because of SAS insistence of taking the lead; the slowness in unloading troops from the helicopters (the machines themselves being described as 'geriatric'); [215, p. 75] disagreement between the SAS and the conventional forces over the deployment of the mortars and the choice of targets – all revealed 'friction' to an alarming degree. It was, moreover, an operation which Sir John Fieldhouse on 17 April had told Brigadier Thompson and General Jeremy Moore was not worth the bother: they should concentrate on recapturing the Falklands. [215, p. 68] The pleasantly archaic language in which London was informed of the success of the operation ('Be pleased to inform Her Majesty that the White Ensign flies alongside the Union Flag at Grytviken'), [215, p. 76] and the Prime Minister's call to the nation to 'rejoice' (which John Nott found 'marginally embarrassing') [44] covered up the ominous shortcomings of Operation Parquet. And it was with this first victory achieved that the Government assessed the last phase of General Haig's shuttle diplomacy.

This phase was marked by two significant developments. The first was Argentina's success at a meeting of the Organisation of American States which on 18 April resolved that Britain must cease her 'hostilities' and that both parties should proceed with negotiations aimed at a peaceful settlement of the conflict 'taking into account the rights of sovereignty of the Republic of Argentina over the Malvinas (Falkland) Islands and the interests of the Islanders'. Argentina interpreted this as a diplomatic success, though the support offered was less than full; there was no mention of collective measures in support of Argentina. [90, pp. 228–9] The second was that the Prime Minister was increasingly determined to dislodge anyone – especially the Opposition in Parliament – from sitting on the fence (as she saw it), that is, of agreeing to send the Task Force and yet demurring its use. [203, p. 207] She was, by now, growing increasingly certain that Argentina would neither withdraw from the Falklands, nor concede what she regarded as fundamental to the British case; that any settlement must be agreed to by the Islanders, and that it must not be taken as leading inevitably to Argentine sovereignty over the Islands. [19, p. 22] In this she was right: Haig's proposal of 27 April went a long way to meet the British desire to place the right of self-determination at the heart of the matter, referring to the 'will and wishes of the Islanders'; it also left the British in possession of the Islands for an unlimited period. [90, pp. 229–33] Mrs Thatcher feared that Francis Pym's desire to avoid war and its damage to Britain in South America would lead him not only to recommend the Haig proposals, but to give Haig this impression before the War Cabinet had considered them. [203, pp. 205–6]

If Francis Pym was a worry to the Prime Minister, then the Haig proposals were even more of a matter of concern, for by now Mrs Thatcher had apparently placed the Islanders' wishes at the centre of any settlement plan. On 26 April, in a BBC Panorama programme, she declared that the 'sticking point for us is the right to self-determination'. The Falkland Islanders' loyalty to Britain was 'fantastic'. 'If they wish to stay British, we must stand by them. Democratic nations believe in the right to self-determination…The people who live there are of British stock. They have been for generations, and their wishes are the most important thing of all. Democracy is about the wishes of the people'. [96, p. 110] Thus, if Haig's latest proposals seemed in essence to fulfil this principle, Mrs Thatcher would find it hard to resist them. The War Cabinet had on 26 April declared a 'Total Exclusion Zone' around the Falklands, which applied to aircraft as well as ships; this edged the Task Force closer to what Admiral Woodward regarded as a key question: who and in what conditions was to 'start' the war by firing 'the first shot'? [236, p. 108] Haig's mission was now taking place in parallel with this important military development.

The War Cabinet waited for Argentina to make the first move in responding to Haig's plan. It seemed to Mrs Thatcher that she was now failing to get the support she believed she deserved from the Opposition in the Commons. James Callaghan urged that the Islanders' views and interests should be defined more closely than had so far been done, recommending a blockade of the Islands by sea and air, perhaps for months. [114, 29 April 1982, col. 994] Robin Cook identified the position towards which the Government, he believed, was moving. As the Task Force approached the Falklands, 'it becomes evident that however effective it may be in putting pressure on the Argentines to reach a diplomatic solution, it is much more effective in putting pressure on ourselves to adopt a military solution'. [114, col. 1033] Indeed, Mrs Thatcher in her Panorama interview insisted that 'I have to keep in mind the interests of our boys who are on those warships and our navies. I have to watch over the safety of their lives, to see that they can succeed in doing whatever it is we decide they have to do at the best possible time and with minimum risk to them'. [203, p. 209]

These were significant words, for they suggested that military necessity and the safety and success of the Task Force might become paramount; or at any rate must not be jeopardised by fruitless negotiations. That the Haig negotiations proved fruitless was, fortunately for the Prime Minister, because of Argentine obduracy. The British had been appraised of the substance of Haig's proposals before 27 April; Argentina had not, and the Junta asked for more time to consider what it described, not unreasonably, as 'prima facie…elements that help towards the progress of the negotiations, though there are other elements that are not adequately treated and that we believe are essential for the satisfactory solution of the issue'. These were the clauses on the administration of the Islands 'after the lapse of negotiations proper';

the terms and minimum references for these negotiations 'and the consequences of an eventual prolongation without results further than the date assigned for the end of the negotiations'. For the Junta, the 'present elements are not balanced and prejudge in favour of one of the parties of the dispute'. The Argentine response referred to what it called 'the growing threat of an aggression by the United Kingdom that today indicates an imminent attack on the Malvinas Islands': a reference to the British occupation of South Georgia (which Argentina regarded as a rebuff for one of her negotiating principles, that Britain should not move further south than Ascension Island), and the declaration of the Total Exclusion Zone. [90, pp. 234–5]

The Argentine doubts about British commitment to Haig's attempts at brokering a settlement had some foundation: as one member of the War Cabinet put it, 'we were quite happy to have negotiations continue because the ships were chugging on down and there was nothing we could do in the meantime'. [186, p. 130] But Mrs Thatcher had moved some distance from her first position on the Falklands, in particular, by accepting a role (however minor) for Argentina in the administration of the Islands and the flying of the Argentine flag. Had Argentina accepted the Haig proposals of 27 April, then the British might have found it hard to avoid being drawn into further negotiations to try to resolve in detail their differences with Argentina; and this, in turn, would have compromised their military policy. As it turned out, the Junta 'obligingly' rejected the Haig proposals. [186, p. 135] On 30 April Haig declared that the Argentine refusal to compromise meant that the United States must make effective its opposition to the use of unlawful force to resolve disputes. John Nott saw the significance of this statement: it was 'very important with the memory of Suez when we hadn't had international support'. [186, pp. 142–3] It was important to note, however, that the memory of Suez haunted at least some parts of the American administration as much as it did the British. America wanted to avoid the 'worst possible outcome' for the United States, which was that Britain would try and fail to recover the Falklands, and fail because the United States had withheld or withdrawn support.

The Americans had found it impossible to resist one early British call upon their loyalty: the release to the British of the airstrip on Ascension Island. Britain owned the Island but the United States operated the airstrip, and the American agreement to Britain's request that she should be allowed to use it as a forward base was a vital concession. [132, p. 90] The delicate position in which the United States found herself was shown in Mrs Jeane Kirkpatrick's decision to attend a dinner with Argentine Government members on the night of the invasion of the Falklands, which she later explained was because of her fear that to cancel the engagement would be seen as an act of hostility towards Argentina (though she admitted that, in retrospect, she 'felt personally rather exploited'). [19, pp. 26–7] Less excusable in British eyes was her claim that a government which used force to pursue a claim that it believed to be justified on historical grounds was not committing aggression; if this line of reasoning were followed, Denis Healey observed, we could see Mexico attacking Texas, which also had a disputed history. [114, 14 April 1982, col. 1200]

The American response to the crisis was not one dictated or decided by a single-minded administration. President Reagan, for his part, found it hard to believe that anybody would fight over an ice cold bunch of land, and hoped on one occasion that the British might sink an Argentine ship and then go home with honour satisfied. [90, p. 181] But more determined minds were at work in American official circles. Alexander Haig assured the British Ambassador in Washington that the United States was 'not at heart impartial'. [108, p. 50] This the British found hard to believe, but it was demonstrated by the line of action described by the Chairman of the Joint Chiefs of Staff as giving help to the British, 'but not to get caught doing it'. [186, p. 125] The United States provided Britain with supplies, weapons, and intelligence, drawing up a 'shopping list', and never denying anything that the British asked for. They supplied the 'most successful weapon of the war', the Sidewinder AIM-9L missile and the adapted plates to fix them to the GR2 Royal Air Force Harriers, which forced the Argentine pilots to deliver their bombs from a low altitude without adequate time for defusing – which resulted in the large number of Argentine bombs which hit their targets but failed to explode. They provided intelligence co-operation, though they were unable to offer useful satellite photo-reconnaissance until late in the war. The Royal Navy used American communication channels, enhancing the confidential communications between the Task Force and Northwood. The prime mover in all this was Casper Weinburger, Secretary of Defence, who proved to be the strongest supporter of Britain in the crisis, and who held what were dubbed 'what-can-we-do-for-Britain-today meetings' every day. [186, pp. 123–8] In early May he went so far as to offer to replace any British carrier sunk by Argentina with the USS *Eisenhower*. [186, p. 147] The British tabloid newspaper, the *Sun*, repaid American help with a typical headline, 'Yanks a Million'; *The Times* responded after its fashion, saying that America had proved 'a friend indeed'. [186, p. 143] This reflected the sense of relief in Britain that the United States had come close to 'letting Britain down', and the effusion of thanks contrasts with the indifference shown by the United Kingdom Government to the European Community's important support at a time when it was locked in dispute with Britain over the British contribution to the EC budget. [199, pp. 184–5]

The agreement by the ten states of the European Community to place an arms embargo on Argentine was of the greatest importance, for it meant that France, the supplier of Super Etendards and Exocet missiles to the Argentine, complied – willingly – with the embargo. This was quickly followed by an import ban for one month on Argentine goods on 16 April. [72, p. 41] Not all the member states were as single-minded as their action so far implied. Italy was a special case, because of her historical links with Argentina; the Republic of Ireland, under the (at least nominal) Republican leadership of Charles Haughey found it hard to disguise the innate doubts of a former 'British colony' about the behaviour of her evicted rulers. But the European states could hold the line as long as the peace-seeking efforts of the United Nations and the United States continued, and while serious hostilities had not yet begun. The Community went so far as to assert that 'since the Falklands are part of the overseas territory associated with the Community, it is the Community which has been attacked'. There were special resonances in this for Germany (with her concerns about the East and the safety of Berlin) and the French (with the remains of their colonial empire). [72, p. 44] The British made adroit use of the Treaty of Rome. Article 224 required member states to implement common action through common legislation. This was time-consuming. The British therefore resorted to Article 113, in which sanctions would 'arise as trade policy' and would be a Community matter rather than one of national responsibility. [211, p. 10] And although economic sanctions were applied for only one month, this decision gave Britain a moral as well as economic weapon, but one which they could best exploit by moving quickly in both diplomacy and military action.

There were two dangers for Britain. If efforts to reach a settlement moved too slowly, then the European Community might become absorbed by more pressing domestic concerns, and the (qualified) support afforded so far might crumble. But if the British Government seemed less than interested in a settlement, and more committed to the use of force, then, again, the Community might find it hard to sustain a united front. There was another consideration: was it Argentina's action (the use of force to occupy the Islands) that was to be condemned; or was it her ultimate goal and long-standing claim (that the Islands were historically part of Argentina, and that she had used force merely to claim what was rightfully hers)? The dispute over Britain's budgetary contribution inserted itself as well; the British Government regarded attempts to get them to focus on the budget as a form of blackmail, with the rest of Europe seeking to take advantage of British preoccupation with the crisis. [73, pp. 49–50] It is doubtful if Mrs Thatcher, her War Cabinet, her Party, or the British media and public regarded the European Community as having any right to exercise a major influence over British aims in the Falklands crisis. But if European solidarity disintegrated, then this would make it harder for the United Kingdom to sustain what, as the more militarily powerful state in the conflict, she needed: the moral upper hand. Any evidence that Britain was a bully, seeking a neo-colonial role at the expense of what (rather improbably) was called by some a 'third world power' would run the risk of compromising her diplomatic victories, which up to 29 April and the ending of the Haig shuttle mission were impressive.

But military imperatives could not be set aside. There were some major difficulties confronting the War Cabinet, Northwood, and the Task Force as the Haig shuttle went on its way. The first was the, perhaps inevitable, suspicion that could never be eliminated from the relations between politicians and military people. There was, to be sure, always the satisfactory reflection on the part of the military that the armed services would now put a stop to the consequences of decisions made by a 'spineless government' in the early 1970s; and to the wobblings which existed even in Mrs Thatcher's Cabinet. [206, pp. 551–2] Commodore Michael Clapp, Commander Amphibious Warfare, shared Brigadier Julian Thompson's contempt for politicians who sent out the message that 'the lion was thought to be an amiable pussycat'. [46, p. 10] There was the grim satisfaction that the armed forces were needed, not for the first time, to do the dirty work reserved for them by political failure. But for the soldiers there was always the uneasy suspicion that if they did not behave themselves, or show themselves as willing as the politicians wanted them to be, they could be replaced. The Commander of the Task Force, Admiral Fieldhouse, felt obliged to reassure the Task Force commanders that, 'while there had been efforts back home to replace the commanders at sea, he had managed to resist attempts by other senior officers and the politicians to get their own men in place'. [46, p. 78]

Matters of this kind, however, paled beside the vexatious question of what the politicians wanted from the Task Force Commanders, and how what they wanted could be shaped into practicable tactics. The Chiefs of Staff had ordered the Ministry of Defence on 8 April to prepare an Amphibious Operations Appreciation; this came to the conclusion that the Task Force should be able to establish sea control and a reasonable degree of air superiority over the Falklands. It acknowledged that the Landing Force might not in itself necessarily achieve the political aim, which was the re-establishment of the presence of British Armed Forces on the Islands, and the provision of the means to effect military pressure on the Argentine forces to surrender. The paper also surmised that operations subsequent to a landing might have to be confined to attacks on selected Argentine positions and possibly to special forces operations. A direct assault on Argentine positions could not be conducted without risk to civilians. 'This ambiguity', wrote Michael Clapp, 'was to influence our planning in later days'. [46, p. 79] They were never told of the second part of the Appreciation, that of 'actually taking possession of the Islands', though they made plans for this 'privately'. But they did not envisage an opposed assault; a landing without bloodshed followed by a firm base on the Islands would be a very strong diplomatic and military bargaining counter. [46, pp. 79–80] Their doubts about the belief of the Chiefs of Staff that the war was even winnable were reinforced by the delay in sending the second brigade of troops, and then its ad hoc construction: it would not consist of a brigade, trained on BAOR near-operational duties, but one that had 'not worked together apart from a hastily conceived exercise in the Welsh Mountains where command and control had not been the strong points'. [46, p. 86]

Some of these criticisms were surely ill-founded. There is no reason to believe that the delay in sending 5 Brigade was because of any sense of defeatism among the Chiefs of Staff. But there was indecision and prevarication, which meant that the new Brigade had to be prepared for its task, and there was little enough time for this. [22, p. 72] The choice of this Brigade is explicable in that its commander, Brigadier Anthony Wilson, had had his two parachute battalions taken from him and sent to the South Atlantic; his remaining unit, a Gurkha battalion, was now despatched (though this aroused criticism from some 'third world' states over its use for a 'colonial war'). The choice of the Guards battalions could be justified in that they were, like the Gurkhas, an elite unit, whose reputation alone might serve to overawe the enemy. There was as yet no clear purpose for this brigade: they might be deployed as front-line attacking troops – and certainly Brigadier Thompson requested the reinforcements because he did not feel he had sufficient forces to take Stanley – or they might act in a support role: defending the bridgehead established by the front-line battalions, or garrisoning it if the break-out were achieved cleanly and successful advance took place. [46, p. 97]

Just as political decisions were influenced by military considerations, such as the need to create 'Rules of Engagement', so military actions were shaped by politics and diplomacy. On 20 April General Haig telegraphed the British Government to say that 'It is imperative that you maintain military pressure. I see no other way of bringing the Argentines to a position satisfactory to you'. [46, p. 90] This occasioned the sending of the Task Force south from Ascension Island, before it had 'unscrambled the politically induced chaos of loading'; [46, p. 90] after representations were made about the impossibility of loading stores and equipment, and securing training in small arms fire, sailing was delayed. Northwood still hoped that a successful landing on the beachhead (estimated for 16 May) would be enough to 'convince the Argentines that their own position is militarily untenable and that they can honourably agree to withdraw..'; but the bridgehead position must be one that allowed for a 'decisive battle' to be fought should this not be the case. [46, p. 94] The Task Force Commander, Admiral Fieldhouse, believed that the notion of holding a bridgehead and awaiting an Argentine response was unrealistic: there must be a break-out from the beaches 'as soon as we, on the ground, thought fit'. [46, p. 79]

But at least one, and that one of the most controversial decisions of the crisis, was made as a direct result of the final breakdown of the Haig shuttle diplomacy. On 30 April Fieldhouse spoke directly to Admiral Woodward, telling him that he now had authority to enter and enforce the Exclusion Zone, which the Government had declared on 28 April, to take effect from 11.00 GMT on 30 April. This announcement stated that:

> Any ship and any aircraft whether military or civil which is found within this Zone without due authority from the Ministry of Defence in London will be regarded as operating in support of the illegal occupation and will therefore be regarded as hostile and will be liable to be attacked by British forces.
>
> Also from the time indicated, Port Stanley will be closed; and any aircraft on the ground in the Falkland Islands will be regarded as present in support of the illegal occupation and accordingly is liable to attack.

> The British Government reserved its right also to self-defence under Article 51 of the United Nations Charter; and the possibility of action taken outside the Total Exclusion Zone was not ruled out. [90, pp. 249–50]

Admiral Fieldhouse told the Task Force in blunt terms what this meant: 'The Argentines had rejected Haig's peace plan late on the 29th and on the 30th CTF (Fieldhouse) spoke directly to Sandy (Woodward) telling him that he now had the authority to enter and enforce the Exclusion Zone the following day with enhanced, almost unlimited, Rules of Engagement…' [46, p. 115]

And, as Michael Clapp put it flatly, 'As we now know these events culminated in the sinking of the *Belgrano* on 2 May'. [46, p. 115] It was this event that tested both the resolve of the British Government and the state of public opinion, and revealed that the scales between military and diplomatic action were most finely balanced.

5

From the *Belgrano* to San Carlos

The failure of the Haig mediation attempt did not render armed conflict inevitable; but it pushed the initiative closer in the direction of confrontation. Mrs Thatcher feared that persistent attempts at mediation would remove the power to make decisions out of her hands. She was particularly concerned about the role of the United Nations: 'in the longer term', she wrote, 'we knew that one had to try to keep our affairs out of the United Nations as much as possible'; there was a real danger that, given the anti-colonialist attitude of many nations, that the United Nations Security Council would 'force unsatisfactory terms upon us' [203, p. 182]

For the commander of the Task Force, Admiral Woodward, and his military colleagues, initiatives and suggestions were troublesome diversions from the job in hand. He was aware of the vulnerabilities of his position; as he put it, 'Lose *Invincible* and the operation is severely jeopardised. Lose *Hermes* and the operation is over'. [236, p. 99] 'Basically', he noted, 'we were operating a small air force out of a large tin box'. [236, p. 89] The declaration of the Total Exclusion Zone was not as helpful as it might seem. 'London', he mused, 'had put me under orders to go towards the two-hundred-mile-radius Exclusion Zone and make aggressive noises, but only when I got there'. 'Militarily not very sharp', since 'should the opposition decide to the contrary, they will be able to carry out a co-ordinated pre-emptive strike on my aircraft carriers and ruin any chances we had of retaking the Falkland Islands'. He saw the War Cabinet's military policy so far as one of bluff, which the Argentines might call. [236, pp. 98, 99] The fine distinctions between war and peace were revealed in Operation Parquet. Captain Brian Young, commanding the destroyer HMS *Antrim*, did not open fire on Argentine planes as they were unarmed; this was done on order from Northwood, which was insistent that the planes were not attacking so therefore should not be shot at. [32, p. 337]

While the Haig shuttle was in motion, the Task Force deliberated on the best way to re-take the Falklands; as Michael Clapp put it, they assumed that they would have to land, somehow, somewhere, when conditions were favourable. This was a formidable task, one that Clapp's understatement could not disguise. The Task Force commander and his colleagues needed to know all the options of time and place. They needed to know more about the Argentine opposition, the country, its beaches and the sea approaches to those beaches. Could they be defended against air, surface, sub-surface and Exocet attacks? Were they suitable for slow transports and logistic ships? [46, pp. 65–6] There were the perhaps inevitable frictions between the Task Force commanders, which were partly personal, partly because different arms of the Services had different, and sometimes clashing, priorities. [46, pp. 71–3] Clapp's instincts were steadily moving towards San Carlos Bay as the best, or least worst, landing place. It was within striking range of Darwin and Goose Green should these enemy bases require 'elimination'; it was believed to be unoccupied; it was suitable for the deployment of British military equipment, such as the Rapier weapon; it could be defended against surface attacks. There were also the danger that San Carlos was within range of un-refuelled Argentine aircraft, vulnerable to submarines, and a long way from Stanley. Its approaches could be mined before and after a landing. Above all, since the Task Force wanted to avoid an opposed landing, the Argentine army must be absent. [46, 100–1]

While these plans were being worked out, Admiral Woodward had other, more immediate, military operations to press for. He wanted to tempt the Argentines into engagements, partly to test their strength, partly to initiate a process of attrition of their naval forces. He needed to know more about the enemy's dispositions; information would be gathered by the Special Air Service and Special Boat Service landing on the Islands. [236, pp. 31–3] The sharpening of hostilities on 1 May involved a single Vulcan bomber attacking Stanley air-strip; Sea Harriers attacking Stanley and Goose Green airfields; and the bombardment of Stanley by a small naval force. Two frigates and several Sea King helicopters went on the alert for Argentine submarines. Several Argentine aircraft were shot down. Stanley airfield was sufficiently damaged to deny its use to the Argentines as a forward operating base, or an emergency landing ground for their high performance jets. But the Argentine assessment of these engagements was that they, and not the British, had come off best: in particular, the naval attack on Stanley was seen as part of an imminent British landing which had been frustrated. The Argentines believed that two Sea Harriers had been shot down; they had attacked and damaged British ships, the *Glamorgan* and the *Arrow*. [90, pp. 254–7] The morale of the Argentine pilots was high. Argentina was encouraged to take the initiative, and in particular, to deploy its naval forces to 'find and destroy the British fleet if the Islands or the mainland were attacked'. This conditional order was altered on 1 May: now the fleet was given 'freedom of action to attack'. [90, pp. 257–8]

The operations of the Task Force were increasingly governed by the 'astronomic proportions' of the signals exchanged between London and the fleet's communications office. [46, p. 113] War waged from a distance was never easy; it was now time to simplify its inevitable complexities. For Admiral Woodward, the end of April was, realistically, the end of the negotiation process; it was now time to get on with the war.

The difficulty of fighting an undeclared war would not go away. Francis Pym believed that the British position would be strengthened if the warning to the Argentines of 23 April (that 'any approach on the part of Argentine warships, including submarines, naval auxiliaries, or military aircraft, which could amount to a threat to interfere with the mission of the British Forces in the South Atlantic will encounter the appropriate response') were given more clarity. Argentina should be warned that her carrier would be attacked if it were to move out of Argentine territorial waters, and constituted a threat to the Task Force, or if any British naval or air forces were attacked anywhere in the South Atlantic. [90, p. 253] This would have strengthened the British political position; but Admiral Woodward would have found it unacceptable. He was concerned about the ambiguity already existing over the enforcement of the Exclusion Zone. Was the navy to wait until the Argentines fired the first shot? If so, 'then the first shot must clearly arrive on board one of my less-valuable frigates – not too easy to arrange'. [236, p. 108] Thus the Exclusion Zone, far from putting pressure on the Argentines, might prove a liability for the Task Force.

Admiral Woodward pressed Northwood for permission to take direct command of the three submarine vessels in his fleet, but this was refused. [236, pp. 122–4] On 29 April he was given the new Rules of Engagement, which authorised him to open fire on any combat ship or aircraft in the Exclusion Zone identified as Argentinian once the Task Force had entered it. [236, p. 126] His assessment of his overall position was this: up to the north-west was the Argentine carrier, the *Veintecinco de Mayo*, with her two escort destroyers; on her deck would be some ten A4 fighter bombers, and possibly some Exocet-armed Super-Etendards. Down to the south-west was the heavily armed cruiser, *General Belgrano*, with her two escorting destroyers, each carrying Exocets. These formidable ships were manoeuvring into what Woodward believed was a pincer movement. His purpose was to keep the submarine *Conqueror* in 'close touch with the *Belgrano* group to the south, to shadow the carrier and her escorts to the north with one of the 'S' Boats up there'. On the word from London, he 'would expect to make our presence felt, preferably by removing their carrier and the aircraft she contained'. [236, pp. 126–7]

Woodward was frustrated by the consequences of the divided command between London and himself. The submarine *Spartan* was close to the best estimate of the carrier, *Veintecinco de Mayo's* position, but had been diverted by Northwood to look for other targets. Now it was close to the 'edge of her patch', and was forbidden from crossing the line beyond which the fleet believed the Argentine carrier was steaming. The submarine *Splendid* was too far away to do anything. [236, p. 127] Woodward was concerned that the *Veintecinco de Mayo* or the *General Belgrano*, or both, could move comfortably within range for a decisive battle which 'would give them, tactically, all the advantages'. The enemy could attack his force from different directions, using different weapons that required varied responses, 'all in the half-light of a dawn which would be silhouetting us'. He concluded that he must 'take one claw of the pincer', which, since the submarines *Spartan* and *Superb* were not in contact with her, could not be the carrier; therefore it must be the *General Belgrano*, though he would have preferred taking out both ships. [236, p. 149]

The *General Belgrano* was no insignificant or obsolete vessel. She was elderly, having been the United States Navy's *Phoenix* between 1938 and 1951, when she was sold to Argentina. But she was well armed and well armoured, and has been described as 'potentially a highly dangerous adversary for the British surface fleet'. [31, pp. 130, 134] She was being tracked by the submarine *Conqueror*, whose commander Christopher Wreford-Brown, regarded what he was doing so far as 'a bit of a waste'. [236, p. 150] He was hoping for a signal to change the Rules of Engagement which would give him permission to attack outside the Exclusion Zone.

Woodward believed that, as he put it, he could not 'let that cruiser even stay where she is, regardless of her present course or speed. Whether she is inside or outside the TEZ is irrelevant. She will have to go'. [236, p. 152] His assessment was later vindicated by Argentine

Naval Officers, who agreed that there was as much danger 'in or out of the (Exclusion) Zone', and that the Zone would have been entered if the conditions for a successful action arose. When the *Belgrano* and her escorting destroyers, the *Hipolito Bouchard* and the *Piedra Buena*, were ordered to head away from the Zone towards the Argentine mainland, they were, as the Captain of the *General Belgrano*, Hector Bonzo said, 'not going to the mainland: we were going to a position to await further orders'. [152, p. 105] Woodward was anxious to sink the cruiser, before she turned away from her present position, 'because if we wait for her to enter the Zone, we may well lose her, very quickly'. [236, p. 153]

It was at this point that long-range communications posed some dilemmas. Woodward clearly saw himself as the man on the spot, and therefore most fitted to take a decision; but the process of requesting, and receiving, a change in the Rules of Engagement would, he estimated, take some eight hours and 'it might not be the reply I wanted or needed'. He therefore issued a direct order for the *Conqueror* to attack the *Belgrano* at 04.10 (08.10 BST) on the morning of 2 May. Woodward reflected that his signal would give Northwood an 'interesting jolt at six o'clock in the morning'. He was right. When Northwood received the signal, he was ordered to rescind his command to the *Conqueror*, and Northwood removed it from the satellite, so that Wreford-Brown could not receive it. Woodward had, he himself acknowledged, exceeded his authority by altering the Rules of Engagement; but he believed that by sending his signal to *Conqueror* he had at least protected himself against any accusations that he had put his fleet at risk from the *Belgrano* by doing nothing; a consideration reinforced by his acknowledgement that politicians would shrink from approving the sinking of the cruiser with much loss of life. They could now 'let it run and blame me' if it proved convenient; and if it went right, they could take the credit. Woodward could at least enjoy the satisfaction that his signal would 'ginger up' Northwood. [236, pp. 154–6] Northwood did not, as it happened, need 'gingering up'. Woodward later acknowledged, what he did not know at the time, that 'I and Northwood and reaching upwards into the Ministry were all of the same mind', and that the military and naval chiefs, fortified with British Intelligence intercepts, had 'already set in motion the negotiations to change the rules of engagement' (200, p. 31)

The Foreign Secretary, Francis Pym, had left for Washington on 1 May, and when he arrived he announced that the British had taken their military operations so far in order to 'concentrate Argentine minds', which suggested that diplomatic pressure might now be resumed. But he also said that no further military action was envisaged, 'other than making the Total Exclusion Zone secure'. [182, p. 84] This could imply that Argentine ships would be prevented from entering the Zone; but, in Woodward's interpretation of what it meant to make the Zone secure, this could mean a more offensive, forward posture in the interests of defending his command. In this sense, an agreement by the War Cabinet to authorise an attack on an Argentine vessel outside the Zone would not be more than the logical extension of a 'defensive' posture. But it would be a serious extension, one not of degree but of kind, in its consequences: a large ship sunk must mean a considerable loss of life.

To justify this escalation of the crisis, it would be necessary to prove that the *Belgrano* constituted a real and present danger to the fleet. Admiral Woodward was by 11.30 fairly sure that the carrier group had 'in some way withdrawn', but, he claimed that the *General Belgrano* was heading back to the west in a 'gentle zig-zag'. [236, pp. 157–8] The submarine *Conqueror* was still tracking the *Belgrano*. Woodward's signal to the submarine, ordering it to attack the *Belgrano* would cut through the babble of messages passing between London and the Task Force, and concentrate Northwood's minds. Admiral Lewin and Admiral Fieldhouse went to Chequers and told the Prime Minister of the situation and requested a change of the Rules of Engagement. Mrs Thatcher then met her Ministers and officials who had gathered for the War Cabinet meeting in the afternoon, and it was agreed that the rules should be altered, to permit attacks 'on all Argentine naval vessels on the high seas, as had previously been agreed for the 25 de Mayo alone'. [90, pp. 266–7] Admiral Lewin had no doubt that 'this was the right political and military thing to do'; the decision was taken because there was a military threat, which could be eliminated. The Argentine commander of the carrier *Veintecinco de Mayo* agreed with this professional assessment. [45, pp. 211–12, 216] John Nott described the decision to change the Rules of Engagement as 'one of the easiest…of the whole war'. [172] William Whitelaw (not a man who welcomed conflict) asked Admiral Lewin, 'Can you be in contact with the *Belgrano* and just choose the time, if we are going to give permission for an attack when she may obviously be moving towards the Falklands? Can we follow her in the South Atlantic and just choose the moment?' He said: 'There is no chance of doing that. You may lose contact and may never get contact again'. 'One came hard up against the very simple decision'. [19, p. 299] *Conqueror* was still trailing the *Belgrano*, and the changed Rules of Engagement were sent to the submarine at 13.30 (BST) but a defective radio mast prevented her from reading the signal until 17.30 BST , when *Conqueror* acknowledged the signal and informed Woodward that he intended to attack. At 20.30 BST Wreford-Brown reported to Northwood that the *Belgrano* had been hit. It sank with the loss of 321 lives. It was a 'textbook operation', in Woodward's words; the Argentine crew sang their national anthem as they abandoned ship.

The sinking of the *General Belgrano* was the most controversial action of the whole Falklands War. In one sense, it was an understandable, even necessary, act of war. The British Task Force was now engaging the enemy. It was preparing to land troops on the Islands in what must be one of the most fragile and vulnerable operations, an amphibious approach and landing. It had been and still was under threat of an attack from two formidable Argentine naval vessels, the *Veintecinco de Mayo* and the *Belgrano*. It had the chance to remove one of those threats, which, if it failed to do so, might in the end be blamed on the Task Force Commander's lack of will – and the War Cabinet's also. But the difficulty was that Britain and Argentina were not at war. Pym was in Washington, and diplomacy was not yet dead. The two sides had only skirmished so far, with little loss of life. Wreford-Brown, for his part, did not do what he would certainly have done had he been in the South Atlantic or anywhere else in the Second World War; he did not attack the *Belgrano's* escorts, knowing, as he put it wryly, that 'Mrs Thatcher would not have thanked me all that much if I had reloaded and hit the other two ships'. [236, p. 163] John Nott's explanation in the House of Commons (based on information from Northwood) that the *Belgrano* was sailing towards the Task Force ('closing on elements of our Task Force') when she was attacked was wrong; Mrs Thatcher gave the impression that the *Belgrano* was heading towards the Task Force. The Government chose not to correct this version of events and the cover-up that later provoked a major trial when the civil servant, Clive Ponting, leaked documents contradicting the official explanation. It would have saved the Government much obloquy if Nott had been in a position to explain that the *Belgrano* was not proceeding towards the Task Force, but, as Woodward claimed, that she still was seen as posing a threat. His account of his House of Commons statement was that it had been 'knocked…together' in the car on the way to the House. [172]

Apart from the Government's misinforming the House of Commons about the sinking of the *Belgrano*, two major criticisms were made of the British escalation of the conflict. One was that she had, indeed, escalated it; that she had crossed a line, and that, as Haig put it, 'people might say that Britain was over-reacting'. [90, p. 287] The second, more serious, criticism, was that Mrs Thatcher had deliberately sanctioned the sinking of the *General Belgrano* in order to subvert an initiative taken by the Peruvian Government to engineer a peaceful compromise to the dispute.

The first of these is more of a criticism than a condemnation; it can be met by reference to the fine line that, in this kind of confrontation, divides diplomacy from conflict. Robin Cook in the House of Commons on 29 April, shortly before the sinking of the *General Belgrano*, set out the dilemma with characteristic precision. He identified the position towards which the Government was moving, almost inexorably: as the Task Force approached the Falkland Islands 'it becomes evident that however effective it may be in putting pressure on the Argentines to reach a diplomatic solution, it is much more effective in putting pressure on ourselves to adopt a military solution'. [114, col. 1033] Haig wondered whether 'hitting the Argentines was the only thing that brought them to negotiate or whether it made them more inflexible'. (90, p. 187) This general predicament was compounded by the exigencies of the British military situation. Admiral Woodward had no doubt in his mind that he must seize the initiative, if necessary from the British War Cabinet itself. It was unfortunate from the British perspective that the Foreign Secretary, Francis Pym, who flew to Washington on 1 May, announced that the British attacks so far launched on the Argentine positions on the Falklands had been intended to concentrate Argentine minds in the direction of seeking a solution, and that 'No further military action was envisaged at the moment except to keep the exclusion zone secure'. But it could be argued that keeping the zone 'secure' was by no means incompatible with attacking the *General Belgrano*. However, Pym on the morning of 1 May suggested that the Government could all the more effectively defend and justify any attacks without warning on the Argentine carrier outside the exclusion zone if it would give a warning to the Argentine Government, to be conveyed to them by the Swiss. [182, p. 82]

Pym was, in the light of what happened in the next 24 hours, right in his assertion that this course of action would 'greatly strengthen our hand in dealing with criticism at home and abroad once an attack on the carrier had been carried out'. [182, p. 82] His focusing on the *General Belgrano* is important, for while the War Cabinet's authorisation was not specifically to attack the carrier, but to attack any Argentine warship outside the exclusion zone, the *General Belgrano* was the only vessel with which Admiral Woodward was concerned, and the only one with which the British submarine, *Conqueror*, was in touch at that time. The specificity of the change to the Rules of Engagement cannot be contested. As Vice Admiral Sir Terence Lewin put it (in an interview on 11 September 1983), 'Here was an opportunity to knock off a major unit of the Argentine fleet'. [182, p. 86; 45, pp. 211–12; 95, p. 100] Moreover, Woodward's action in sending his signal to the *Conqueror* was deliberately designed to push events along faster than Pym's suggestions for careful preparations for a change to the Rules of Engagement ever envisaged.

Pym's cautious approach to further British military action was justified by the criticism that was levelled against the British Government over the sinking of the *General Belgrano*. Sir Anthony Parsons, a man adept at feeling the pulse of international opinion at the United Nations, believed that the incident made the British look 'more like bullies' than the victims of aggression. [19, p. 37] On 4 May in the Commons, Michael Foot asked the question, was this particular action really necessary? [114, col. 15] Others asked and answered the question in terms highly unfavourable to the British. The European Economic Community was already concerned about the retaking of South Georgia on 25 April; now it seemed as if European support for the British so far had been taken as a 'blank cheque'. The British Prime Minister was seen as 'neither personally nor politically disposed towards compromise'. The Community also noted the discrepancy between the 'dovish' Francis Pym and the 'hawkish' Mrs Thatcher. The Community's sanctions against Argentina were now perceived in a different light: they were, it was held, seen by the United Kingdom, not as a means of exerting pressure on Argentine, but as a reinforcement of her desire for a military solution. There was public disquiet, especially in Italy and it was thanks to France and Germany that the Community agreed on 24 May to renewing sanctions without limit. [199, pp. 48–50] The Community states in the United Nations, especially the Republic of Ireland, led attempts to refresh conciliatory methods, and a growing number of Community states tended to abstain on Falklands resolutions. [199, pp. 141–8]

The Government was aware that it had indeed taken what many regarded as one military step too far. They sought to defend their action by stressing that the Government had a prime responsibility to 'protect our boys'. Mrs Thatcher reminded the Commons on 4 May of the Government's communication to the United Nations and the Argentine Government on 23 April that any approach by Argentine warships which could amount to a threat to 'interfere with the mission of the British forces in the South Atlantic will encounter the appropriate response'. She referred to Argentine claims to have sunk HMS *Hermes*, and to have brought down 11 Harrier aircraft as 'clear evidence of Argentine aggressive intent'. The *Belgrano* carried heavy armament, and had the Government 'left it any later it would have been too late and I might have had to come to this House with the news that some of our ships had been sunk'. [114, 4 May 1982, col. 16]

The sinking of the *General Belgrano* can be put in context of the difficulties and dilemmas that inevitably arise in a 'no war no peace' predicament. A civilian government must keep control of military operations, especially in the light of potential diplomatic repercussions. Yet it could hardly ignore serious and urgent military requests, which, if refused with troublesome consequences for the armed forces, could seriously jeopardise the whole mission. John Nott's doctrine of 'minimum force' and his desire to achieve 'the diplomatic objective' [114, 5 May 1982, col. 156] hung by the most slender of threads.

More serious was the condemnation of the Government for having allegedly contrived the deliberate sabotage of any possible peaceful outcome to the crisis, specifically an initiative inaugurated by the Government of Peru. This initiative arose from the Peruvian concern that the conflict might escalate, and the hope that Peru might intervene to break the diplomatic deadlock – one that was attributed by Alexander Haig as arising from 'intransigence on both sides'. [90, p. 274] The possibility that a fellow South American state might have some influence over Argentina at a time when Francis Pym on 1 May had stolen a march on Argentina by claiming that he came to the United States to visit, not a negotiator, but an ally, was not lost on Washington; it would be harder for the Argentines to dismiss an initiative from Peru than they could from the United States. Indeed, the former Assistant Secretary of State, Thomas Enders, claimed that the initiative was really an American one. '*We* drafted that proposal and negotiated it with the British...Belaunde made it his own...'. [45, p. 174]

At midnight on 1 May the Peruvian Prime Minister Manuel Ulloa, contacted the United Nations Secretary General and told him that Peru was about to offer mediation, beginning with Argentina; Costa Mendez recommended that the Peruvian President, Fernando Belaunde Terry, contact General Galtieri at once, and at 01.30 Belaunde spoke to Galtieri who accepted the mediation. [90, p. 276]

The Peruvian peace proposal was one that aimed at simplifying the essentials in the hope that this would prevent any negotiations becoming mired in detail. It was that there should be an immediate ceasefire; that British and Argentine forces should withdraw from the area; that third parties would temporarily govern the Falklands; that the two governments, British and Argentine, should recognise the conflicting viewpoints about the Islands, and that they should take into account both the interests and wishes of the Islanders; that an initial 'contact group' which would start at once to implement this agreement would consist of Brazil, Peru, West Germany and the United States, which would be responsible for the arbitration, supervision and interim administration of the Islands; and that a final solution must be found by 30 April 1983, under the contact group's guarantee. [90, p. 278] This was a set of proposals that must be viewed by Britain and Argentina in the light of their own assessments of their military situation. Argentina believed that the British raids on the Falklands amounted to a failed invasion attempt; [90, p. 277] Britain, for her part, was still determined to apply diplomatic and military pressure in equal amounts, and was encouraged by what she saw as a United States 'tilt' towards her, given a shrewd push in the right direction by Francis Pym's 'ally' claim. The notion that General Galtieri was in some sense on his way to accepting the Peruvian initiative was most strongly put by Arthur Gavshon and Desmond Rice, in their book, *The Sinking of the Belgrano* (1984). But their transcript of a telephone conversation between Galtieri and Belaunde, in which Gavshon and Rice claimed that the initiative was making progress, hardly bears out that claim. Galtieri warned that 'we're not going to change. You voted in TIAR (the Rio Treaty which stated that "Any aggression against an American state should be considered an aggression against all American states"), we're not going to change sovereignty for anything…'. [95, pp. 87–8] Since sovereignty was also the sticking point for the British, it seems clear that no breakthrough was imminent. The Argentine 'acceptance' of the Peruvian plan on 1 May, 12 hours before the sinking of the *Belgrano*, was a very conditional one. As Douglas Kinney put it, 'neither then nor at any time did Argentina agree to the plan firmly. It was still considering trade-offs and other options when military events intervened'. Argentina accepted the 'negotiation process' in principle, but not the terms of the plan which, inter alia, called for Argentine withdrawal and the factoring in of the Falkland Islanders' wishes. [133, p. 153] Ruben Moro likewise acknowledged that Argentina would not concede on the term 'wishes' of the islanders; there was 'no blank cheque' to do the bidding of 1,800 islanders. Argentine agreement on the terms of peace would be (at least) conditional on this being made clear, that the local administration would not be retained. [158, pp. 138-9] This again would be unacceptable to the British. There was, then, no imminent breakthrough that was destroyed with *the Belgrano*. The most that can be said on this head is that the British War Cabinet's decision to sanction an attack on the vessel (or any other Argentine warships that posed a threat to the Task Force) showed that it was, as Robin Cook claimed, putting military pressure on itself. And that any chance that Galtieri might change his position on sovereignty – hardly likely – was made more unlikely by the *Belgrano* attack, which, as he put it in elliptical terms, had 'caused the study of such reasoning to be set aside and has become the central focus, which is psychologically and politically transcendental, even beyond military considerations, in the eyes of the Argentine public'. [158, pp. 139–40]

The belief, nonetheless, that the War Cabinet had, to say the least, paid scant attention to the diplomatic and moral consequences of its authorisation of an attack on Argentine warships outside the Total Exclusion Zone was reinforced by its failure to contact Pym before the decision was made; the differences that existed between Pym and his Prime Minister over the resolution of the crisis reinforce the notion that Mrs Thatcher was anxious to keep control of British policy, and to deny any significant contribution from Pym, whom she appears to have disliked personally as well as politically. But when Pym met Alexander Haig on the late morning of 2 May, when he was still unaware of the sinking of the *Belgrano*, he told Haig that what was outlined in the Peruvian plan was in essence not very different from Haig's own earlier scheme, which Argentina had already totally rejected. [90, p. 280] There was always in these matters, as in those prior to and subsequent to the Peruvian initiative, a core consideration for the British Government: they must calculate whether or not any Argentine response was compatible with the British diplomatic and military investment in sending a fleet to the South Atlantic in the first place. This calculation was made more difficult by what Haig noted about the Argentine Junta: its lack of a clear directing head. [90, p. 214]

The sinking of the *Belgrano* had a profound effect on Argentine opinion, even though it was not the cause of the failure of the Peruvian initiative. Argentina could hardly proceed with its interest in the proposal when so many of its sailors had died: this would appear to be ignoring a tragic national loss. But military disaster can exert different and contrasting effects: it can undermine the possibilities of peace; it can also revive them. On 4 May two Argentine Super-Etendards carried out a skilful attack on HMS *Sheffield*, firing Exocet missiles when *Sheffield's* radar system was inoperative. Only one of the two Exocets fired hit the target and failed to explode, but its fuel ignited. Twenty of the *Sheffield's* crew were killed and 24 injured; the ship was abandoned after efforts to save her failed.

This – what Admiral Woodward called the 'first major missile strike on the British Fleet in forty years' [236, p. 170] – caused him much anxiety: was there a technical or a human failure which allowed the Exocet to penetrate the *Sheffield's* warning system? But, whatever the human disaster involved, he must maintain his type 42 frigates as 'pickets', since his carriers were 'not expendable'. [236, p. 174] '*Sheffield*' as he put it, 'told us that you can get badly hurt out there'. [236, p. 177] For Mrs Thatcher, the spectacle of British sailors being 'badly hurt' could not be regarded with the same necessary detachment as a serving officer. As Cecil Parkinson put it, 'The most important thing about it was that the military and a lot of us had been wanting to see what Margaret Thatcher's reaction would be to really major British casualties, because there was a feeling she might find this unbearable, the idea of all those lives lost'. She was 'very shaken, very concerned', but 'she didn't waver at all'. Her reaction was influenced by the service reassurance that 'these sorts of things happen in war', with Admiral Fieldhouse reckoning that the British might lose 'up to 3,000 people'. (200, pp. 34–5)

The element of luck in warfare, never to be discounted, seemed to be deserting Woodward: on 6 May two Sea Harriers took off on a routine air combat patrol and were never seen again; this cost Woodward ten per cent of his Harrier force, 'gone at a stroke'. The weather remained 'murky all day'. [236, p. 179] His anxiety about the War Cabinet's intentions (which to him seemed far from the belligerence depicted by Mrs Thatcher's critics and enemies) resurfaced. He could not 'hit anyone outside the TEZ', he could not take risks. He was feeling 'very hassled and suspicious of Cabinet'. If he could not take risks, then the enemy could strike from safe havens, and 'the strength we came with will be whittled away'. He made a long signal to the Commander-in-Chief 'giving a list of the riskier possibilities for the next week or so' but really pointing to the need for Woodward to know whether the Cabinet would 'actually decide to land, on the day'. And, 'to cap it all, the submarines have been stopped from doing anything nasty in the area of the main Arg [sic] surface force'. Some of his ships developed engine and other technical faults. Nerves were on edge: 'too many Ops Rooms were over-reacting to a flock of seagulls'. [236, pp. 180, 182]

Woodward's frustration reflected, again, the gap that was opening between the civilian and the military mind. The War Cabinet's decision to authorise Woodward to attack Argentine warships outside the TEZ, far from initiating a ruthless assault on the enemy, had reinforced, in political minds, the need to keep alive the hopes of a peaceful resolution of the crisis. The War Cabinet now saw much virtue in Francis Pym's arguments for the primacy of diplomacy. The British public needed to be convinced that their Government must go to war. The Government revived its interest in the Peruvian plan on 5 May, accepting an interim administration of the Falklands made up of a small group of countries, excluding the United Kingdom, to supervise the withdrawal of Argentine forces and to be involved in negotiations for a 'definitive agreement on the status of the Islands.' [90, p. 296] Pym on 4 May, referring to the Peruvian initiative, had acknowledged (rather ominously from the Falkland Islanders' point of view) that if they wanted a different solution than that of remaining under British sovereignty, the British Government 'will not stand in their way'. [114, 4 May 1982, col. 25] On 7 May Pym said that the British Government was considering yet another peace initiative, this time emanating from the United Nations Security Council. This would involve the withdrawal of Argentine troops from the Falklands, the withdrawal of the Task Force, the opening of negotiations on the future of the Islands, the ending of European Community sanctions and the institution of a joint administration of the Islands under United Nations' auspices. The British, Pym claimed, had 'no desire to escalate military action'. [36, pp. 118–19] But this was contradicted by the British Ministry of Defence media spokesman on 7 May, when at six o'clock he warned that British forces would, following the *Sheffield* disaster, treat as hostile any Argentine ships and aircraft located more than 12 miles off the Argentine coast, a declaration which Argentina described as 'a belligerent action which can only escalate the conflict'. [36, p. 120] Field Marshal the Lord Bramall later praised the lack of 'excess of back-seat driving' [26, p. 8] in the conduct of the campaign, but Woodard's anxieties did not confirm this. The problem for both the military and the politicians was whose back-seat should predominate at any given time; and from 4 to 16 May diplomacy again came to the fore.

The British were, however, always nervous about the implications of the United Nations' intervention, insisting above all that, as

Mrs Thatcher put it in the Commons on 13 May, the Argentines 'do not enter into any settlement at the outset on the understanding that they have sovereignty at the end'. [114, 13 May 1982 col. 942] Divided counsels seemed to resurface when on the same day Francis Pym stressed that the Government was not ruling out the discussion of sovereignty: 'we still remain willing to discuss it as one of the factors in negotiations about the long-term future'. He noted that the Islanders' wishes for that future 'may or may not be the same as before' – a hint that he hoped that the crisis as it had so far unfolded might have changed their minds on the choice between the dangers of war and the security of peace, even of a peace that left them under Argentine sovereignty. The Islanders, he went on, needed to consider how their prosperity, economic development and security could best be organised: 'These questions at present are some way ahead and the Government retain an open mind'. [114, cols. 957–8] He was given support by Edward Heath, who warned against the Islanders having a 'veto' on any solution as they did in 1970–74: 'We did not fight Hitler or Mussolini because they were dictators or because of their internal policies. We fought them because they had reached such a state of power that they were a menace to vital British interests'. [114, 13 May 1982, cols. 966, 968] Enoch Powell immediately attacked what he saw as the drift towards compromise, warning that no definitive agreement could be made without the consent of the Islanders. The Prime Minister must restore the unity of the Government and that clarity of purpose upon which basis the whole operation began. [114, col. 978]

The chances of the United Nations' initiative succeeding depended largely on the same factors that had dominated the previous peace proposals: the wishes of the Falkland Islanders; the administration of the Islands; and the eventual outcome of the negotiations, that is, the sovereignty question. They also depended on the balance of the military situation, and the suspicions held by both sides about their respective intentions. Britain's military position was the most vulnerable; and it was harder for her to accept proposals for a ceasefire or any other 'restraint' in the conduct of military operations. Argentina still held the initiative: she occupied the Islands, and she could launch air attacks on the British fleet. Yet when the British sought to bolster up their position on 7 May by announcing the extension of the Exclusion Zone up to 12 miles from the Argentine coast, this could be presented by Argentina as mere provocation.

Perez de Cuellar identified the heads of a possible compromise: a ceasefire, withdrawal of forces, the lifting of sanctions and exclusion zones, and the start of negotiations. Britain conceded on the administration of the Islands, accepting some United Nations' role in the interim administration; Pym agreed to talk about sovereignty. Argentina offered to omit the offensive word from its proposals, which was now an 'objective' of the talks, not a prior condition. [90, pp. 295–8] Sir Anthony Parsons and the British War Cabinet went through the documentation so far on 15 and 16 May. The British proposal was that the United Nations would administer the Islands with equal Argentine and British representation alongside it, for a period of six months, which could be extended. Negotiations would continue under the United Nations' Secretary General's auspices to reach a definitive solution to the dispute. During the administration of the Islands by the United Nations the two states' claims to sovereignty would not be affected by any development (such as Argentine immigration or settlement) that might take place after the agreement was signed. None of the points of the provisional agreement would affect the rights, claims and position of each of Argentina and Britain in the final peaceful agreement over the Islands. There would be no preconceived position regarding the results of negotiations, but Britain still stood firm on the importance of Article 73 of the United Nations Charter, which made the interests of the peoples of non-self-governing territories paramount, and insisted on taking into account the political aspirations of the inhabitants. The dependencies of South Georgia and the South Sandwich Islands would not be part of the settlement. Before any parts of the process could begin, Argentina must withdraw her forces from the Falklands. [90, pp. 204–6] This, Sir Anthony Parsons later claimed, was an 'absolutely serious offer' which 'any sensible government' would accept; though he noted, quite rightly, that Mrs Thatcher would have had difficulties with the Conservative Party if the terms had been accepted. [19, pp. 39–40]

This document was handed to Perez de Cuellar as the British 'final offer' to which Argentina must reply within 48 hours. Britain was aware of the passing of time, and its implications for its final decision to mount, or not to mount, a landing on the Islands. Argentina still felt, quite rightly, that any delay was on her side: the British position had softened; there were signs of disagreement in the British War Cabinet. [90, p. 306]

Argentina's final position was that Britain must withdraw completely from the South Atlantic (to 'their normal bases and areas of operation'), that the interim administration of the Islands should be the exclusive responsibility of the United Nations, and with the administration of the Islands made up of individuals of nationalities other than Britain and Argentina. There would be no restrictions on Argentine immigration or settlement, which might end in a kind of Argentine sovereignty by stealth. When considering the British proposals, the Argentines rejected the exclusion of the dependencies, the continuation of the Islands Councils, the open-ended character of the temporary administration, the deployment of Article 73 of the United Nations Charter and the inaccessibility of the Islands to Argentine citizens. [90, p. 310] Sir Anthony Parsons later described the Argentine response as a 'flood of rhetoric' which was not directed to the points at issue. [19, pp. 38–40] Perez de Cuellar suggested a few small changes to the text of his proposals, but the vexed question of 'mutual force withdrawal' was not addressed. [90, p. 317] Argentine later claimed that she had not rejected the process, but had merely wanted 'clarification'. [36, p. 129] This was disingenuous; but there could be no doubt that the British Government was treating its proposals as a kind of ultimatum, and as a means of putting Argentine sincerity to the proof. On 20 May Mrs Thatcher denounced the Argentine response as a rejection of the British peace proposals. She told the House of Commons that the 'key sentence' of Articles 8 and 9 of the British proposals for a draft agreement with Argentina was that 'these negotiations shall be initiated without prejudice to the rights, claims and position of the parties and without prejudice to the outcome'. The wishes of the Falkland Islanders would be paramount, though Mrs Thatcher moved closer to Pym's position, that if the Islanders wished to go under Argentine rule she believed that 'this country will uphold the wishes of the Islanders'. Argentina, she claimed, had rejected 'proposal after proposal' and was still bent on occupying the Falklands, leading eventually to sovereignty. The British proposals were 'no longer on the table'. [114, 20 May 1982, cols. 480–1]

But the table was not yet swept clean, as least as far as the United Nations' Secretary General was concerned. Perez de Cuellar sought to revive the negotiations, [19, p. 41] but it is hard to see how the British and Argentine differences could be reconciled. The problem for Argentina was, paradoxically, not unlike that which faced the British negotiators in their 1921 negotiations with representatives of Sinn Fein for an Anglo-Irish treaty. Then, in 1921, the British were prepared to make concessions on detail; but they would not budge on their insistence that the Irish must accept an oath of allegiance to the Crown as symbolic of their common citizenship of the British Empire. Now, in 1982, Argentina was prepared to make concessions on detail, such as the administration of the Islands, but was determined that the original purpose of its invasion of the Falklands, the transfer of sovereignty, could and would not be abandoned; indeed, it is hard to see how Argentine opinion generally could have retreated from this position, one increasingly strengthened by its continuing occupation of the islands: possession was, if not nine tenths of the law, then a significant proportion of tenths. Moreover, the fundamental Argentine fear – one shared by the British, as it happened – that her opponent was stringing out the talks in order to buy time for military operations, still governed events. The British decision to publish its response to the proposals, which Argentina denounced as a breach of the procedures agreed with the Secretary General, [90, p. 318] seemed like, and indeed was, a sign that the War Cabinet, and certainly the Prime Minister, believed that the negotiating process was at an end. Even as Perez de Cuellar produced more proposals, on 20 May, Admiral Woodward's landings on the Islands began; and Sir Anthony Parsons, feared that Argentina would 'somehow reverse the diplomatic situation to our discredit', and while he would welcome any initiative there was 'one unattainable condition: immediate and unqualified Argentine agreement to withdraw from the Islands'. [19, p. 41] At dawn on 21 May British Forces landed at San Carlos Water.

6

From Bridgehead to Goose Green

The diplomatic efforts that had continued and intensified after the sinking of the *General Belgrano* were, in the opinion of Admiral Woodhouse, almost another dimension of what he feared most in the days and weeks before he received his orders to proceed with landing on the Falklands: the attrition that was threatening to undermine his command. On the day that HMS *Sheffield* was lost a Harrier was shot down by a 'Blowpipe' missile while strafing Goose Green airstrip. Two days later he lost his two Harriers in what was believed to be a mid-air collision. Fortunately, additional Harriers had been converted, at speed, for in-flight refuelling and these now flew directly to Ascension Island, taking nine hours to cover the journey. Some were embarked on the *Atlantic Conveyor*, but others flew on south, again being refuelled in flight, to bring the Task Force's air element up to strength. The air war continued in a desultory fashion. Harriers attacked ground targets and engaged in brief clashes with Argentine Mirage fighters. There were a few minor British successes, such as the shooting down of a Puma helicopter near Stanley; Vulcans made bombing runs from Ascension Island. Argentine Skyhawks on 12 May attacked HMS *Glasgow*, damaging but not sinking her. [179, pp. 90–1] But all the time Woodward chafed at his static position, one imposed on him by the War Cabinet. [236, pp. 179–80] And from 6 to 20 May, while discussions were taking place about what the Task Force should do, now that it had reached the Falklands (John Nott, for his part, favouring a blockade of the Islands, and showing again his lively awareness of the consequences for Britain of a permanent military presence there), [90, p. 323] the fleet was preoccupied with defending itself. This was not easy to do. Woodward was concerned about poor or misleading information; the Royal Air Force, he claimed, was making 'best guesses' about the character of, for example, fishing vessels that might turn out to be somewhat more dangerous items. These and similar errors 'kept on happening' and Northwood felt obliged to censure

Woodward for upsetting the RAF high command. [236, pp. 209–10] Woodward remained unimpressed. On 11 May he wrote feelingly in his diary, 'weather finally cleared so started high bombing Port Stanley airfield. Probably very inaccurate'. [236, p. 216] The Commander-in-Chief of amphibious landing operations mused on the attrition worked on his 'precious Wessex 5 helicopters', in what he regarded as the 'off line of march' recapture of South Georgia. [46, p. 93]

Woodward was aware of what he discerned as a 'high degree of caution and scepticism in the Ministry of Defence', and in particular of the Army Staff's doubts about the necessity and likely success of an amphibious operation. [236, p. xvii] Yet he had to plan to repossess the Islands, even before he had been ordered to do so. On 16 April Woodward met Clapp and Julian Thompson and suggested several possible options: one was to use Carcass Island or possibly 'somewhere in Byron Sound' as a 'stone frigate' or stores dump from which the army could move out towards Stanley. 'Clearly', Clapp remarked, 'he had no idea of the amount of equipment that would have to be landed, only to be moved forward again over a very considerable distance'. Another suggestion was to construct an airstrip in the valley that led eastwards from Stevelly Bay in West Falkland from which to operate Phantom Air Defence fighters during the opening stage of the assault; but Clapp complained that Woodward did not accept that the 3rd Commando brigade had not the plant, equipment, men or time. Other suggestions were met with an equally sceptical response by Clapp, the Army and the Royal Marines. [46, pp. 71–3]

These disagreements were all part of the friction of war, and of an inevitable degree of inter-service rivalry; it was not surprising that each branch of the service felt that it knew its own business best. More troubling was the question of what the War Cabinet wanted its services to do. On 26 April an 'outline plan' set out various tactical considerations, putting the case for and against the possible choices of a landing place. The 'Executive Paragraph' read:

> A strong and sustainable British presence ashore will be achieved by landing 3 Cdo Bde RM augmented by two Parachute Battalion groups (about 5,500 men) on or about the 16 May. The force will establish a bridgehead close enough to exert direct military and psychological pressure against the main Argentine force in the Port Stanley area. This may be enough to convince the Argentines that their own position is militarily untenable and that they can honourably agree to withdraw but the possibility that the enemy may

> advance for a decisive battle must be allowed for in selecting the position for the bridgehead. [46, p. 94]

This paragraph bears closer study. It adumbrated two possibilities: an Argentine withdrawal or an Argentine attack. This was a perfectly logical, if somewhat obvious, prognosis. But the gap between these two was more profound than the text seemed to suggest. To put 'psychological' pressure on the Argentine forces merely by landing might well be achieved; but 'pressure' might best be exerted by a landing that put the Argentine forces in Stanley in more direct harm's way. A landing force on the bridgehead would be in a vulnerable position for several reasons: it would be open to Argentine air-strikes; it would probably have to wait for an indeterminate time to see if the 'pressure' was working; or it might be asked to make a demonstration against the nearest Argentine military presence to show that British patience was wearing thin. Clapp was doubtful if a landing at San Carlos Bay (the recommended place in the Options paragraph of the 'Outline Plan') was the most effective means of 'exerting direct pressure' against Argentine forces in the Stanley area. [46, p. 94]

A brief analysis of one historical amphibious operation, that in 1778 against Saint Lucia, exposes some of the difficulties involved. During the passage to the landing site the division of responsibility was clearly delineated between the Navy and Army commanders. But once at the landing site the troops had to be moved ashore, and here the question of responsibility arose, and a clear 'chain of command' had to be established to ensure that 'at a given and agreed point in the operation command moved smoothly from the sailors to the soldiers'. No-one must have any doubt about their part in the plan. [83, pp. 12–13] Once the ships had arrived off the landing place their anchorage had to be protected. In 1778 they were vulnerable to fire-ships. Once the landing had taken place the Navy's task was logistical; it had now to make a secure communication between land and sea. [83, p. 115]

These considerations were as vital in 1982 as in 1778, though the security of the anchorage was even more pertinent in an age of air warfare. There was another modern danger, that of mines laid by the Argentines in Falkland Sound; the Task Force had no minesweepers to deal with this threat, and Woodward was obliged to despatch HMS *Alacrity* to test for mines. [236, pp. 201–3] The question of command proved to be a vexatious one. The Command and Control paragraph of the 'Outline Plan' implied that the task organisation was to be changed back to that under which the Task Force had set forth: that Clapp and

Julian Thompson were 'task units' operating under Woodward's command. This did not accord with the present command structure under which all three officers were co-equal Commanders Task Group. [46, pp. 94–5]

The choice of a landing site was governed by certain fundamental considerations, those dictated by military, naval and amphibious requirements. The British, Julian Thompson explained, no longer had the equipment (such as tracked landing vehicles, swimming tanks and gun-armed landing craft) to make an assault on a well-defended beach. [206, p. 561] The anchorage must be one offering a difficult approach for, or an easy defence against, Exocet or submarine attack. The land surrounding the anchorage must be low enough for ship's radar to detect distant aircraft or so high that the approaching aircraft would have little time to identify and select a target. Defending ships must be able to lie 'hidden' behind some form of land obstacle. The 'Amphibious Objective Area' had to be taken by surprise with the minimum of loss en route. This would require a night approach. The site must offer waters easy for the merchant ships accompanying the Task Force and warships to navigate without using systems detectable by the enemy. A calm anchorage was needed so that the roll-on/roll-off vessels could unload without hindrance from sea-swell. The beaches must be capable of accepting a brigade landing quickly into at least four different areas so that the commanders and battalions could swiftly achieve an all-round and mutual defence for themselves, and the anchorage as a whole. Each beach needed to be within a short march to the dominating ground which would have to be occupied against counter-attack. The beaches needed suitable gradients for landing craft and one beach at least must be co-located with a suitably large flat space for a 'beach support area'. Dry landings were required to prevent foot disease among the troops. The beaches must have good infantry and tank exits, and must be out of enemy gunfire range. The surrounding area must be suitable for Rapier anti-aircraft missile sites, and the routes from the beaches to Stanley should, if possible, be suitable for men on foot and light vehicles. The distance to Stanley should, if possible, be short and not dominated nor easily blocked or vulnerable to ambush by the enemy. [46, pp. 99–100]

Special Forces gathered vital information about the most suitable landing place for British troops. [80, p. 89] San Carlos Bay was perceived to possess most, but not all, of these essentials. For example, it was believed to be unoccupied, but within striking distance of Darwin and Goose Green, where Argentine troops were placed; but these were off the 'line of march' and could be contained by methods other than direct attack. Moreover, the bay was well-sheltered. But it was vulnerable to un-refuelled Argentine aircraft and submarine attack. And there were few if any convenient areas where helicopters or Harriers could hide: 'it was a long way to yomp to Stanley if helicopters were not to be employed'. But in any case helicopters were too few to operate beyond an 'ammunition forward and casualties back' function. [46, p. 101; 236, pp. 189–90]

On 12 May Admiral Fieldhouse had obtained an operational order 'to repossess the Falkland Islands as quickly as possible'. [46, pp. 108, 133] This was more energetic than the original order to land 'with a view to repossession'; but the ambiguities of the previous order seem to have overshadowed the second. Fieldhouse saw the original order as a delaying tactic so that the infantry reinforcements (5 Brigade) would be available to help meet the aim of repossession. Julian Thompson and Michael Clapp took it to mean that, once landed, the landing force would be largely confined to consolidating a beachhead until 5 Brigade arrived, after which the force would break out and advance on Stanley using the newly arrived 5 Brigade mainly as a reserve and a rear-guard. The new, 12 May Order still left this latter question unanswered ('were we to wait for the second brigade before breaking out? Was 5 Brigade to be used as reserves or in the front line…?). The phrase 'repossession of the whole Islands' offered no detailed plan as to how this was to be done. The 12 May Order referred to the need to 'push forward from the bridgehead area, so far as the maintenance of its security allows, to gain information and to forward the ultimate object of repossession'. [46, pp. 133–4] Admiral Woodhouse sought to clarify the landing force's task by explaining that the concept to continue operations was to destroy the enemy reserves at Darwin and Goose Green 'as soon as possible to allow freedom of manoeuvre and if opportunity offers for you to achieve this during phase 4 (Land Operations before the arrival of 5 Brigade) I will welcome that'. However, he stressed, 'we must still aim to close with the main enemy at Port Stanley'. [46, p. 136]

The execution of the order to repossess the Falklands was preceded by British attacks on the Argentine forces there. The SAS raided Pebble Island on 15 May, destroying 11 Argentine aircraft; Vulcans and Harriers delivered over 51 tons of ordinance on the Islands, though with less effective impact by the Vulcans. [83, p. 161] The success of any landing would depend mainly on two factors: good intelligence work, which would define the task at hand; and a well-co-ordinated, and above all unopposed landing, which would enable the troops to establish their bridgehead and set up anti-aircraft defences. The first of these proved hard to get. The British did not have the capability to obtain air photographs of the enemy until nearly the end of the campaign. They could only estimate the strength of the opposition. [90, pp. 332–4] There was the danger that Argentine morale and the character of their soldiers would be underestimated; the SAS carried out a night deception raid on Darwin-Goose Green on 20 May, reporting that the 'enemy soldiers had little stomach for a fight and that whenever they met SAS patrols they ran away, nor were they particularly staunch in prepared positions'. [93, p. 44] However, Brigadier Julian Thompson was more realistic: this affair, he told his officers just before the British landings, would be 'no picnic'. [215, p. 97]

The second hazard, that of confusion at the landing stage, was one that particularly concerned Michael Clapp. The problem, he stressed, 'was complex and so inundated with variables that it was easier to conclude that the fog of war might be at its thickest, making instant decision-making the only correct action'. [46, p. 127] This concern was shared by the military. The technical aspects of the landing craft arrangements had been rehearsed on 13 May, but one officer later admitted that 'Although I am sure they (the instructors) understood it, I had the general impression that no one had a clue what they were talking about'. [215, p. 97] In the event, the British landing on 21 May at San Carlos Water was relatively easy. It was unopposed; Special Boat Service parties were on the beaches to guide the troops ashore; naval gunfire on Berkeley Sound provided a diversion, as did an SAS attack on Darwin. The only contact with the enemy was the SBS rooting out of a small group of Argentine soldiers at Fanning Head, overlooking the entrance to San Carlos Water. The only British losses were three aircrew of two Gazelle helicopters, which were shot at by Argentine soldiers withdrawing from Fanning Head who had not been involved in the fight with the SBS. [90, pp. 340–1]

Nevertheless, the landing did not go without mishap. The leading landing craft picked up the men intended for the second craft, while the second craft collected those meant for the first. This necessitated a revised order of march once ashore. The landing was slower than expected, with a gentle swell causing the craft to heave up and down. The lifeboats, lowered to the halfway position, snagged on the head-ropes, creating more confusion, with no ship's hands to help. One soldier's gun went off accidentally, wounding one of 2 Para's men in the foot. When the coxswain shouted 'off troops', nobody moved; soldiers, soon to face enemy fire, proved reluctant to get their feet wet. [93, pp. 29–30]

Serious difficulties lay ahead. Perhaps the most troublesome was the British failure to gain mastery of the air. The fleet anchored in San Carlos Water was vulnerable to Argentine attack; and, as Field Marshal Lord Bramhall put it, in something of an understatement, a 'favourable air situation would normally have been an essential precaution'. [26, p. 11] Admiral Woodward took refuge in the hope that the Argentine Air Force 'would prove no braver than the Navy'. [236, p. 246] He was mistaken. Michael Clapp felt that the Operational Directive was too vague, omitting as it did any strategy for a subsequent land battle ('secure a bridgehead' and then 'push forward from the bridgehead area, to gain information and to forward the ultimate objective of repossession'). There was still no definition of the task of 5 Brigade, of how the operations of this Brigade should be linked to those of the landing force. [46, pp. 134–5] There was a general appreciation of the enemy strength on the Falklands, which was estimated at 11,000 troops, and a reasonably clear picture of the Argentine forces around Stanley, including their air defence system and their heavy weapons; but information about the enemy strength at Darwin and Goose Green was less comprehensive, and accounts of this varied. [206, p. 565]

The landings on 21 May were the beginning, not the end, of one of the most – perhaps the most – testing periods for the whole British campaign in the South Atlantic. This was for two reasons. First, the Task Force ships anchored in San Carlos Water were soon attacked by the Argentine Air Force. By the end of the first day *Argonaut* and *Antrim* were both badly damaged; *Brilliant* and *Broadsword* were hit, and took casualties. Of all the frigates only *Plymouth* and *Yarmouth* escaped unscathed. [46, p. 183] On 25 May HMS *Coventry* was sunk, when she slewed across the path of the *Broadsword*'s Sea Wolf missile launcher, thus depriving Woodward of the last of his 'original picket ships'. [236, pp. 286–7, 290] The troopship, *Canberra* (the 'Great White Whale') escaped, despite her conspicuous appearance. More effective air support for the anchored vessels could only be given if Admiral Woodward moved his carrier *Hermes* nearer the scene of battle, but this he felt he must not do: 'Carrier group cannot risk half our long-term air defence force by coming much further than 56″30′W′.' [236, p. 188]

Woodward, contemplating the losses so far sustained in this battle, drew comfort from the example of history: 'little had changed since the eighteenth century', he confided, except of course for the hardware and the speed of the conflict: the people were just the same, the spirit in the ships was just the same, the courage of the men was just the same. Was not the *Argonaut* facing incoming Skyhawks comparable with the best of Britain's naval traditions? What difference between *Ardent*, crippled and burning, still fighting and Sir Richard Grenville's *Revenge* all those centuries ago…'. [236, p. 265] There can be no doubt about the Royal Navy's traditions and their importance in shaping the outlook of its officers and men; but this must be set beside the reality of the sinking of the *Atlantic Conveyor*, with the loss of five Chinook heavy-lift and six Wessex medium-lift helicopters. These, plus 11 Sea Kings and five Wessex helicopters, would have been sufficient to move the bulk of the British brigade to Mount Kent, overlooking Stanley; the sinking of the *Atlantic Conveyor* by an air-launched Exocet missile destroyed all but one of the Chinooks. This setback, on D Day plus Four (25 May), did not spell disaster for the Task Force. Argentine airpower, inflicted serious but not decisive losses on the fleet, and Argentine aircraft losses were severe: the Argentine Air Force was 'clearly unable to maintain the attrition rate the British imposed'. [99, pp. 105–7]

John Nott had surmised that the fleet might lose 'up to five or six ships'. [172] Mrs Thatcher seems, for once, to have lost her coolness under fire; on hearing of the loss of the *Atlantic Conveyor* she spent what she later called 'one of the worse nights of the war'. [203, pp. 226–8] Her anxiety was shared by Admiral Woodward who asked himself, 'can we live with that? Answer: obviously not, because if it went on for a few days after that, at the same rate of destruction, we'd lose all the reinforcements as well – there would be no protection for the amphibious ships, or for the carriers, and the rest of the Royal Navy is weeks away'. He later acknowledged that 'the nearest I came to ringing up home and saying "Hey, boss, I think we're losing this" was on the 25th May when we lost both *Coventry* and *Atlantic Conveyor*' [237] The Argentine Air Force's attrition was to him small consolation: the Royal Navy was not winning what he called the 'prize fight'. Woodward placed much reliance on the Rapier batteries which would be set up on land; meanwhile he looked to his Sea Harriers which, however, were only excellent so far because the Argentines had not sent in high level escorts to take them on while their bombers 'do the business below'. [236, pp. 269–71]

But there was another, if paradoxical, issue confronting the British campaign: that its very success so far was intensifying diplomatic and international opinion pressure for Britain to hold her hand, suspend hostilities, and look once again for a peaceful resolution of the crisis.

Some delegates at the United Nations called for a standstill and a ceasefire. As John Nott put it, 'It was just as possible for us to lose the war in London as it was to do so on the battlefield of the Falklands'. The Government, he acknowledged, was 'in severe trouble both with domestic and international opinion, and it was urgently necessary for our troops to establish early contact with the Argentine forces'. [172] A new Peruvian initiative was launched suggesting a ceasefire, mutual withdrawal of forces, and an interim administration, which Argentina formally accepted on 21 May. [90, p. 346] Latin American support for Argentina gathered momentum, with the Rio Treaty meeting on 28/29 May condemning the 'disproportionate and unjustified British armed attack'. [290, p. 344] Alexander Haig thought the moment opportune for the British to 'show readiness to negotiate'. The European Community still maintained sanctions against Argentina, but with unease, and with Ireland and Italy's opting out. [90, pp. 346–8]

It is difficult to understand why those in the international community who favoured further negotiations after the successful landing of British troops at San Carlos Water felt they had much chance of success. It was easier for Argentina to agree to a proposal that involved a ceasefire and a mutual withdrawal of forces, even back to Buenos Aires; their initial seizure of the Falklands had been almost bloodless, and certainly easy. The British were in a different position. Their progress to, and landing on, the Falklands was a hard, risky and dangerous affair; it would be as hard to withdraw from the Islands as it had been getting to them in the first place. As the British Ambassador in Washington put it 'the establishment of a bridgehead in the Falklands was bound to have a major effect on our diplomatic position. We could not in present circumstances consider the idea of British withdrawal from the Falklands or the establishment of an interim administration'. [90, p. 346] The loss of the *Belgrano* was a shock to Argentina; but British losses, while fewer in number, had a profound impact on British public opinion. When the *Coventry* was sunk, John Nott was advised by the Admirals not to name the ship for fear it might disclose important information to the enemy. The result was that the telephone exchanges were 'jammed all night by calls from relatives of the entire Task Force, worried about their sons and daughters'. [172] It would be hard to accept losses and then abandon the bridgehead in the Falklands for which they had been accepted. On the other hand, if the losses continued to mount, then the public might waver in its support of the war.

It was this pressure that the War Cabinet in London felt keenly. Nott acknowledged that Julian Thompson was 'understandably concerned to consolidate and build his bridgehead at San Carlos'; but the international and domestic political situation made it 'urgently necessary for our troops to establish early contact with the Argentine forces'. [172] Mrs Thatcher described the frustration felt in the War Cabinet at what 'appeared to be little movement by our troops out of the bridgehead'. [203, p. 228] Nott claimed that the decision to 'move forward' was made by the armed forces chiefs themselves, Admirals Lewin and Fieldhouse. [172] Admiral Woodward was concerned that the bridgehead troops were becoming spectators in a war of attrition fought by his ships. San Carlos had been a 'high risk' affair, and 'It must now go high risk on land'. [236, p. 301] Brigadier Thompson attributed his lack of movement to the loss of his helicopters on the *Atlantic Conveyor*. He was unsympathetic to instructions from London that the 3rd Commando Brigade was to start moving out of the bridgehead. The Brigade was well dug in and able to protect the beachhead while its supplies were landed; there was no point in advancing until this was completed. Thompson had a lively awareness of the classic danger of an army outstripping its supplies. Contact with the enemy meant a swift depletion of ammunition: 'more and more has to be transported further and further'. As the Brigade advanced, its line of supply would be vulnerable to air attack, and it would be abandoning its air defence perimeter in San Carlos Water. [205, pp. 68–9]

But this was not a simple case of the political at odds with the military priorities, though this was certainly part of the disagreement. Field Marshal the Lord Bramall ascribed the delay to the failure to put the commander-in-chief land forces, Jeremy Moore, ashore during the 72 'crucial hours' after the bridgehead had been established. This meant that he was 'out of touch with the battle and unable to provide the immediate impetus and direction which was required'. [26, p. 8] There was in this remark at least an implied criticism of Julian Thompson. Admiral Woodward was aware too of the limited time available for the land campaign to be conducted; and he feared that the Argentines would find a way to replenish their supply of Exocet missiles. The inventory of British losses so far was daunting: 'Harriers (five); several SK4s and 5s; Chinooks (three) Wessex (five); *Ardent, Antelope, Sheffield, Coventry* and *Atlantic Conveyor*. Badly damaged: *Argonaut, Antrim and Glasgow*, LSLs (two); *Arrow* (defective)'. [236, p. 301] The War Cabinet had its own concerns, which William Whitelaw explained as 'having got a beach-head at San Carlos, we were going to get stuck there…There were memories of the time we took to break out of the beach-head at Normandy…just to be stuck in a very small area and confined there, we've had all sorts of trouble. In every way not least on the diplomatic front because...all the proposals for cease-fires would become stronger...So a breakout was very important'. [19, p. 102]

It is inappropriate for a lay person to criticise military decisions, the arguments for and against which are finely balanced (though there are, it is true, fewer inhibitions about lay criticism of decisions taken by politicians). Major General Jeremy Moore's order to Julian Thompson of 13 May instructed him to 'push forward from the bridgehead area so far as the momentum of its security allows, to gain information to establish moral and physical domination over the enemy...'. Thompson estimated that the nearest enemy position was on Darwin and Goose Green, some 19 to 21 kilometres respectively as the crow flies; but, as he noted wryly, not even paratroopers or commandos fly like crows. [205, pp. 73–4] Moreover, although he knew 'there wasn't anything between me and the higher ground west of Stanley, that wasn't the point. The point was that we had to have proper logistical support and especially we had to move guns forward if we were going to start fighting in the area of Mount Harriet'. 'Logistics' was a common military term, but what it meant was, for example, about '60 to 70 Sea Kings to move one battery of artillery plus all its ammunition'. As he put it, 'there was absolutely no point in rushing out of the beachhead with a packet of sandwiches in one pocket and 5 rounds of ammunition in the other to engage the enemy, who were some 50 miles away, until we had our logistics ashore'. (200, p. 43) A 'raid' on Darwin and Goose Green looked to be the most promising way of initiating 'domination' over the enemy. On 23 May 2 Para was formally notified that they were to raid Darwin and Goose Green, and began to prepare for this operation. But the weather prevented the helicopter lift of artillery to support 2 Para and the mission was cancelled on 24 May. [205, p. 77]

London remained impatient. On 26 May instructions were issued that the operation be revived: 'more action was required all round'. [205, p. 81] Thus the attack on Darwin/Goose Green seems on the face of it to be a classic example of political demands forcing the military pace. There is much to be said for this interpretation. Mrs Thatcher believed that 'what was wrong was to snatch diplomatic defeat from the jaws of victory'; [203, p. 230] and 'diplomatic defeat' was more likely to happen if the army remained static, since proposals for a ceasefire would gather momentum. But Field Marshal the Lord Bramall, while noting that the 'acute shortage of helicopters...had slowed down the logistical build-up' reaffirmed that the Brigade had misunderstood its tasks and objectives, and that there had been a 'tactical hiatus'. On this occasion, he added the 'wider intelligence picture' helped Whitehall see the tactical dangers of 'getting stuck halfway across East Falkland by weather' than could be observed on the spot. [26, p. 16] Brigadier Christopher Dunphie, chief of a 'small, hastily gathered staff' (appointed when Major General Jeremy Moore and his headquarters left Northwood to take command of the Falklands landing force) claimed that 'among our deductions were that the major battle would be in the hills west of Stanley and that every available unit would be required'. The enemy at Goose Green 'could pose a threat to the logistical base once the majority of the fighting units had been deployed. It would probably need to be masked or eliminated'. Leaving a battalion to 'mask' the Argentine garrison would, Dunphie argued, reduce the units available for the major battle. The army staff briefed Admiral Fieldhouse on these findings. 'The morning after the *Atlantic Conveyor* and *Coventry* were sunk, the C in C came into our office'. The Navy was suffering both from attacks by the Argentine Air Force and the South Atlantic weather: 'he wanted action on land'. Admiral Fieldhouse spoke to Brigadier Thompson, who submitted his plan: to move three units to the hills west of Stanley, while 2 Para 'raided' Goose Green. Fieldhouse advised one change: 'delete "raid", insert "destroy" the enemy at Goose Green. The C in C agreed. [56, 17 Jan. 2002]

Brigadier Thompson later believed that he had made mistakes in his choice of operations at Goose Green, 'perhaps symptomatic of his belief that it was an unnecessary diversion from the aim of seizing Stanley'. He should have commanded in person; he should have taken another battalion or commando with him; he should have taken at least a troop of CVRT (Combat Vehicle Reconnaissance Tracked) Scimitar or Scorpion light tank. He reflected that he 'asked more of 2 Para than he should have done'. In the Falklands battles, and especially this one, the attacking troops did not enjoy the prescribed (minimum) ratio of 3:1 advantage over the defenders. He was mistaken in his calculation, but it was a plausible one. In the end, 'good came out of it', but 'this could not have been foreseen, nor the credit claimed, by those who ordered the attack from 8,000 miles away'. The 'good' was that British determination was illustrated, and that the Argentines were convinced that the main attacks would come from the South-West, instead of the North and West. [223, pp. 26–7] But these were, he held, incidental advantages. His military assessment was that Goose Green was not a major threat to his overall operations: 'You can see why if you look at a map; Goose Green does not lie on the road to Stanley and the garrisons there could easily have been masked or contained from making a flank attack as we pushed out for Stanley; Goose Green stands on a narrow isthmus, a real bottleneck, so a raid on the airfield was all was needed…'. He was, however, 'not at all opposed to attacking it if we could provide sufficient support'. [166, p. 256]

When the commander of 2 Para, Lieutenant Colonel 'H' Jones was given his orders to attack the enemy at Goose Green he was to use the originally agreed plan. He was given an estimate of enemy strength (two companies 12th Infantry Regiment, one of the 25th Infantry Regiment, a platoon of the 8th Infantry Regiment and possibly an amphibious platoon, together with artillery and helicopter support). An SAS briefing shortly afterwards advised that one company held the Goose Green position. [205, pp. 81–2] This raised another question for the attacking force: Brigade HQ was steadily accumulating information, but the SAS was on the spot and providing what seemed to be much closer, up-to-date intelligence detail. There was no definitive intelligence available. 2 Para's post-offensive report was critical of the lack of authoritative intelligence at this stage of the campaign. [215, pp. 119–20] But the soldier who would plan and lead the attack, Colonel Jones, was not concerned too much about intelligence-gathering and dissemination. He was eager to fight the battle for which he felt he had been prepared all his career. He had been furious when the first offensive had been cancelled, [3, p. 101] and felt that the army was 'not winning. We are losing'. He was delighted when the attack was again authorised; for he was to lead his men into battle. [3, pp. 104–5]

But it is important not to surrender to the notion that 'H' Jones was a kind of latter-day Lord Cardigan, demonstrating in equal measure physical courage and military stupidity. Jones planned his assault meticulously; indeed, even a very sympathetic commentator criticised it as 'quite simply, too complicated. It required company commanders, who in the prevailing conditions had enough difficulty working out their own locations, to keep abreast of the progress of the other companies so that they would know when to trigger particular phases of the operation'. [127, p. 102; 215, p. 128] The original plan soon disintegrated as fighting began. Jones's second misapprehension was that, as he put it 'if the enemy is hit hard he will crumble'. [215, p. 82]

The Argentine forces were not as strong in numbers as some have supposed. One authority puts its effective strength at 684 personnel.

[4, p. 45] At the start of the battle the Argentines had about the same number of effectives as 2 Para. The Argentine commander, Lieutenant Colonel Italo Piaggi, claimed that his shortage of equipment and weapons meant that he was fighting the battle 'on…shirt-sleeves'. His original task was to repel a British landing from the sea; now he had to move out of his first defensive positions to defend a longer perimeter. [152, pp. 177–80] But this was no weak or poorly motivated force. It was, as one officer put it 'going to defend something that was ours'. [4, p. 44] Among the Argentine troops was C Company of the 25th (Special) commando-trained regiment, and 25th Signal Company, well armed, trained and led. The Argentine defensive positions were well chosen. Lieutenant Colonel Piaggi briefed his men regularly and explained his military priorities. [4, pp. 44–5]

It can be said that Brigadier Thompson could hardly have paid his men a higher compliment than asking them to attack these Argentine defensive positions without tank or artillery support. His intelligence staff had difficulty calculating the enemy's strength and order of battle, but it was believed that at least one Argentine infantry regiment was present. Major Philip Neame, commanding D Company contrasted the attacking force's insufficient resources at Goose Green with those in the later battle of Wireless Ridge: 'Had we had something similar at Goose Green we would have walked it. As it was…well…'. It seems that Thompson was told that he 'did not need support' and that he was 'bloody furious' but that Northwood 'insisted on having their way'. He remembered coming away from the telephone call thinking 'I shall win this one for them, and then I will go'. [166, p. 257]

2 Para's attack on Goose Green, whatever the unhappy nature of its origin and planning, was one of the most important battles of the war. A set piece battle could not be presented as a sideshow; for, if lost, it would result in the British offensive stalling even before it was properly begun, with the consequence that London would be under serious and sustained pressure to call a ceasefire and reopen negotiations. A defeat for the Argentine forces, though troublesome, would not have the same consequences; they could still hold that their main objective was the defence of Stanley, and that this fight was indeed not central to their overall strategy. For the British, therefore, much rested on H. Jones and his men.

The battle – really a series of actions – lasted from 27 to 29 May. It seemed to be dogged with unforeseen problems from the start. On the morning of 27 May the BBC World Service broadcast that British Paratroops were approaching Darwin – a settlement of a few houses about a mile from Goose Green – infuriating Jones, who believed (wrongly) that the enemy was alerted to his offensive. The Argentine command held that the broadcast was a bluff, and in any case there had been speculation in the British press about the Army's objectives. [158, p. 259] Jones was even more angry when at his 11.00 a.m. briefing a number of his officers, including at least one company commander, did not turn up. This was simply a failure in communicating information to what was a scattered military force, but the result was that the attack was postponed for four hours. [3, pp. 135–6]

Nevertheless, the battle began with a disaster for the Argentine 12th regiment, which consisted of young soldiers with little military training. 2 Para was able to sweep through their position on Burnside Hill. The Argentine commander ordered that his forces hold their position on Coronation Ridge 'at all costs', [4, p. 46] but this was lost by 6.00 a.m. on 28 May. Now the issue would be decided on Darwin Ridge, but with the British attacking in daylight. 'A' Company began to withdraw from their exposed position. [4, p. 47] Jones's six-phase plan began to falter. 'D' Company, which had initially lost its way, was ordered to attack the enemy, but did not know where the enemy was. [215, p. 130; 3, pp. 199–200] When it advanced it made contact with the enemy, some of whom fled; but others defended their position, killing two paratroopers. The advance slowed down, but the whole tactical plan depended upon precise timing. By 9.00 a.m. the British advance was halted, and an Argentine counter-attack, had it been mounted, might well have resulted in a serious British reverse. [215, pp. 133–4; 3, p. 194]

Colonel Jones' plan was now in danger of degenerating into a serious of confused separate actions, fought with varying degrees of success, but without co-ordination. His anxiety and impatience surfaced when Major Philip Neame suggested that instead of continuing with the attack on Darwin Ridge, his D Company should carry out a right-flanking movement along the western beach of the isthmus; Jones replied, 'Don't tell me how to run my battle'. [3, p. 222, 242–3] Jones ordered an attack on the spur of Darwin hill, only to see it turn into a 'disjointed scramble up the slope', [3, p. 247] with the loss of three more men. Jones was the kind of officer who led from the front. He was alleged to have shouted 'come on A Company, get your skirts off'; [3, p. 247] certainly he urged his men to follow him. In more formal military phrasing, Major Dair Farrer-Hockley described Jones' action thus: 'seeing our predicament and the immediate need to exploit a situation…he made a valiant attempt to get in among the nearest trenches with a small tactical party and disrupt the enemy'. [93, p. 76] Jones was killed. He was subsequently awarded the Victoria Cross.

These British reverses occurred between 9.00 a.m. and 10.00 a.m. It took two hours for 2 Para's second-in-command to reorganise the attack. Gradually 2 Para began to prise the enemy out of their positions, using mortar and small-arms fire; there was little evidence of tactical control at battalion level. [3, p. 305] One officer, platoon commander and two of his NCOs were shot in a confused attempt to persuade Argentine soldiers to surrender. [3, pp. 315–16] But by late afternoon the 2 Para were supported by three Harriers from HMS *Hermes*, and were reinforced with field guns and fresh supplies of ammunition. The following day the Argentine positions were bombarded from the sea, and by 10.45 a.m. on 29 May terms for an Argentine surrender were agreed. [152, pp. 189–92]

The battle cost 2 Para sixteen killed, half of them from D Company, and 33 wounded. A Royal Marine pilot and a commando sapper also died. [215, p. 140] Fifty-five Argentines were killed and about 86 wounded. [4, p. 49] A recent biographer of Colonel H. Jones attributed the victory to his fine example in leading his men in battle, at the cost of his own life, [231] and certainly his behaviour, however it is judged in military terms, can be said to have epitomised the best traditions of the British, or any other army, in taking the same risks as his men, and even accepting greater risks. But it is doubtful if Jones' example alone explains 2 Para's victory, though it may have reinforced their already powerful sense of their reputation as fearless and dedicated soldiers. There was a more prosaic explanation: that the Argentine forces were defeated 'by the devastating effect of direct-fire weapons, particularly the Milan (an anti-tank missile gun) which had at last been brought into action, albeit in an unusual role'. [3, p. 364] And there was an even more prosaic explanation, offered by the Argentine commander: that 'the battle had turned into a sniping contest. They could sit well out of range of our soldiers' fire and, if they wanted to, raze the settlement'. He had no chance of reinforcements. [215, p. 139] None of these need be discounted; but the battle was essentially one of attrition, and therefore a battle in which what soldiers liked to call their 'professionalism' (self-regard, fundamental belief in themselves and their fighting abilities, and the ferocity instilled into an elite regiment) enabled 2 Para to prevail. As an officer put it, it was 'a classical Parachute Regiment punch-up – a gutter fight – but then our blokes are bloody good at that…'. [5, p. 147]

The battle of Goose Green has been dismissed as 'tricky and pointless'; [215, p. 141] but it encapsulated several important aspects of the war. It was, as Major Christopher Keeble put it, an example of 'the full orchestration of war'; whereas the British army's most sustained campaign, that against IRA terrorism in Northern Ireland, despite its 'very violent periods' had nothing to compare to a 'full-scale battle…the noise of a sustained battle…the intense loneliness and fear that results from such an experience'. [5, p. 146] The political significance of the battle was appreciated by Mrs Thatcher: 'a famous battle had been won'. [203, p. 229] William Whitelaw claimed that it 'gave us great hopes for the future'. [90, p. 376] The death of Colonel H. Jones provided a truly British hero. Jean Rook in the *Daily Express* described him as 'steel-eyed. Square jawed. He lived Kipling's "If" line by line'. Only one 'can match with pride, what he did for his country. His wife Sara…captured the spirit of all that is bravest and best in British women by facing the cameras only hours after his death'. [167, p. 117] Even if the battle was, as Brigadier Thompson believed, militarily unnecessary, even if its critics portrayed it as a modern version of the charge of the Light Brigade, still it was significant; for, like that famous charge, it showed what the British soldier could do, the fighting qualities that gave him his reputation. In this sense, the battle of Goose Green was a perfect victory for the British, and, whatever its uncertain origins, a considerable feat of arms.

7
Victory

When Mrs Thatcher heard of the beginning of the fighting at Goose Green she remarked, 'Now that the battle has started on land, there will be an international demand for a ceasefire, which may include some of the countries that have hitherto supported us'. She added that the Commander-in-Chief should be told that 'I can hold the political arena. There will be no political meddling in the conduct of the war. It is up to him to conduct operations as he thinks best', though, she added in an important afterthought, 'I would be grateful if he does not delay things longer than necessary'. [56, 17 Jan. 2002] The Prime Minister's instinct was right: for there were many and good reasons, in the minds of the states and institutions observing the conflict why compromise might yet be tried again. Alexander Haig was anxious that Britain should not humiliate Argentina. The United States suffered strong criticism from the Organisation of American States. A meeting was called to consider the imposition of hemispheric sanctions on 27 May, and the United States had to use its influence to prevent the imposition of mandatory sanctions; but it did not vote against a resolution, which was passed by 17 votes to nil (with four abstentions) two days later, which condemned the 'unjustified and disproportionate armed attack perpetrated by the United Kingdom' on the Falkland Islands, and called for the United States to halt aid to Britain, and to lift its own sanctions against Argentina. [37, pp. 69–78] Haig still hoped to take the edge off what was seen as a hardening of British attitudes, and on 31 May President Reagan telephoned Mrs Thatcher to register concern about Latin American opinion, and to float the idea of another peace initiative. A further attempt was made during President Reagan's visit to Europe on 2–4 June. [108, pp. 58–9]

The United Nations was not yet done with the crisis. On 2 June it met again to consider the implications of the failure of the Secretary-General's efforts at mediation; a ceasefire resolution was proposed by Spain and Panama which many non-aligned states endorsed. Spain had been obliged to adopt a non-aligned position in the crisis, supporting decolonisation but condemning the use of force; she was influenced by her own dispute with Britain over Gibraltar. [10, Ch. 8] Ireland, increasingly disenchanted with the British response to the Argentine invasion of the Falklands since the sinking of the *General Belgrano*, supported the resolution. [209, p. 148] On 4 June the Security Council reaffirmed resolutions 502 and 505, while asking the parties to the dispute to call an immediate ceasefire in the region, under United Nations' supervision. Argentina agreed, and obtained nine favourable votes. The resolution was opposed by the United States and the United Kingdom; there were four abstentions. The French abstention was particularly significant, for France had been one of the British Government's most useful and committed supporters so far. [185, pp. 62–3] Fortunately for the United Kingdom, her veto, which signalled the very lack of British flexibility that was troubling her European Community and United States' supporters, was overshadowed by the United States' Ambassador's remarkable statement that, if the United States could change her vote, she would abstain. [90, p. 355]

The American Ambassador's hypothetical volte-face reflected the United States administration's anxiety that, while it had its pro-British element, it feared that British policy was endangering American interests in the region. As Sir Nicholas Henderson, British Ambassador in Washington, put it 'Nothing assuaged the American concern at this stage – that is to say at the end of May and the beginning of June – about the dire consequences that would flow from overwhelming military defeat inflicted on the Argentines'. [108, p. 59] There was concern that Argentina, with whom the United States had been forging good relations, was now warning that if America should join with the United Kingdom in vetoing the resolution then Argentina might regard this as endangering diplomatic relations with the United States. Argentina suggested that the United States could abstain in the vote on the resolution. Alexander Haig hoped that the way forward could be found in a settlement that would establish a British military administration of the Falklands, which would then cede to a self-governing administration, under international supervision and a small armed force. The umbrella states would be the United States and probably Brazil. Argentina would have a liaison officer. The umbrella group would also have responsibility for considering the ultimate status of the Islands. If no agreement were reached in this, then the self-government umbrella arrangements would remain. [90, pp. 352–3]

This was, at least in the light of hindsight, an equitable solution that would have saved British and Argentine lives; and the hard fight at Goose Green, and the Task Force's losses in San Carlos Bay, suggested that it was worth pursuing. But the British had won an important round in the contest; and the blood so far shed could not be wiped off the map of the Islands. The result of losses in battle is more often to toughen the antagonists than to soften their quarrel; for it there were a compromise, then these losses so far sustained might be in vain: worse still, might be betrayed. Certain sections of the British Press, and the Conservative Party, would have been outraged at such a denigration of the British dead and wounded; and Mrs Thatcher, for her part, though she went along with the United States' mediation, was anxious, as she put it, not to do the wrong thing: and that thing was 'to snatch diplomatic defeat out of the jaws of military victory'. [203, p. 230] President Reagan on 31 May argued the opposite: that it was time to 'strike a deal' now that Britain had, militarily, the upper hand. Mrs Thatcher told him 'that we could not contemplate a cease-fire without Argentine withdrawal. Having lost ships and lives because for seven weeks the Argentines had refused to negotiate, we would not consider handing the Islands over to a third party'. [203, pp. 230–31] This line of argument, though perfectly understandable, ignored Ministry of Defence and Foreign Office concerns over the troublesome legacy of a British victory: the need to spend considerable sums of money holding on to the Falklands, the continuation of the dispute with Argentina over their eventual fate, the unremitting commitment of British diplomacy to what Mrs Thatcher herself had before April 1982 regarded as a dispute of marginal importance.

Britain was still not allowed to pursue her military campaign unhampered by international intervention. On 5 June Perez de Cuellar made further proposals for a ceasefire and an Argentine withdrawal of troops over 15 days, with Britain required only to inform the Secretary General of her plans for troop reductions, with the study of possible security arrangements under the auspices of the United Nations; this was rejected by Argentina. Britain saw no need to pursue this course of action now that she was moving towards military victory. The army was advancing towards its objective of investing the Argentine forces on the high ground around Stanley, defeating them, and bringing the war to a decisive conclusion. [90, p. 356]

The army had demonstrated what it rightly called its 'professionalism' in the battle at Goose Green. But now a series of mishaps and mistakes, inseparable from the conduct of war, intervened, resulting in the highest single cluster of casualties in the campaign. The advance to Stanley was demanding: the territory over which the soldiers advanced was uneven, and without shelter. Rain, sleet and snow fell frequently, and winds were gale force. There was frost at night. The logistical problem was formidable. HQ 3rd Commando brigade made the strongest efforts to ensure that supplies of food, water, and ammunition reached the troops, but this was not always possible. Clothing and equipment were not adequate for the conditions. Trench foot and blisters were common, but, as Captain Ian Gardiner of 2 Company, 45 Commando put it 'one hardened' (216, p. 161). 45 Commando marched to Douglas Settlement, then to Teal Inlet, and then towards Mount Kent, overlooking Stanley. 42 Commando moved by helicopter to Mount Simon, then to Mount Kent. 2 Para was taken by helicopter from Darwin to Fitzroy. The recently arrived 5 Infantry Brigade was to move (as it turned out, by sea) to Fitzroy, where it would consolidate and establish a 'Forward Maintenance Area' prior to an advance to catch up with 3 Commando Brigade on the defensive ring of hills held by the Argentines to the west of Stanley. [46, p. 281]

This flanking movement may not have been part of the original military plan; one authority ascribes it to the success of the Goose Green battle, which opened up a route that would otherwise not have been taken. [46, p. 248] While attention is naturally, and rightly, focused on the endurance shown by the troops moving overland on foot, demonstrating the infantry's independent (and oldest) asset, the campaign still rested on its logistical foundations. This was not always appreciated by the land forces: the Scots and Welsh Guards of 5 Brigade showed what to Commodore Clapp was an alarming degree of slowness in disembarking from the troopship, *Canberra*, their 'unhurriedness' increased by fog, the insufficiency of Landing Craft Utilities, and the necessity to oblige *Canberra*'s crew to form a 'chain gang' to move the Guards' front line stores which they had not taken with them. [46, pp. 276–7]

Slowness, a deficiency in warfare, was accompanied by its opposite, and sometimes equally troublesome characteristic, dash. This was shown in the Marines' occupation of Mount Kent, high ground overlooking Stanley. A small British force was to be flown there on the night of 29/30 May to support the SAS 'D' Squadron, which had been flown in on 24/25 May. Bad weather aborted this mission, and when finally the Commando force was able to land below Mount Kent, it found the SAS engaged in a fight with the enemy. The Commandos were able to land successfully because the SAS had encountered the

Argentines, despite Admiral Woodward's advice that no such reconnaissance party was needed. As Brigadier Thompson put it, 'Without 'D' Squadron's presence around the LZ (Landing Zone) the enemy special forces would have had a "turkey shoot" on the vulnerable helicopters and the troops as they jumped out, temporarily disorient-ated in the darkness; the operation would have been a disaster'. [206, pp. 268–9] However, the SAS Squadron had no idea if there were enemy on the crest of the hill, or, if there were, in what strength. Fortunately for the whole enterprise the Argentines did not attack the isolated hill position. This was the consequence of the Argentine effort at Goose Green, and their decision to move to the west, away from Mount Kent and up to the Goose Green area. Luckily, this enabled the Marines to consolidate a vital vantage point, supported by helicopter lifts which Brigadier Thompson removed from unloading duties. The loss of the Chinook helicopters in the *Atlantic Conveyor* was now making itself felt. [46, p. 272] Brigadier Thompson now confronted the dangers of his success so far: 'Knowing how thinly spread my men really were on the ground, I was furious when I was told that boastful remarks were being made back in England by those who should have known better to the effect that the British were now holding the high ground overlooking Stanley'. [205, p. 109]

The Goose Green victory cleared the way for the dash to Mount Kent and the acquisition of a forward artillery position and a starting point for the final assault on Stanley, [80, p. 90] but it also initiated the 'second flank' that was to cause most logistical difficulty. The 'long southern route' [46, p. 136] was to surface several times before the Goose Green battle was fought, and always in negative terms; now that it was opened, 5 Brigade's Welsh and Scots Guards were to move along it. But the diversion of helicopters to Mount Kent meant that, as Brigadier Jeremy Moore noted in his report covering the landing, the off-loading of 5 Brigade was inevitably delayed. On 2 June the Brigade's movement began 'in earnest', although Commodore Clapp concluded that the first phase was conducted with too much impetuosity and with too little consideration for long-term plans. [46, pp. 272–3] The process was hurried along by an advance party of 2 Para moving to Swan Inlet House in 656 Squadron (Army Air Corps) Scout helicopters. They ascertained that no Argentine forces were in Fitzroy. Part of 2 Para was flown forward to Fitzroy and Bluff Cove which it occupied at dusk on 2 June. [46, p. 278]

Major General Jeremy Moore and his staff were ignorant of this development; the result was that 'we now had a weak, unsupported battalion with no guns [that is, artillery support] strung in penny packets for thirty miles across the southern flank', possessing no defences against Argentine counter attack by land or air, or even by sea had the enemy been prepared to brave the consequences'. Now, 5 Brigade must be moved forward as quickly as possible, by land or sea; and clearly to move by sea would be the quickest way. Jeremy Moore's report on these events implied that the Brigade was 'unbalanced' – a dangerous predicament in the face of the enemy – and that the rest of 5 Brigade (whose physical fitness was doubted by some) must get into the Bluff Cove area and 'pass through' 3 Commando Brigade 'in due course'. [46, p. 278]

5 Brigade was under the command of Brigadier Tony Wilson, whose decision it was to send B Company of 2 Para to Swan Inlet in the first place. The story of Swan Inlet had all the elements that appealed to the British Press and public, which welcomed any familiar sign of the British genius for improvisation, and in imposing a certain kind of domesticity on any situation. 2 Para's company commander telephoned from Swan Inlet to Bluff Cove, spoke to a civilian there, and confirmed that there were no Argentine troops present. He was then reinforced by A Company in a Chinook helicopter on 4 June. This audacious move, adorned with the now famous telephone call, convinced Wilson that it was 'now or never, because they (the Argentines) could come back during the night. I decided that unless I took this chance, I might end up fighting for Fitzroy and Bluff Cove, and only a fool would fight for something he could have for nothing'. The problem was, as Commodore Clapp pointed out, that this had a knock-on effect on the rest of the Brigade's operations. They must move quickly; but there were 'insufficient logistical resources to sustain such an operation'. This he described wryly as a 'formal way of saying that one piece of improvisation must now be followed, inevitably, by another'. [83, p. 186]

Moreover, the task of defending the British position was now a very demanding one. There were five areas now needing protection: the carrier battle group in the eastern sector of the TEZ; the Tug, Repair and Logistic area, that is, the 'mobile home for damaged warships', and merchantmen awaiting convoy into San Carlos; San Carlos itself, with its main land force base and harbour where nightly convoys of supplies were discharged; Teal Inlet, the new advanced base for 3 Commando Brigade; and Fitzroy/Bluff Cove, the new forward base for 3 Brigade. The demands made by these bases were all equally important, but were also potentially at least equally conflicting. Woodward was always aware of the significance of time in the campaign; the land forces must 'get their skates on', lest the enemy find a way to hit the British carriers 'and remove half our air force'. He was never able to forget the tyranny of his 'little bar-chart' drawn up at Ascension Island: 'As forecast, the Battle Group was now well on its way to falling apart: aside from the losses, we were coping with daily breakdowns in equipment and, as the land forces prepared for the break-out from Carlos, we faced an almost overwhelming workload'. [236, pp. 307–9]

Admiral Woodward was unhappy with Major General Jeremy Moore's request that the Welsh and Scots Guards be transferred by sea (apparently he had concerns about their fitness to march overland). [83, p. 187] Woodward doubted the advisability of a move by sea: such an operation would require several amphibious ships, and their frigate and destroyer escorts, 'effectively another complete landing well clear of Carlos Water and its air defences', which he believed would 'have little appeal back at Northwood'. But he did not want to oppose the operation, since he had expressed impatience with the land force's progress so far. Northwood approved the move, thus relieving Woodward of a decision he did not want to make: as he noted on 4 June, 'you don't put two battalions back into such hazard, just because the opposition seems to have taken a day off'. [236, pp. 312–13] Commodore Clapp was told by Woodward that the man on the spot, that is Clapp, must decide. [46, p. 290]

While Commodore Clapp was pondering on his next mission, General Jeremy Moore was deploying one of the key skills of the modern soldier: keeping the politicians happy without telling them more than they needed to know. His report to London on 3 June contained the useful phrase 'as always, a period of rapid movement is having to be followed by one of logistic consolidation'. He praised Brigadier Anthony Wilson, commander of 5 Brigade, for his 'daring dash' to Fitzroy, noting the men's 'excellent heart' and using the stirring phrase '45 Cdo. Have been marching to the sound of guns for some 40 miles and will I hope get into the front line tomorrow'. [46, p. 284]

The question for some units of 5 Brigade was not the marching, but the sailing. Admiral Woodward on 4 June suggested moving 5 Brigade to Teal Inlet, instead of Bluff Cove; but this would not resolve the problem of 2 Para 'being out on a limb', and there would be difficulties in fuelling the helicopters. That night Clapp and Moore signalled Northwood that the only feasible route for 5 Brigade was by the south. [46, p. 291] This would be a complex operation. On 5 June General

Moore and Commodore Clapp sent signals to Northwood explaining why the move by sea was the best option. They decided that the *Intrepid* should sail east at dawn and launch her landing platform deck in two waves with a battalion of the Guards in each, as far as Bluff Cove; but the Commander of the Task Force signalled that no landing craft was to be risked out of San Carlos in daylight, as the loss of such a ship would force Ministers to think in terms of a ceasefire. [46, p. 292] Woodward was anxious about what he called a proposal for 'a mini D-Day all over again at Bluff Cove on the 6th. Perhaps they do not understand how fortunate we were on D-Day when the Args went for the wrong targets...Above all they appear to have forgotten that Bluff Cove is in open country and not a bit like Carlos Water'. 'It seems daft', he concluded 'to take this size of a risk for the sake of a two-day march', The 'essence of the problem' was that such a move 'could blow the entire operation'. [236, p. 313]

The dilemma was resolved by Clapp and Southby-Tailyour deciding to transport the Scots Guards in *Intrepid* as far as Lively Island, and then embark the 600 men of the Scots Guards in their landing craft to Fitzroy. [46, p. 298] The *Intrepid* was protected by HMS *Plymouth*, while the *Avenger* bombarded Fox Bay, West Falkland, as a diversion. [236, p. 313] At dawn on 6 June the Welsh Guards were embarking on the *Fearless* which would sail at dusk for Lively Island. The plan was for *Fearless* to have two of her LCUs offloaded, and that two of *Intrepid*'s LCUs would be brought in, loaded up, and then all the LCUs would land at Fitzroy. [46, pp. 302–3]

This plan was disrupted by the failure of the four *Intrepid* LCUs to make their rendezvous with *Fearless*. Commodore Clapp alleged that three of these had been highjacked by 2 Para and had sailed to Fitzroy. [46, p. 308] Admiral Woodward believed that it was 'scarcely surprising' that the LCUs which had taken the Scots Guards on the previous night had not arrived back. [236, p. 317] The result was delay. Shortly after dawn on 7 June the two empty *Fearless* LCUs sailed for Fitzroy from Bluff Cove to join the original four in offloading the newly arrived landing ship *Sir Tristram*, which was carrying 5 Brigade's equipment. On the same day the Welsh Guards were moved from *Fearless* to the landing ship *Sir Galahad* at Fitzroy, not Bluff Cove. The second in command of the Welsh Guards did not want his men to be separated from their equipment; nor did he want to be embarked at Fitzroy for a 16-mile march, when waiting on board the *Sir Galahad* would enable his troops to be conveyed to Bluff Cove. [46, p. 316] The Guards remained on board the *Sir Galahad*. When a staff officer from 5 Brigade ordered the Guards ashore the instruction was countermanded by the Royal Army Medical Corps Lieutenant-Commander of the field ambulance, who needed to get to Fitzroy and who felt that he should have priority. Further delay followed when a landing craft developed a hydraulic failure in its ramp mechanism. [46, pp. 316–17] While the Guardsmen waited the *Sir Galahad* and the *Sir Tristram* (carrying stores) were attacked at 17.10 by two waves of Argentine Skyhawks. Fifty men on the *Sir Galahad* were killed and 57 wounded. The disaster was the result of bad luck, and poor communications within 5 Brigade and between 5 Brigade and Divisional Headquarters. Brigadier Thompson attributed at least some of the blame to what he called 'yet more back-seat driving from Task Force HQ at Northwood, forbidding Clapp to send either *Fearless* or *Intrepid* to the south of Fitzroy again'. [206, p. 571]

This incident was regarded by Northwood as of no military significance; indeed it offered a slight advantage to the British, because the Argentines believed they had inflicted much heavier casualties, and therefore enjoyed a false comfort that British military preparations would be delayed by the disaster. [90, pp. 388–9, 393] But it seemed to the British media to exemplify the less than glorious side of war. Surgeon Rick Jolly recalled that he 'gave up counting [badly burned soldiers] at about a hundred'; all he could do was the 'best you can do for the biggest number'. He was struck by the Guardsmen's concern for their comrades: 'Don't worry about me, look after my mate'. [128] And it showed too how the original uncertainty about 5 Brigade's role in the campaign, compounded by logistical difficulties and poor communications could jeopardise what should have been, on the face of it, a straightforward operation. The friction of war had indeed manifested itself. Admiral Woodward fumed at what he called the 'ceremonious duffers' (the land force commanders) who 'take two months for a recce', showed no improvisation abilities, but who must 'go now and accept the risks' – a judgement that he later regretted, when he acknowledged the significance of the loss of the *Atlantic Conveyor*'s helicopters 'which could well be laid at my door' and 'which had a major effect on land-force mobility'. [236, p. 325]

Woodward's impatience stemmed from the 'chilling consciousness that the Battle Group was running out of steam' (he also admitted to 'substantial ignorance of conditions ashore'). [236, p. 325] The need to act with reasonable speed was real. The Argentine Joint Chiefs of Staff considered their options after the *Sir Galahad* strike, including an immediate attack on the British ground forces, but rejected this because of lack of sufficient transport and the impossibility of moving heavy artillery pieces. The British still had air and naval superiority (though not supremacy). General Galtieri talked of an advance from Stanley against the San Carlos beachhead, and Darwin; but the Argentine air and naval forces were insufficient for this option. Thus Argentine plans veered between the large, and rather unfocused, and the well-focused but almost fatalistic: General Menendez must be 'prepared to fight to the end, even if we had to die. We were not to surrender'. The Argentine Cabinet seems to have believed that time was on their side, and still had hopes of a diplomatic and international opinion shift that must favour their position. [90, pp. 389–92]

These illusions were given a rude awakening by the British attack on the Argentine defences around Stanley on 11 June. The Argentine forces defending these positions have been put at between 8,500 and 9,000 men, of whom 'maybe 5,000 could be classed as fighting troops'. They had 45 field guns (three 155mm and 42 105mm) to the British thirty 105mm guns, though the British could also bring naval gunfire to bear. The Argentine troops had little or no air support, and few helicopters, and no naval support – 'no fleet effectively' as Rear-Admiral Lombardo put it. [152, pp. 216–17] The Argentines could therefore only offer a static defence. Their deployment was defective. The Argentine command in Stanley expected a British landing from the south or east, and their defences were pointing in the wrong direction; re-deployment was slow and ill-organised, and there were too few troops defending a wide series of fronts. No reserve was prepared (though sufficient troops were available to constitute one). [90, pp. 382, 395] The British forces' attacking strength was at a ratio of 3:2 , with the exception of Mount Longdon, where it was 3:1. [90, p. 396] Their attacking strength comprised almost all the British fighting units; if they suffered a reverse there were no significant reserves to throw into the fight. Like the Argentines, the British soldiers were suffering from the harsh climate and were physically run down. What they had were the advantages of determining never to launch attacks in daylight again, following the Goose Green experience; and their elite units, which could sustain tough and close order fighting.

Brigadier Thompson's 3 Brigade consisted of 42 and 45 Commando, 2 Para and 3 Para, to which was added the First Battalion Welsh Guards, as well as two companies of 40 Commando which replaced the Welsh Guards companies which had suffered losses in men and equipment at Fitzroy. The British plan of attack was to unhinge the

Argentine defenders on three key points: Mount Longdon, the Two Sisters, and Mount Harriet. These would be attacked by 3 Para, 45 Commando and 42 Commando respectively, each with about 600 men, with 2 Para and the Welsh Guards in reserve. 3 Para's task was perhaps the most difficult. They must fight along the spine of the Mount Longdon ridge; they were also vulnerable to fire from Argentine positions that they had passed; 6 Platoon suffered casualties from an Argentine bunker as well as Argentine positions along the ridge. [127, p. 130] The attack stalled several times, once when a heavy machine gun held up B Company; 'A' Company, moving from the east, suffered losses and was forced to pull back to the western end of Mount Longdon, from where they fought their way forward with artillery support, 'clearing the enemy positions with rifles, bayonets and grenades'. [196, pp. 100–1] As always in such fights, there were individual acts of bravery, as when Sergeant Ian McKay gathered together a few men to attack a position which was defended by a machine gun, 'still going on'. [127, p. 138] He was awarded a posthumous V.C. The paratroops were assisted by artillery fire which adopted the Great War 'creeping barrage' tactics of firing just ahead of the advancing soldiers. [152, p. 235] The Great War generation would also have been familiar with the percentage of casualties suffered in the fighting (though the actual figures of course bear no comparison): on the western end of the ridge these came to 50 per cent. In all, the Mount Longdon battle cost 3 Para the lives of 19 men; 35 were wounded, in the most costly battle of the war. [152, p. 236]

The attack on Two Sisters, a formidable ridge of two prominent hills about 1000 feet high was no easier, though here the Argentine defenders were fewer in number. The attack envisaged a kind of hill-hopping assault, with the taking of the western hill being used to support the next phase of the offensive on the saddle between the two hills. Then the attack would move on to the eastern hill. The plan was disrupted by the late attack on the first objective because of one company's being burdened with heavy weapons and ammunition, but it met lesser resistance than 3 Para had encountered and was assisted by artillery. [205, pp. 150–1] Argentine soldiers did not fear naval gunfire, describing it as 'zonal fire', but the British artillery was considered a much greater danger; and the Argentine soldiers suffered the exhausting, as well as dangerous, experience of coming under fire by day 'so that the hitherto quiet and safety of daylight hours no longer existed'. [152, pp. 228–97] The British Brigade Commander attributed the paratroops' success to a 'combination of good control, fitness and the proper use of fire power'.

[205, p. 158] The third battle of the first night of the fight for Stanley was the attack on Mount Harriet over minefields. This position was defended by about 300 Argentine soldiers. [152, pp. 239–40] 42 Commando's Lieutenant-Colonel Vaux had the ingenuity and opportunity to execute a rare operation in the Falklands War: an outflanking movement. He decided that two companies would march south from the western end of Wall Mountain, cross the Fitzroy-Stanley track, and then go south-east until they reached a point almost 1,000 metres south of the track, then swing in a north-easterly direction, cross the track again, and form up on the south-east shoulder of the mountain. He attacked the eastern end of Mount Harriet, and an hour later another company (L) would attack the western end. Then Vaux's company (K) would attack Goat Ridge, while J Company would carry out a diversionary attack from the eastern end of Wall Mountain. To distract the enemy and encourage them to 'keep their heads down' 42 Commando shelled Mount Harriet before the attack, thus forfeiting surprise but complementing the overall tactical plan. [205, p. 160] This worked well, as the Argentine troops could neither counter-attack nor escape; they surrendered. British losses were one killed and ten wounded; the Argentines lost about ten men with 250 prisoners. [152, pp. 242–3]

The detached, unemotional language used to describe these battles disguises a whole series of complex, confused and bloody incidents. There was tension at the start line (one soldier crying). [127, p. 127] One officer admitted losing control of himself and being told by a Corporal to 'keep it together'. [127, p. 151] There were 'bodies everywhere', the 'smell of morphine and blood'. [127, p. 153] Wounded Argentine soldiers, it is alleged, were shot. There were acts of great bravery, such as that of Sergeant McKay. Men cursed, fought stubbornly and brutally. At the end, the men were not even certain whether the battle was won or not. [127, p. 156] But one Argentine officer saw the British victories as the end of the campaign: 'I realised that the war was as good as lost after that night; I didn't think the rest of our defence would hold. We were being encircled, the ring getting tighter and tighter'. [152, p. 244]

The final battle for Stanley was begun on 13 June. 2 Para attacked Wireless Ridge in the north and the 2nd Battalion Scots Guards from 5 Brigade attacked Tumbledown Mountain in the centre. The Guards were opposed by the 5th Argentine Marine Infantry Battalion, whose rank and file were conscripts, but with a better level of training. [152, pp. 254–5] The Scots Guards' plan was to make a diversionary action along a track south of Tumbledown, while the real assault would be a three-stage attack along the thin ridge, from west to east. The first sign that Argentine resistance would be determined was experienced by the diversionary force, which was forced to abandon its attack and withdraw. The main attack encountered no Argentine forces on their part of the ridge; the second phase of the attack met a stubborn and skilful resistance: 'slightly shocking' was how one Scots Guards officer described the Argentine weight of fire, but a frontal attack led by Major Kiszely, supported by a short barrage, and using 'fire and move' tactics carried the position. The last engagement was equally difficult, and saw another rare event in this war: a well executed Argentine counter-attack, from which the Argentines retired only when they were reduced to 16 men. Their defence, which lasted ten hours of combat, upset the British timetable and caused the proposed Gurkha attack on Mount William to be postponed. [215, pp. 197–203]

The Guards' experience was by now a familiar one to any troops engaged in the Falklands War: attacks on Argentine foxholes, supported by machine guns and light mortars. Again, British persistence and training, supported by in this instance naval gunfire from HMS *Active* and *Avenger*, were vital. However, the ships had to leave before dawn, and again the only way for the British to fight was by close order combat, hand to hand fighting. It was at this phase of the battle that the Scots Guard Officer, Lieutenant Richard Lawrence, was seriously wounded, an incident which provided one of the most fierce anti-war narratives of the campaign. Meanwhile, 2 Para attacked Wireless Ridge. The area had been heavily bombarded the previous day and attacked by Harriers. Its natural defences were less strung out than the other positions, and the defenders fewer in number. 2 Para did not repeat the dangerous tactics of Goose Green; now they followed a well thought out plan, supported by four light tanks and artillery. The use of field and naval gunfire was effective. The northern ridge was captured and the tanks lined up to fire on the southern range, which the paratroops then attacked, rolling up the southern hill. [152, pp. 263–7]

The night battles of 13–14 June ended the Falklands War. The feeling that this had been a risky business lasted until the end; General Jeremy Moore told the Royal United Services Institution on 20 October 1982 that, 'By the morning after the final night attacks, some of my batteries were down to only six rounds per gun'. [155, p. 31] The last struggle took place with 45 Commando's attack on Sapper Hill, supported by the Welsh Guards and was in progress when a ceasefire was announced between 1.00 and 1.30 p.m. Three Argentine conscripts were killed, leading to Argentine accusations that the British killed them after the ceasefire. [152, pp. 271–2] Jeremy Moore negotiated the surrender, accepting Argentine objections to the word 'unconditional' and the Argentine Army piled its arms and filed out of Stanley under an escort of Marines and Paratroops (complaining of rough treatment by the latter). [152, p. 277] The Argentine forces lost 655 men of all services in the war; British losses were 255 (including two Falkland Islanders killed by shelling). The Falklands War was, as Brigadier Thompson put it suggestively, 'an example of joint operations par excellence – eventually'. [206, p. 580]

In an age where blame is apportioned for almost any act that is deemed appropriate for such a response (and some that are not), it was inevitable that there should be repercussions, investigations and criticisms of the armed forces involved. These were not levied at the 'brass hats', nor at 'unacceptable losses'; even the *Sir Galahad* disaster was regarded as one of the misfortunes of war. The fighting was brutal, but was accompanied by calls for surrender, white flags and the like, by actions 'designed to save life rather than taking it with cold efficiency'. [133, p. 241] But there was criticism of the behaviour of British soldiers after the Argentine surrender. Commodore Clapp alleged that discipline in some cases broke down. A member of his staff wrote in his diary of finding Stanley

> Utterly depressing. The troops are in a post war mood and very selfish. Grab, Grab – transport, houses, equipment, food, etc. – gone is the spirit of selflessness in the field. It will return but at present all is filth, squalor and (the) looting instinct prevails. Quite the worst aspect of the whole campaign. [46, p. 344]

Nicholas van der Bijl, who criticised Commodore Clapp for his comments ('from someone who spent the campaign fed, watered, warm and comfortable') noted that, 'During the afternoon (of 19 June) 2 Para barged three abreast along the sea front to hold their famous church service in the cathedral. Royal Marines escorting prisoners sat on the grass to let them past. The Paras had arrived but it seemed a little ostentatious and unnecessary'. [215, pp. 220, 223] 3 Paras' behaviour in battle was investigated ten years later by Scotland Yard detectives following publication of a memoir by a former Paratrooper; descriptions of war crimes were investigated, but no action was taken. [127, pp. 177–9]

All this contrasted with Brigadier Thompson's elegiac account of the post battle scene.

> So it was all over...So with luck all the young men now alive in my Brigade would go home alive, the soldiers of B Company 2 Para lying asleep in heaps all over the house we shared, so that every square inch of space was covered in bodies, still clutching rifle or machine gun, only sentries alert; the gunners of 29 Commando Regiment Royal Artillery, asleep beside their now silent guns, only the gun sentries awake, one at each gun, ready to fire the loaded pieces on the target on which they were laid; 45 Commando shivering with cold on Sapper Hill; 42 Commando among the rats and debris of the sea-plane hangar; 45 Commando about to go to West Falkland; 2 Para and 3 Para in deserted houses, sheds and the racecourse grandstand in the west end of town; the Sappers who had taken part in every attack; my logisticians working through the night, as always, preparing loads at Teal and Ajax Bay for the morrow; Major Armitage missing and with a broken back being kept warm by his driver, Gunner Inch, lying out in the dark and snow all night by the wreck of their Bandwagon...He, and about five thousand others like him in my Brigade, had done what we had come 8,000 miles to do. [205, p. 186]

None of these accounts or descriptions are contradictory; nor do they cancel each other out. They are aspects of the myriad faces of war, which even a short, relatively bloodless campaign like the Falklands exemplified. And they were to be further exemplified away from the scene of battle, in the war of words that accompanied, surrounded, and outlived the conflict itself.

8

The MOD, the Media, and Public Opinion

The first parliamentary and public reaction to the Argentine invasion of the Falklands gave the British Government a fair wind as the Task Force was assembled and set sail for the South Atlantic. *The Times* claimed to speak for the nation when on 3 April it declared that Argentina's action was 'as perfect an example of unprovoked aggression and military expansionism as the world has had to witness since the end of Adolf Hitler', and one that 'threatens the right of self-determination of all island peoples throughout the world'. On 5 April it issued a ringing call to arms, declaring that, 'We are all Falklanders now', warning that to oppose aggression 'will not be easy' but recalling that 'in 1939 we stood by Poland and went to war'. No-one would say that the Poles did not suffer the consequences of that decision; but 'a moment had come in Europe when the consequences of not standing up to the aggressive policies of a dictatorship would have been worse than not standing up to them'. Moreover, 'the Poles were Poles; the Falklanders are our people. They are British citizens (sic). The Falkland Islands are British territory'. Such a cause had positive, invigorating effects: 'The national will to defend itself has to be cherished and replenished if it is to mean something real in a dangerous and unpredictable world'. The British were 'an island race' and 'one of our islands inhabited by our islanders' had been attacked.

This, almost euphoric, reaction to the crisis might be expected to have created a relaxed attitude to the war for hearts and minds on the part of the Government; but seasoned politicians and even more seasoned civil servants of the Ministry of Defence did not underestimate the potentially fickle nature of public opinion; nor were they unmindful of the example of the American war in Vietnam, in which initial public approval turned in the end to persistent and at times violent protest. [97, p. 128] The Vietnam analogy was inescapable, but hardly appropriate: the United States did lose public support, but it had a lively awareness of the importance of public opinion; its difficulty was that it became engaged in a protracted war with no decisive battle that could attain its goal of defending the sovereignty of South Vietnam. The Falklands crisis seemed at least to call for a less complex reaction: Argentina must surrender to British sovereignty. But the detail of achieving this objective, the diplomatic exchanges that must accompany (or bedevil) it, could turn what seemed like a straight forward good cause into an uncertain enterprise; and public relations was 'regularly on the agenda of War Cabinet meetings'. [149, p. 17]

The Government and the Ministry of Defence appreciated that, while public and media support could not of course win the war, they could very well help the Government to lose it. There were several issues to be addressed: the release of information that might damage public support, jeopardise the safety of the armed forces, or be prejudicial to the success of military operations; the contextualising of the war, which might be presented as a kind of colonial campaign, and not one for justice and morality; the scrutiny of the conduct and morale of the armed forces, and their shortcomings revealed; and the vexatious issue of how, when and in what detail to release the names and numbers of British casualties.

These issues were scrutinised by television, radio and press commentary on the campaign, and the reports of journalists from the front line, filed by those who were not necessarily sympathetic to the campaign. And there was the overarching philosophical issue, summed up in the accreditation papers which were issued by the MOD to journalists sailing to the South Atlantic: 'The essence of successful warfare is secrecy; the essence of successful journalism is publicity'. [42, pp. 5–6]

This was an oversimplification of the case. Openness can be useful for the military; publicity as well as secrecy can assist a campaign. There was an early example of this in the Task Force's departure for the Falklands. The fleet sailed before all was ready. *Hermes* left with its Harrier aircraft and Sea King helicopters 'crammed into the deck for all the world's TV cameras to see'. But one Admiral admitted that 'to tell the truth we were not ready to leave, but it was very important to back up the diplomatic effort. It was very much a PR show – to show the Fleet leaving, both for British opinion to rally them behind the ships and as an expression of power for world opinion and, of course, the enemy'. [149, pp. 18–19] On 6 April Northwood's Public Relations staff sent a signal stressing the 'intense public interest' in Operation Corporate and the need to 'maintain a high level of public support, and understanding of, your task by offering all facilities to the press, radio and television personnel who will be with you to do their job well'. [149, pp. 20–1]

The Ministry of Defence was less enthusiastic about the media. It assumed that the public had both an interest and a right to know about defence matters. But these rights were, it announced to the House of Commons Defence Committee on 21 July 1982, 'not unlimited', and so the 'fullest possible flow of information' must be 'compatible with the overriding dictates of national and operational security' and the protection of servicemen's and servicewomen's lives. Speculation, disinformation and propaganda were coming from Buenos Aires and elsewhere; but at no time were the Government Information Services involved in psychological operations or 'disinformation'. [115, p. 1]

The Government explained that 'three critical points' must be borne in mind: that events were taking place 8,000 miles away; that the Task Force was assembled and deployed extremely quickly; and that 'we were dealing with an operational situation where Commanders, their staffs, and their communications were inevitably and rightly preoccupied with the military tasks in hand'. [115, p. 1] The Government's first instinct was to nip the journalistic problem in the bud. The civil servant dealing with the media, Ian MacDonald, convened a meeting at the Reform Club in Pall Mall attended by editors of BBC Television news and Independent Television, and technical experts. It was agreed that they would send one correspondent; share the same cameraman and sound recordist; and carry an engineer to test the possibilities of transmitting pictures back to London. Since the original total of journalists accompanying the Task Force was to be ten, this left only five places. The Director of the Newspaper Publishers' Association, Jack le Page, was called away from his Sunday lunch to telephone almost every newspaper in Fleet Street, all of whom insisted that their correspondents should go. Le Page put all the names in hat and let his wife draw the winners. [104, pp. 18–19] Indignant pressure from the unlucky editors finally won over the Prime Minister's Press Secretary, Bernard Ingham, who put pressure on the Royal Navy, which had objected that there was not enough room for more correspondents on their ships. With six hours to go before the fleet sailed the remaining journalists scrambled on board. [104, pp. 19–23]

The improvisation so far seen was criticised by the journalists. There was more to come. MOD press officers accompanied the Task Force and these 'minders' bore the brunt of the journalists' frustration. Michael Nicholson, an ITN reporter, complained that 'these men were not only unqualified. They were afraid: they were looking over their shoulders: they were constantly worried about London'. [104, pp. 27–28] Peter Archer of the Press Association listed a series of complaints, such as inconsistencies in vetting copy, copy being censored twice (sometimes three times) the intervention of a 'mystery man' who censored a colour piece describing flying exercises, 'striking out adjectives, altering style and taking out passages already passed by the MOD representative'. [115, p. 311] Early one evening, he explained:

> I handed copy to the *Hermes'* MOD man who was sitting in the wardroom drinking a glass of port. I told him the story was urgent and asked if it could be dealt with immediately. I returned half an hour later to find the unvetted copy soaking up port and other spilt liquids on a wardroom table. The copy had to be retyped and was delayed for over an hour. [115, p. 312]

The Government's publicity work was hampered by staffing cuts in the military public relations sector. The Army had only 111 Public Relations Officers outside the MOD; the Royal Navy had 31; the Royal Air Force had ten. Almost one third of the Army's Public Relations staff were military personnel. But the Army at any rate had the advantage of learning, often under the most difficult circumstances, about the importance of media scrutiny in the Northern Ireland conflict. Only one commanding officer in the Falklands had not held command there. The Royal Marines also had public relations experience. As Major General Jeremy Moore put it, 'We have all had to face cameras…we have learnt that whether a thing is a success or not is seen not in terms of its undoubted military achievement but what the PR effect had been'. [149, pp. 66–8] The Royal Navy was less happily prepared. Unlike the Army, the Navy had conducted no significant active service operation since Suez, was the 'most inward-looking of the services' and was 'ill-equipped' to deal with public relations demands. PR was seen as 'low priority', 'about the same as looking after the laundry'. [149, pp. 69–70] Admiral Woodward was given an early lesson on the dangers of approaching war equipped merely with weapons. He encountered what he called ruefully his 'unforeseen, though probably unwitting enemy, the British Press'. Woodward had been issued with a complicated written briefing from Headquarters which instructed him to give the Press 'every co-operation', but then proceeded for the next page and a half to give all the details of what he was not to tell them. This could be summarised as 'co-operation, yes; information, no'. Woodward had to face a general interview with reporters on board *Hermes*, in addition to the television interview he had with Brian Hanrahan and Michael Nicholson a few days previously. Both interviews reached the public simultaneously. The result was a 'minor catastrophe in the eyes of the Foreign Office and on downwards'. Woodward was quoted as having said, 'South Georgia was the appetiser, now this is the heavy push coming up behind. My Battle Group is properly formed and ready to strike. This is their run-up to the Big Match which in my view should be a walkover. I'd give odds of 20 to 1 on, to win'. His words were boiled down to the headline 'Walkover Woodward'. He complained that it did not 'sound' like him, and his tape of the interview, he added ambiguously, 'does not contain the word "walkover", though I do remember using the word in a slightly different sense'. [236, p. 109]

Woodward may have shown his naivety in handling the media; but his dilemma was real. The question in any public interview given by the armed services was to calculate the extent to which his words were directed at the media, or to his own personnel and their families. He must not give the media the opportunity to read its own meaning into his words; but he must also endeavour to imbue his 'team' with the conviction that they were going to win, and 'maybe also to frighten the Argentinians a bit at the same time'. Hence his words, 'But frankly, I'd really rather be given a walkover', by which he meant that 'strictly in a tennis sense, that is, a walkover when your opponent fails to turn up for the match'. He was not to know the 'subtleties such as that are rarely respected in the newspaper world'. [236, p. 110]

There was another difficulty facing the Task Force and the Government. What might seem trivial information to the media was regarded as dangerously revealing by the military. The 'classification' of the weather was an example. Correspondents accompanying the Task Force could not report that helicopter operations had been grounded by fog, for a description of the fog, which was confined to barely 40 square miles, would alert the Argentines to where the Task Force was. [148, p. 38] Some inhibitions on the media were mutually acceptable, such as the 'cardinal principle' that the names of casualties should not be announced until next-of-kin had been informed. [115, p. 2] But even here the issue was not as clear-cut as it seemed: the Government had the advantage of delaying the transmission of military setbacks, such as the explosion of HMS *Antelope* for three weeks. The *Economist* complained that 'no news is bad news', alleging that the MOD allowed information that HMS *Superb*, a nuclear-powered submarine, had left for the South Atlantic. Official confirmation was never made, but the MOD 'clearly wanted the story published, in the hope of inhibiting Argentine actions'. A few weeks later, the vessel turned up in Scotland, occasioning 'some red faces in Fleet Street'. It was, the *Economist* maintained, 'the duty of a free press to avoid being used to spread false information'. This, the *Economist* held, meant that subsequent MOD statements had less credibility. [*Economist*, 15 May 1982]

The War Cabinet had different, and contrasting, opinions about the media. Francis Pym urged that it was the duty of the Government to help its forces win the war, and denied that there was a public right to know information which reduced the possibility of the war being waged successfully; but he regarded presentation of policy as crucial and made himself available to the media. [115, pp. 22–3] But he wished that pictures and film extracts of the Argentine forces 'had a caption indicating their source, rather than a picture merely showing that something was happening'. [114, 19 April, col. 28] Mrs Thatcher, characteristically, simplified the issue. Setting aside Pym's judicious words, she expressed anxiety about what she saw as national unity, and concern over the 'even-handedness' of journalistic reporting. [203, p. 181] On 6 May at Prime Minister's Question Time, Mrs Thatcher replied to a question from John Page about television and radio coverage of the crisis. She replied

> Judging by many of the comments that I have heard from those who watch and listen more than I do, many people are very concerned indeed that the case for our British forces is not being put over fully or effectively. I understand that there are times when it seems that we and the Argentines are being treated almost as equals and almost on a neutral basis.

She understood that 'there are occasions when some commentators will say that the Argentines did something and then the "British" did something'. 'I can say', she concluded, 'that if this is so it gives offence and causes great irritation among many people'. [114, 6 May, col. 279]

But there was a further dimension of the Falklands War that irritated journalists. That was geography. The distance from home at which the war was conducted meant that journalists were 'shipbound'. Official resistance to providing adequate facilities for the media added to the difficulties: as one photographer put it, 'It wasn't a news war, it's as simple as that. It was in the wrong place'. [42, p. 121] The war would not be a television spectacle, nor even a pictorial one. Despatches sometimes took longer to reach London than had W. H. Russell's reports of the charge of the Light Brigade in 1854. [42, p. 121] Television pictures were not transmitted live, though TV film and some still pictures were shipped to Ascension Island and then flown back to Britain. In the later stages of the war still pictures were transmitted by wire on commercial links, but access to this was still controlled by the military. [149, p. 145] Radio reporting was mainly conveyed through the medium of television. The Falkland Islands were five hours behind British Summer Time, and when news broke it was either in the late afternoon or early evening in the United Kingdom, when television was the dominant medium. Yet it was unable to receive pictures from the Falklands. Allegations that this was deliberately engineered were unfounded: commercial satellites could not be used for ships at sea, and there were no ground stations nor terminals designed for TV transmission on land. Thus broadcasts were dependent on military channels. These technical considerations did not, as it happened, displease the military. Pictures of the *Sheffield*'s burning were taken on 7 May; the date of transmission was 28 May. The attack on the *Sir Galahad* was on 8 June; the date of transmission was 24 June. [159, p. 169]

Some spoke darkly of journalists being chosen on the basis of their likely attitude to the campaign, while others were excluded for the same reason. But the MOD was alert to the need to lay down ground rules covering all the media and its relations with the Task Force. On 7 April the Permanent Secretary issued guidelines for editors in London on what they could not cover: these were

a. Speculation about future possible action.
b. Plans for operations.
c. Readiness state and details about individual units' operational capability, movements and deployment.
d. Details about military techniques and tactics.
e. Logistical details.
f. Intelligence about Argentine forces.
g. Equipment capabilities and defects.
h. Communications. [115, pp. 13–16]

This involved changing words to render them neutral in meaning, if not altogether meaningless. 'Bracketed Signal' transformed 'Marines and Paratroopers' into 'Assault Forces'. Copy thus amended was transmitted to the MOD and it was again vetted by Press officers to decide if it did not breach three specifically issued 'D' notices. [42, p. 124]

Journalists believed that the 'minders' were deliberately obstructive, 'mislaying' copy or destroying it, while the MOD withheld certain facts on grounds of copy or images that might reflect poorly on the troops. [42, pp. 124–5]

There was also the question of deliberate untruth. When Sir Frank Cooper was questioned by the Defence Committee about the accuracy of information released by the Government Information Services, and in particular about the statement that there would be 'no D-Day type landing' on the Falklands (prior to the San Carlos landings), Cooper replied, with some satisfaction, that he did not 'unveil the whole picture', that he was 'delighted' that there was a good deal of speculation and that it was 'very helpful to us'. 'We did not tell a lie', he claimed, 'but we did not tell the whole truth'. [115, pp. 22–3] When it was put to him that he had worked on the principle of '*suppressio veri*' and '*suggestio falsi*' he bridled, suggesting that 'we did not produce the full truth and the full story. And you, as politicians, know as well as anyone else that on many occasions the news is handled by everything in politics in a way that redounds to their advantage'. [115, p. 35]

Cooper conceded the difficulty in conducting a war of information and propaganda, and the distinction – or lack of it – between the two: especially in a war which, as one member of the Defence Committee put it, was 'referred to as a war situation, variously described as a conflict and so on'. [115, p. 39] In a 'war situation' (as distinct from a war) Government could not define its behaviour on the basis of a formally declared war, and the issue of national survival. Cooper remarked that he did not think it 'obnoxious in any sense to contemplate deceiving one's enemies. One should conceal one's decisions and policies on occasion. Of that I have no doubts or reservations whatsoever'. When it came to 'deceiving one's own people', he added, 'I think one is on very much tender ground because at the end the truth will out'. [115, p. 39] But Sir Frank did not draw the conclusion, which from his own words would have been a reasonable one, that 'deceiving' one's enemies necessarily involved deceiving one's own people, as his example of the San Carlos landings indicated. Cooper remarked in considering a question about deceiving or not deceiving 'your allies' that he was 'not sure that I like these philosophical questions'. [115, p. 37] But, as one Committee member, Dr Gilbert, pointed out, 'they should inform the basis of policy, should they not?' [115, p. 37]

Gilbert identified a serious issue. The Government was not in a war, but in a war-situation; and it needed to adjust to this Orwellian world and develop some philosophy of how to define, explain and justify its actions. Since it was feeling its way, it found itself managing on an ad hoc basis, and the result was an almost amateurish mode of operation, shown in the selection of the MOD official in charge of public relations. This was Ian MacDonald, who was by 1979 the assistant secretary in charge of Division 14, the Ministry's recruitment and pay section: a post, as Robert Harris wryly remarked, 'not...renowned for requiring a detailed knowledge of the world's media'. He was moved across to become the MOD's deputy chief of public relations when the Defence Minister, Fred Mulley, was photographed asleep at an RAF ceremony; it was felt that a 'personal shield' was needed. [104, p. 95] In 1981 MacDonald applied for the post of chief of public relations. He was unsuccessful, but when the head of public relations fell ill and burdened with a backlog of work MacDonald took over as acting head of public relations at the MOD until June 1982. And thus it was, as Robert Harris put it, 'in this state of bureaucratic confusion that the Ministry of Defence public relations department suddenly found itself caught up in the most hectic crisis in its history'. [104, p. 96]

When he was asked by the Defence Committee chairman if he had any training for the role of public spokesman for the MOD, MacDonald replied 'As a spokesman, no', adding (with admirable and revealing frankness) 'If you mean by "training" television camera technique and so on'. [115, p. 398] The Permanent Secretary gave him peremptory instructions ('Ian, you will have to make these announcements on television, there's the chair'), and a PR man with some experience in broadcasting said, 'Well, there are these rules: sit well back in your chair; don't move your eyes about because it makes you look shifty, and speak slowly, don't gabble'. MacDonald admitted that he was 'terrified'. [201]

MacDonald explained that during the first part of the Falklands crisis, up to the landing at San Carlos, 'we were in a situation where we were restricting ourselves really to the spokesman and to the on-the-record briefings'. When the landings took place, 'the whole of the PR changed...and we had various briefings...So there were two quite distinct periods which had their own rules and their own rationale'. [115, p. 398] However, the Press reacted unfavourably to the first phase of MOD public relations, claiming that the MOD suffered from the loss of credibility from which it never recovered. [104, p. 97] MacDonald was also caught in the trap of promising not to tell an untruth, and yet not saying anything that might prejudice the success of the Task Force or jeopardise the lives of its men. To sustain the second objective might very well prejudice the first. [104, pp. 98–9] On

24 April he told the press that the Task Force 'has not landed anywhere', when newspapers were already claiming that the operation to recover South Georgia was under way. In his defence he argued that the SAS was not the Task Force. [104, pp. 99–100] He admitted to the Defence Committee a difficulty that might be seen as of the department's own making. When asked about the reports of the British intention to attack Goose Green, which were broadcast on the BBC world service just before 2 Para moved to its starting line, he replied that there was 'tremendous public interest'. There were many people saying, 'unless you say something you will only encourage speculation'. [115, p. 403] This was exactly what MacDonald had been doing – or not doing – and thus encouraging speculation. It was, he explained, because there was a 'general feeling that something was happening' that the speculation was so intense, 'particularly on Goose Green, that for once we relied only on a telephone conversation between Northwood and the Task Force to tell the world that Goose Green had been taken. We discovered subsequently – and this was purely a mistake in the communication from the Task Force to Northwood – that Goose Green had been surrounded (sic) but not taken and it was under the kind of pressure to get news out that we deviated from the normal practice of waiting…to ensure that you got confirmation'. [115, pp. 403–4]

MacDonald's television appearances were, in the eyes of many, bizarre. His appearance – black hair severely parted on the left side, his square black glasses – may have 'appealed to women all over the country'; [201, 24 May 2002] but his curious way of speaking – what General Jeremy Moore called his 'Humanoid "I-speak-your-weight Machine" style of diction [156, p. 146] – seemed at odds with the necessities of smart public relations. And yet there was a positive side to MacDonald's broadcasts. His very lack of training, indeed his willingness to, so to say, have a go, seemed to 'personify British truthfulness; his civilian status to symbolise a democratic nation at war with a be-medalled junta'. [149, p. 183] His decision to announce the final sinking of HMS *Sheffield* after the television cameras had been switched off was a curious means of communication; it lacked the polish of the professional PR man. But his motive (that it was not right to announce this news in front of all the lights and cameras because 'it was like announcing the death of a child') [97, p. 10] was, perhaps, more in tune with the public feeling about the loss of a Royal Navy vessel.

The Government's difficulties in straightening out its public relations offensive were compounded by the plethora of sources it deployed. There was the faithful MacDonald; the ubiquitous Bernard Ingham, the Prime Minister's Press Secretary (who chaired daily meetings of the Information Co-ordination group); and a 'variety of interested officials', including Nicholas Fenn, head of PR at the Foreign Office; an official from the Cabinet Office, and the private secretary of Cecil Parkinson, a member of the War Cabinet. MacDonald read the newspapers and prepared a short summary of their contents. When the meeting of this group ended MacDonald would then attend the daily meeting of the Chiefs of Staff Committee, which included public relations as a permanent item on its agenda. This committee consisted of Admiral Lewin, Frank Cooper, John Nott and representatives from the Intelligence Services and the Foreign Office. MacDonald would outline what he thought should be released to the media. At 12.00 he would meet the press and take 20 minutes of questions. There was, as Robert Harris noted, a mildly eccentric atmosphere on these occasions, with MacDonald fond of using quotations from literature to support – or even to make – his point. [104, pp. 101–3]

The Ministry of Defence's public relations were troubled by internal dissension. The designate chief of public relations, Neville Taylor, and MacDonald, were in disagreement because Taylor was barred by his letter of appointment from dealing with the Falklands campaign. [104, pp. 104–5] Taylor was anxious about what he called the Defence public relations staff's 'very responsive and not terribly aggressive PR machine'. [115, p. 374] The Service directors of public relations, for their part, were frustrated at not having control of the 'image' of their activities, which Admiral Lewin later regretted. [104, p. 105] By 11 May Sir Frank Cooper resorted to off-the-record briefings in an attempt to defuse press anger over the paucity of information. On 14 May MacDonald took a holiday, at Cooper's suggestion, and when he returned he found Taylor in control of the MOD's public relations department. By now Cooper was conducting two regular sets of background briefings, one for editors and one for defence correspondents, which seem to have been regarded by neither as useful. [104, p. 109] On 18 May a News Release Group was established under the chairmanship of the Assistant Secretary of State for the Defence Staff, including senior officers of the public relations and service staffs. The views of Fleet Headquarters and Northwood were 'invariably sought' on the release of operational information and on 'particularly difficult questions' the personal view of the Commander-in-Chief was obtained. All releases were approved by the Secretary of State. [115, pp. 1–2]

The press never seem to have been comfortable with its diet of news from official sources. In its official statement to the Defence Committee which reviewed the conduct of public relations during the war, the BBC spoke of the 'considerable praise for the BBC's objectivity', in contrast to that of the MOD which, it claimed, 'came close to losing its credibility'. [115, p. 41] The BBC argued that MOD reticence not only did not help the British military campaign, but hindered it; for example, the BBC began to perceive that, while most Argentine claims of damage inflicted on the Task Force were 'patently hysterical, self-evidently propaganda', some were 'possibly true and accurate'. Journalists realised that they should not be rejected out of hand, but the MOD system, which presented swift rejection or confirmation of such claims, was a self-inflicted wound. It gave the Argentines, internationally, a credibility they did not deserve. The MOD's information was, too often, the 'runner-up'. And that, it concluded, 'perhaps, was the greatest damage of all'. [115, p. 43]

While the BBC was critical of the MOD's performance, which, it alleged, 'has come very close to the "management" or "manipulation" of news, an idea that is alien to the concept of communication within a free society'. [115, p. 45] It noted with approval that 'between the military and the correspondents with the Task Force, that trust did exist'. Correspondents were kept informed of decisions and plans. Correspondents were told only they should not use certain information in their despatches – and they complied without hesitation. [115, p. 42] There was much truth in this, but there were important exceptions as well. When HMS *Conqueror* torpedoed the *General Belgrano* Michael Nicholson, on board the *Olmeda*, which was equipped with a commercial telephone system known as the Marisat, happened to overhear on the bridge the name of the submarine responsible for the attack. He promptly broadcast the information in a despatch to ITN's News at One. Admiral Fieldhouse was so angry at this exposure not only of the whereabouts of the submarine, but of the possibility of its receiving adverse publicity, that he rebuked Captain Middleton, on board *Hermes*, who never spoke to Nicholson again. [104, p. 108] There were particular tensions on board *Hermes:* Middleton 'did not like the press. He said to us from the very start that we were an embarrassment to him'. [104, p. 30] There was also the distraction, at least in service and operational terms, of Prince Andrew's presence on board *Invincible* as a helicopter pilot, whose captain was besieged by reporters anxious to interview the prince. *The Sun*'s Tony Shaw revealed on 10 April that he had hunted the enemy 'with Andy'. [104, pp. 28–9]

The tensions between military needs and journalistic values was revealed in the aftermath of the Argentine attack on the *Sir Galahad*. The MOD public relations machine told journalists that they 'could report the disaster but had to mention the "good news" first: that enemy planes had been shot down'. Two voice despatches from Fitzroy arrived simultaneously in London that night. In one, Michael Nicholson of ITN spoke of a 'day of extraordinary heroism'. Brian Hanrahan of the BBC gave a 'far more sombre' report, describing survivors from the *Sir Galahad* as 'shaken and hysterical' with hearing the cries of their comrades trapped below. This was objected to by the censors who refused to release the tape until the offending passage was removed. Nicholson's more positive report was released and broadcast by ITV and the BBC. [81, pp. 160–1]

The BBC, in its submission to the Defence Committee after the war, made the unfortunate, but central, point: that the Americans in Vietnam allowed reports and television pictures to be transmitted without vetting; it was a matter of policy that United States and South Vietnamese military depended at least in part on winning the fight for hearts and minds. [115, p. 47] Since it was widely held that the media cost America the war, this was a less than convincing reason for allowing more latitude to journalists. But there was also an element of self-censorship in the BBC's journalism. Alan Protheroe, Assistant Director General of the BBC, defended the BBC's call for more co-operation from the MOD by insisting that it did nothing to jeopardise in any way the objectives of the Government nor the lives of those serving with the Task Force; thus it did not file reports about the number of Argentine bombs which failed to explode – and which, if they had exploded, would have been a serious reverse for the British campaign. [115, p. 50] The Glasgow University Media Group cited evidence of the BBC's reticence, taken from its News and Current Affairs minutes. Protheroe warned that 'to describe a successful British assault on the Falklands (he) favoured "repossession", and objected to the use of "invasion"...(but) discretion of the editors was required to determine the most apposite word or phrase'. [97, p. 13]

Nevertheless, the BBC and the Government found itself at odds. The BBC insisted that its essential mission was to serve its audience: 'The broadcaster's function is to serve that audience and the broadcaster is only in that general sense a protagonist in the pursuit of "the national interest"'. [115, p. 50] The Government had its own concept of the national interest; and in the extremities of war, it naturally felt that these must be paramount. But the Falklands conflict was not a war – but a 'war'. And it was hard to make a distinction between what was legitimate criticism of Government policy, or of the conduct of the campaign; and what was a real danger to the war effort: or perhaps 'war effort'.

There were two main areas of disagreement between the Government and the television media. One was the media practice of inviting military experts to give their analysis of the campaign, and a critique of the tactics of the British commanders. About 30 retired officers and 20 civilian defence correspondents were involved, and the purpose of consulting them was to add 'interest and authenticity' to broadcasts, and to impart some of the 'atmosphere' surrounding the military. The Conservative MP, Michael Mates, complained about 'armchair strategists', while Mrs Thatcher and John Nott alleged that these discussions were putting servicemen's lives in jeopardy. [115, pp. 8–9, 57–8]

The special position of the BBC raised particular concerns in the Government. In 1977 the BBC told the Annan Committee on Broadcasting that it was 'part of the nation', and that it could not be 'impartial between the maintenance and dissolution of the nation'. [115, p. 192] Mrs Thatcher clearly believed that the Falklands crisis was a crisis for the nation; and some even held that it did represent the crisis for the nation, whose future would be decided by the outcome of the war.

The question of whether or not the BBC should be 'on our side', as a Conservative MP put it, or indulge in a 'superior tone of superior neutrality' [207, 14 May 2002] came to a head when on 10 May it broadcast a 'Panorama' programme which closely scrutinised the policy of the Government in the crisis, and included an interview with a member of the Argentine delegation to the United Nations who outlined Argentina's position on the sovereignty issue. The programme also included interviews with Conservative MPs who disagreed with their Government' policy, Sir Anthony Meyer and David Crouch. Crouch said that in fighting we 'may be judged to be standing on our dignity for a colonial ideal'. George Foulkes and Tam Dalyell, Labour MPs severely critical of the move to war, were also interviewed. [81, pp. 162–3] The BBC's difficulties were further compounded when Robert Kee wrote to *The Times* explaining why he had disassociated himself from the programme, asserting that it had confused its own view of the Falklands War with that of the minority view: over half the programme was devoted to an explanation of the minority opinion. The specific suggestion that Mrs Thatcher was warmongering was 'left to a point not far from the conclusion'. Kee explained that he had raised his objections before the programme was shown and that its editor told him that it had been cut and the commentary rewritten. But Kee's objections had hardly been met, and he considered disassociating himself from the programme on the air. The editor, George Carey, defended himself, saying that the purpose of the Panorama programme was to represent the minority view; the majority view had been aired previously on the BBC since the crisis began, but the programme was not 'anti-British', and the introduction stated that Argentina had put herself in the wrong by her aggression. [207, 14 May 1982]

The Government's reaction, and that of the Conservative Party, perhaps surprised even themselves in the degree of their hostility to the BBC. A member of the War Cabinet claimed that there was 'a general hate of the BBC whom we reckoned to be biased and pro-ITN which we reckoned were doing much better'. [149, p. 134] The Panorama programme brought these suspicions out in the open. John Nott described the BBC as 'the propaganda wing of the Argentinians', 'pumping out contrary Argentine propaganda'. [172] Mrs Thatcher told the House of Commons that she had received assurances from the BBC stating 'in vigorous terms that the BBC is not neutral on this point'. The following morning the BBC's Director General reminded editors and producers at a News and Current Affairs meeting that 'the BBC was the British Broadcasting Corporation. It was now clear that a large section of the public shared this view and he believed it was an unnecessary irritation to stick to the detached style'. The following evening's edition of the Nine o'Clock News ended with a report on 'a display of patriotism in Merseyside, where more than 500 people gathered to sing songs as a sign of their support for the British troops out in the South Atlantic'. [81, pp. 162–3]

Nonetheless, the BBC's Director General insisted publicly that 'the notion that we are traitors is outrageous. There is no-one in the BBC who does not agree that the Argentines committed aggression. But this is not total war. One day we will be negotiating with the enemy, so we must try to understand them'. [149, p. 133]

It was difficult to strike a balance between neutral reporting and the needs of a nation that, if not 'at war', was indisputably waging it. Words could take on a new significance. When the MOD's own Ian MacDonald referred to the 'British Task Force', [149, p. 133] the use of the prefix 'British' could be construed as implying a certain kind of detachment: 'our' Task Force or even simply 'the' Task Force had a small, yet significant, resonance. Peter Snow, a 'Newsnight' presenter, explained that he saw himself as 'a citizen of the world, a detached journalist. I don't think it is right to twist things so that you have put the British case over in the most favourable light. Maybe we are not neutral between the IRA and the British Army, but we should be detached'. [148, p. 119] ITN's submission to the Defence Committee after the war seemed, however, to suggest that better co-operation from the authorities on the Task Force, and in particular the better provision of technical facilities, would have had beneficial results. What it called 'flair in high places' could have 'led to nightly offering of interesting, positive and heart-warming stories of achievement and collaboration born out of a sense of national purpose'. [115, pp. 76–7] It rejected the Vietnam analogy as 'totally invalid'. [115, p. 72] The right analogy was found in the Second World War when Ed Morrow was allowed to broadcast the truth to America, and as a result he made it 'decisively easy' for President Roosevelt to assist the British war effort. [115, p. 74]

This was a profoundly important assessment of the relationship between journalism and war: the common experience of military life, the closeness of the journalist to the soldier when in action, helped mould a positive attitude to the Falklands campaign, if not necessarily to the justice of the British Government's cause. As relations between the MOD and the media deteriorated, those between the journalists and the soldiers in the field were enhanced; 'trust was well established with the unit PRO for 3 Commando Brigade…His briefings about each day's events were masterly'. [115, p. 142] Alaistair McQueen, *Daily Mirror* correspondent, found the commanders of the group with which he sailed (40 and 42 Commando Royal Marines; 3 Para) 'delighted to have us with them. They were proud of their units, the capabilities of their men and of their profession. They were prepared to spend much of their precious time with us, educating us, helping us and making sure we understood everything'. [115, p. 144] Not even censorship was irritating, because 'If or when they cut items from our despatches it was not done out of hand. They discussed it with us and tried to help us get round the barrier'. [115, p. 145] When the BBC reporter, Brian Hanrahan, whose name became a household word when he coined the phrase (referring to the safe return of Sea Harriers to HMS *Hermes* after their first attack on the landing strip of Stanley), 'I counted them all out and I counted them all back', admitted that his attitude had changed during the campaign:

> I think there were two contrasting things going on. One was that in personal terms I was surprised at both the humanity and the

> intelligence shown by everybody I met. I think I started off with a stereotype that people in the Forces are rather odd; they have a mission in life, which is to go out and shoot people, and they are really not much more than that...I found that they were very humane, very aware, willing to discuss all-round issues and not to take the military view of them. I think I grew to warm to everybody out there and discovered they are a very bright bunch of people whose opinions are by no means jingoistic and militaristic, although they are in a profession which is military.

He learnt how vulnerable everybody was, and how this apparently 'invincible force' was in danger, not of biting off more than they could chew, but of biting off 'something we were going to have to chew on'. [115, p. 160] Max Hastings was willing to help the British forces in their 'chewing'. He admitted to the Defence Committee what Sir Frank Cooper had originally denied, that he had been allowed to use the SAS direct line to Hereford (their HQ) because senior officers hoped to use his report on 'our guns shelling Moody Brook' to show the Argentines how serious their own military predicament was. In the event his despatch was held up by the MOD for three days and so helped nobody. [115, p. 214]

Hastings attributed the military's positive response to the journalists (compared to that of the Navy) to the Army's experience in the Northern Ireland troubles. All the forces which had served there 'have learnt that the media can be helpful if they are helped and brought along'. [115, p. 215] The Press Association confirmed this, noting that the Army 'learned...the hard way over a number of years that the press is a necessary, and often very useful, evil...'. [115, pp. 303, 307] The danger was, as Patrick Bishop of the *Observer* complained, that 'essentially the journalists were regarded by the MOD as public relations men for the Task Force'. [115, p. 367] But it was nearer the truth to say that the journalists themselves became, if not mere public relations men for the Task Force, then certainly patriotic men. Patrick Bishop acknowledged that 'the situation was that you were a propagandist'. [159, p. 98] Max Hastings filed optimistic copy about the Army's spirit on the San Carlos beachhead, declaring that he would not file any copy that could give the Argentines 'hope or comfort'. [159, p. 113]

It was not, perhaps, surprising that Max Hastings should like soldiers and 'get on well with them'; [159, p. 113] more unusual was the exuberant admission by *The Guardian*'s Gareth Parry that he 'felt a terrific admiration for them. I could put aside the fact that it was ridiculous that we should be doing this. I was terrifically impressed by these guys, and the spirit of friendship as well. It sounds pretty corny now, but I tell you, you could leave a quid in your bunk and it would still be there two days later'. [159, p. 26] He began by referring to 'the British', and within a few days 'I was calling "us" or "we"'. [159, p. 99] Parry's tribute to the troops was all the more striking in that he left the Falklands shortly after the British landings and went home to write about the 'futility' of war. [159, p. 34] David Norris described how 'on shore I dressed like a soldier. I ate like them, I lived with them. I just began to feel part of the whole thing'. [159, p. 98]

Press descriptions of the fighting were cast in the heroic mould. Brian Hanrahan described the battle of Goose Green as one of, 'Troops against a defensive position, storming it, and taking against ten to one odds against them…It was the sort of victory which will live for a long time in the Second Paras'. By contrast the Argentine soldiers were characterised as committing 'squalid and mindless vandalism'. [85, pp. 50, 53] Robert Fox in a 'World Tonight' programme on 2 June described how he had 'made a friend for life…with the RSM, RSM Simpson. We've hugged each other and fallen into trenches together so often now that we can't part from this anything but soul mates'. [85, p. 56] When Fox was asked how he now thought of the armed forces, he replied

> Now, the odd sort of thing that I've found among the Paras, and they've had a fearsome reputation I know, but amongst the officers and many of the men I have found some of the most civilised men that I've ever been in a tight corner with in my life. The standard of personal generosity, of kindness, of respect, strange to say, of respect for human life, is of a very high degree indeed, and I think that says a lot for their efficiency. That is why they are such good fighting troops, because they're fighting troops who care about each other desperately as individuals. [85, p. 60]

Journalists did not want to file stories of soldiers' misbehaviour. One claimed to have seen unarmed Argentine soldiers shot while surrendering, but 'although he disapproved of it, he felt he could understand it. In the tension of battle…it was inevitable'. [159, pp. 121, 123]

There is no reason to dispute this opinion. What is significant is that the Parachute Regiment, which was seen in the context of the Northern Ireland troubles as the perpetrators of 'Bloody Sunday' in January 1972, were now, a decade later, held up as the best example of the

British soldier. John Shirley compared the Falklands experience to that of Northern Ireland, his 'only experience of the British Army previously'. In Northern Ireland he had 'never been very impressed by them. The press officers are appalling, they oil around the Europa Hotel – they are oily. And most of the blokes I haven't much time for. They never seemed to me to be very bright; they seemed to be thoughtless and clearly contemptuous of the IRA, and they didn't consider any political dimension of the Provos at all – whether you agree with the Provos or not is irrelevant – but there is essentially a fairly serious political situation in Ireland as well as a military one'. In Northern Ireland 'you don't know who the enemy is, and everybody wears civilian clothes, and the civilian population insults you in English – they're not wogs you can go and beat up'. [159, pp. 25–6]

So the Northern Ireland conflict was political; the Falklands conflict was not. The Argentine enemy, if Shirley's logic is to be followed to its conclusion, were indeed 'wogs' who, possibly, could be beaten up. The transformation of the British Army from 'stupid blokes' and 'effete' officers to men who were objects of admiration was, again, not a false one; but its significance lies in what it revealed about the impact of a different, and shared, kind of war had on its reporting and characterisation. Soldiers who had lost comrades and friends killed by an IRA sniper would have felt anger and grief; but this was not at the heart of British reporting of the Northern Ireland conflict, whereas after the battle of Mount Longdon the commander of 3 Para was described as watching 'the determined, triumphant but shocked, saddened faces of those who had lost their friends'. [7, p. 121] Journalists reporting Northern Ireland seldom, if ever, associated themselves with the serving soldiers; in the Falklands most of them were, in the words of Patrick Bishop 'seduced one by one, we became Troopie groupies'. [57]

At home, the British Press pursued its own agenda. *The Sun*'s notorious 'Gotcha' headline celebrating the sinking of the *General Belgrano* is taken as typical of the jingoistic style of the pro-war tabloid press. But there was a more serious debate in the Press than is sometimes suggested. The *Daily Mirror* attacked *The Sun* for its trivialising and inaccurate coverage of the conflict, calling it the 'harlot of Fleet Street'. [7, p. 16] The broadsheet newspapers criticised its tabloid rivals for their dubious professional standards. *The Sun* detected treason in the misgivings about the war expressed in *The Guardian* and the *Mirror*. The *Mirror* was a 'timorous, whining publication'. [104, pp. 49–51]

It was significant, however, that despite *The Sun*'s patriotic support of the war, and the *Mirror*'s criticism of it, the former did not increase its circulation, nor did the latter lose it. On the contrary *The Sun* lost sales of 40,000 a day, whereas the *Mirror* added 95,000 (though this was attributed by the *Mirror*'s editor, Mike Molloy, to a successful promotional campaign launched before the war). [104, p. 55] This only reflected the old adage that people bought their newspapers for reasons other than their politics. But it also raised the question whether or not, as *The Times* put it, we were indeed all Falklanders now.

The initial response of the British public to the war was described by the *Economist* as that of a 'spectator's war': 'eager to rally to the flag, but not if it means anybody getting hurt'. [71] Public opinion, as expressed in Market and Opinion Research International (MORI) supported Mrs Thatcher's response to the Argentine invasion of the Falklands and by 1 May reached 76 per cent. Support for the Conservative party rose by 6 per cent: 'rarely has a party registered such a sudden improvement in its standing'. [66] The public appeared to be taking the Government's leadership on trust. It approved of economic sanctions against Argentina; sending the fleet; and, on principle, landing troops on the islands. It appeared that voters, with no casualties so far, 'found the Falklands crisis politically absorbing, militarily exhilarating and a welcome outlet for clannish self-righteousness'. But on the question of going to war if substantial loss of life were incurred, the response was evenly divided: 58 per cent accepted that British servicemen's lives would be lost, 'and no more than that would agree to sinking Argentine ships'. A majority remained against Britain firing the first shot if negotiations were still in train. The *Economist*'s conclusion, that in this spectator war the British wanted 'clear principles' to be upheld, but not if it means anybody getting hurt'. In the case of Northern Ireland, people had grown used to a 'steady trickle of service lives in support of a principle, even where the cause of Protestant supremacy is not a popular one'. The Falklands was a more distinct issue: 'Unlike Ulster, it holds the potential for military calamity', and public opinion was not yet convinced that this was worthwhile. [66]

The sinking of the *General Belgrano*, followed by the loss of the *Sheffield*, produced a varied response. On 8 May the *Economist* reported that support for Mrs Thatcher's Government seemed to have peaked. The MORI poll on the previous Tuesday and Wednesday showed a downturn in Conservative voting intentions and satisfaction with the Prime Minister's handling of the confrontation (67 per cent from 76 per cent). But the news of the *Sheffield*'s sinking did not substantially alter the balance of opinion in the MORI sample, merely continuing the slight trend against the Government, begun before the *Belgrano* sinking. There was no statistically significant change in the proportion which regarded Falklands sovereignty as worth the loss of British service lives (53 per cent down from 58 per cent, but still up on the 44 per cent who felt this way at the start of the crisis a month previously). On the *Belgrano* sinking 46 per cent of the sample was in favour and 44 per cent against. A high 81 per cent approved of the bombing of Stanley airport. The conclusion was that it was the large-scale loss of life involved in sinking ships rather (as against simply bombing targets) that determined the sample's reaction. [67]

This trend continued throughout the remainder of the month, as the Task Force drew nearer to the Falklands. Opinion polls gave the Government cause for satisfaction, but also for concern. There was still, on 25–26 May, strong support for its action; the percentage supporting a landing on the islands rose from 67 per cent to 89 per cent in a week and the proportion of those approving of sinking Argentine ships now stood at 79 per cent. Sixty-two per cent now accepted the possibility of casualties. But the difficulty for the Government was that 51 per cent favoured United Nations trusteeship of the islanders, with 43 per cent against (though 70 per cent were for the retention of British sovereignty). There was overlap here, but the conclusion was that some kind of compromise solution would in the end be unavoidable. [69]

On 2 June Mrs Thatcher showed that she had sufficient confidence in both the public and her backbench MPs to adopt her most determined stance so far: if 'magnanimity' meant granting concessions to the Argentines, this would amount to 'treachery'. [70] As the campaign drew to its close, it was clear that the Government had kept in tandem with public opinion. But it was in some respects fortunate to do so. On 16 April David Watt, Director of the Royal Institute for International Affairs at Chatham House warned that 'if it turns out that the cost is in fact higher in men, in money or perhaps even in terms of world opinion, its patience may run out fast'. [207, 16 April] The loss of life in the conflict was, on the British side at least, gradual and was accompanied by either military success, or continued negotiations, or sometimes both. The loss of the *Sheffield* was the most striking disaster for the Government to surmount, but at this time it was still pursuing negotiations, and, even though the chance of success was slight, it was in tune with the desire of a considerable proportion of the public for negotiations to continue. [97, p. 19]

A survey of public opinion by Mass Observation put some human detail on the polls. It discovered that there was frequent reference to Munich and the appeasement policies of the 1930s. One woman, who was born in 1914, declared that 'people of my age remember Munich and the soft treatment we handed out then'. Some used the appeasement analogy to criticise the Government for its weakness in the dispute with Argentina. But on the whole the 1930s experience rallied support for the mobilisation of the Task Force: 'we have to act'. Some criticised those whose patriotism 'increases proportionately to the distance of the individual to the sharp end of war', but the perception that the crisis 'made people proud to be British' surfaced again and again. But there was also tension and fear on the part of some of those who recalled the Second World War. This, however, was mitigated by the reflection that 'our young men are still patriotic at heart, ready to defend the honour of the land of their birth'. [167, pp. 121–8]

The Glasgow University Media Group attributed much of the state of opinion to the failure of the media to facilitate a more open debate on the Falklands War. It focused on two issues which, it claimed, demonstrated a kind of covert media support of the British campaign. One was the sinking of the *General Belgrano*, in which the treatment of the issue of 'survivors'; and 'casualties' was given a more facile, or at least less critical, account. The BBC and ITN at first played down the number of likely casualties, and stressed the effort being made to rescue survivors. There was a lack of information, but this 'cannot explain the extraordinary minimising of the consequences of the attack'. [97, p. 32] The BBC reported that transmissions from the Argentine commander on the Falklands revealed his saying that the incident had 'opened the way for us to kill', whereas he had said, 'The sinking of the *Belgrano* has opened the door for us to pass through'. [97, p. 35] ITN reported that the *Belgrano* had been 'on the edge' of the 200 mile Exclusion Zone, whereas it had been outside it. [97, p. 36] By contrast, the sinking of the *Sheffield* was described as 'dreadful news' with an emphasis on the casualties incurred. [97, pp. 40–1] There was no consideration of the possibility that the British action had led to a major escalation of the conflict. [97, p. 55] The Glasgow Media Group gave further examples of the managing of public opinion, such as the exaggeration of the impact of the British bombing raids on Stanley airport which, the Group alleged, 'overestimated the ease with which a military operation could be conducted to re-take the Falklands'. [97, pp. 91–2]

The Glasgow University Media Group's evidence is meticulous and impressive, though it is hard to see, for example, how the media's dwelling on the 'dreadful news' of the *Sheffield*'s sinking [97, pp. 40–1] and the casualties incurred could have possibly helped the Government's cause. A brief, but expert, survey by the Department of Politics at Strathclyde University of Scottish media opinion about a crisis that was 'neither Scots nor English' ('the troops that fought in the Falklands were both Scots and English and Welsh and Gurkha'), confirmed that the Scottish media 'like all the English except *The Financial Times* and *The Guardian*, supported a firm response to the Argentine invasion'. Popular support for the Task Force was also high in Scotland, but the difference was 'the party political advantage to the Conservatives simply failed to materialise'. [153, pp. 22–3] There was little of what the authors called the 'mindless belligerence' which characterised the English best-selling newspaper, [153, p. 23] and the *Mirror* Group's *Record* backed 'our boys', but warned that 'win or lose, war is always a tragedy'. But the Task Force were 'heroes'. [153, pp. 24, 26] The Government's anxieties about media treatment of the war, seen in the MOD's cautious attitude to the Press and television, and its attempt to manage the news and reporting of the war, were perhaps over cautious. Moreover, failure in war is, fairly soon, self-evident; propaganda or news manipulation cannot stand up in the face of serious military disaster, as the German experience at Stalingrad in the Second World War demonstrated. For most of the British people the war, as defined, negotiated over, and fought, legitimised itself. It was this that its critics and the official mind alike found hardest to accept.

9

War and the State of 'Thatcher's Britain'

'We have ceased to be a nation in retreat', Margaret Thatcher proclaimed at Cheltenham on 3 July 1982:

> We have instead a new-found confidence – born in the economic battles at home and tested and found true 8,000 miles away. We recognise that Britain has rekindled the spirit which has fired her for generations past and which truly has begun to burn as brightly as before. Britain found herself again in the South Atlantic and will not look back from the victory she has won. [203, p. 235]

And not only the nation had regained its rightful place; one historian argued that the Falklands War which 'so notably revived her political fortunes, was the moment of truth for Mrs Thatcher's political leadership. She was subsequently taken at her own valuation and she subsequently felt an unshakeable confidence in her own judgement, which she was ready to back against all-comers'. Peter Clarke went on to argue that the war's successful outcome fed her 'wild streak of moral authoritarianism', [47, pp. 316–17] temporarily solving all her political problems, but also forming the 'seedbed' for a style of Thatcherite triumphalism that came to caricature her earlier successes: 'hubris was inexorably succeeded by nemesis'. [47, p. 321]

Whether or not this was the case – and the debate on the part played by the war in the Conservative party general election victory of 1984 has been a subject of dispute [191] – it is certain that Mrs Thatcher's response to the crisis gathered and retained an impressive (if by no means unanimous) degree of public support. Many commentators ascribed this to the way in which her will coincided with strong and enduring (and now resurfacing) traits in the British national character. These could be little things – but the things that helped define what Edmund Burke characterised as 'the little platoon' in which all allegiances and loyalties began – such as Brian Hanrahan's recollection of 'moments of peculiar Englishness. In the bar (on board ship) two aristocratic cavalry officers were overheard lamenting the opening of the polo season and the other was more worried about whether his bronze sculpture would be accepted for the Royal Academy summer exhibition than almost anything that might or might not await them in the Falkland Islands'. [85, p. 13] There were endearing eccentricities, ranging from a Marine bandsman going into the ladies' lavatory with a violin under his arm, to the victory signal sent to London from South Georgia after its recapture: 'Be pleased to inform Her Majesty that the White Ensign flies alongside the Union Flag at Grytviken South Georgia'. [85, p. 16] A Marine officer was ordered off the bridge of the *Fearless* for inciting the officer on watch to look for seabirds rather than enemy aircraft, protesting that, 'One must keep a sense of proportion about these things'. [221, p. 42]

There was also the spectacle of the Prime Minister depicted as a 'warrior-queen exhorting the people to battle against a foreign tyranny'; [7, p. 105] and some satisfaction in discovering that one of the senior Argentine officers believed to be on the Falklands was one Major Patrick Dowling, whose 'pathological hatred for the British' allegedly derived from his claim to have Irish grandparents. [86, pp. 60–1] The historian, E. P. Thompson (admittedly a man of left-wing belief) and his wife who were abroad for the first ten days of the crisis complained that 'to return to England on Day 10…was like passing through a time-warp into an earlier imperial age'. They found themselves suddenly 'back in the days of Dunkirk, replayed this time as a nostalgic piece, with parliamentarians "speaking for Britain"'. [207, 29 April 1982] Enoch Powell, one of those who 'spoke for Britain', did not dissent: 'The British are never as formidable than when they are in this mood'; quiet, matter-of-fact, with a unanimity of purpose 'reminiscent of 1939 and 1940'. [207, 14 May 1982]

The tension and excitement of the crisis, the sustainability of public and political approval of the war, the rise to great heights of Prime Minister Thatcher, were soon challenged; those who had a contrary view gathered their strength. The process by which it became possible not only to offer a critique of the war, but a more fundamental condemnation of those who fought it, and allegedly profited from it – notably the Conservative party – did not take long to gestate. Its manifestation can be traced through the story of the young Scots Guards' officer, Robert Lawrence, who was terribly wounded in the battle for Tumbledown in the last days of the fighting. He was interviewed for Max Arthur's symposium, *Above all Courage*, published in 1985.

In this Lawrence's account of his war was distinguished by his willingness to accept his injuries, which cost him his army career.

> I love the Army, I love weapons and loved everything we did...But that's all over now and I'm adjusting to it, though every now and again I think 'Fuck this'. It makes me angry...I used to enjoy doing stupid things – That was me.
>
> A lot of people who are depressed just sit and think and become morbid and upset. When they are happy those problems are still there. So the answer is: don't think about this! Just get on with it! [5, p. 306]

In his own story, *When the Fighting is Over*, the experience of fighting was more graphically (and brutally) told: there is the incident in his account in Max Arthur's book of the Argentine soldier who 'suddenly swung round and he bust my bayonet, so I ended up firing him off'. [5, p. 303] In his second account Lawrence wrote 'I stabbed him and I stabbed him, again and again, in the mouth, in the face, in the guts, with a snapped bayonet'. [137, p. 32] He described how a Scots Guards' officer lost his nerve during the Tumbledown fighting:

> As we pushed on, I remember coming across a very young officer from Left Flank who had only recently joined the battalion and had been caught in the back blast of an 84-millimetre anti-tank weapon. He was being looked after behind a rock by two Guardsmen, and was crying his eyes out. His sergeant had died in his arms. 'Don't go on', he said to me. 'It's too horrific. You'd be better off turning round, and shooting anyone who tried to stop you going back.

Lawrence did not name the officer, but gave sufficient clues to his identity from those who would have known the battalion well: 'he was suffering from shock, I realised, but at the time I just thought, rather unsympathetically, how unprofessional, and pushed on. After the war I was delighted (sic) to learn that he had received a mention in despatches'. [137, p. 28]

Robert Lawrence's description of the battle is sharp and convincing: 'people just don't die in real life the way they do in television...It takes an enormous amount to kill a man'. [137, p. 30] But his autobiographical account stressed that his real grievance was that 'when the fighting was over, nobody wanted to know'. Despite this, despite the Army's neglect of its wounded, Lawrence thought that the war was worth the cost: 'When thousands of fighting troops suddenly march into your house to tell you, with the barrel of a gun stuck in your nose, that you must no longer speak English, but Spanish, you have a right to be defended by any civilised nation'. [137, p. 192]

The third account of Lawrence's tragic experience of battle was a film, 'Tumbledown'. The script was written by Charles Wood, whose screenplays included 'The Charge of the Light Brigade' (1968). For Wood, 'it all started in 1984 when Mark Burns sent me a copy of a *Guardian* article dated Friday, 17 August'. The heading was 'Falklands victims the army tried to forget' (soldiers were now 'victims'). The sub-heading of the article read: 'Seumas Milne meets an officer who was shot in the head in the South Atlantic. He says the sniper who hit him was doing his job but believes the military establishment and Civil Service have not done theirs. He was kept out of the way at the St Paul's service of remembrance, had to pay for a "free" car and was told nothing about how to start a new life…'. Wood wrote to the *Guardian* in 1986 telling the newspaper that the BBC had at last agreed to produce a film he had made about Lawrence, one that avoided any political stance but concentrated on Lawrence's courage when recovering from his serious wound. [235, p. ix]

Controversy about the script, which Wood feared would now be labelled 'subversive', [235, p. ix] was sharpened by the parallel experience of Ian Curteis, who was commissioned to write a play about the Falklands War in April 1983. Curteis approached public figures in the Ministry of Defence and the Cabinet Office to begin his research where he was 'hit by a Force Nine Gale. Tempers still ran hot over the BBC's alleged behaviour during the conflict itself'; he felt that no play could be written in the teeth of such 'gales of hatred'. He began work on the play again in 1985, inspired by the belief that, 'This was not shallow jingoism, but the dramatic rising to the surface once more of values and issues that we on these islands have cared most profoundly about down the centuries, and on which our civilised freedom rests'. [53, pp. 13–14] Curteis gave the first draft of his play to the Director General of the BBC and the Producer in April 1986; it was 'warmly received', and transmission was scheduled for 2 April 1987. [53, p. 17] But the new Head of Plays, Peter Goodchild, objected to scenes revealing the Prime Minister as showing grief over loss of life in the war, though he approved of the 'bellicose Iron Lady' scenes. He was unhappy too with scenes which presented the war as being fought to resist aggression. Michael Grade raised the question of the connection between the *Belgrano* sinking and the Peruvian peace plan. Curteis denied that there was any such link between the two. [53, pp. 25–7] Curteis claimed that he had been asked to rewrite scenes to show Mrs Thatcher and her Government in a 'less good light'; certainly his draft of the last scene in the play, in which Mrs Thatcher shouted at the Leader of the Opposition that he 'would not enjoy the freedom of speech that he puts to such excellent use, unless people had been prepared to fight for it!', and the directions showing the House of Commons roaring 'like the sea. Freeze frame on her triumphant gesture', were, to say the least, consistent with the Prime Minister's self-image. [53, pp. 187–8]

Curteis's play was not produced: Wood's was broadcast in May 1988, and was as controversial in its transmission as Curteis's was in its cancellation. The reason given for the cancellation of Curteis's play on 22 July 1987 was because of the 'next election'. [53, pp. 25–9] He was unconvinced by this explanation, since, he alleged, the Tumbledown play, based on Robert Lawrence's experience, was transmitted in October 1987, which was a possible election date; [53, p. 37] but in fact Wood's play was also postponed until the following May. [53, p. 43] Nevertheless, Curteis complained of left-wing bias in the BBC. Wood claimed that his play had no political stance, but was merely a warning, 'think twice before you elect to serve in an army'. [53, p. 43] But the way in which this was conveyed – and it was of itself not an uncontroversial point of view – raised a storm of protest. Robert Lawrence was depicted much as he depicted himself: as a wild young man who looked forward to active service (though apprehensive about being disabled in battle), and whose savage frustration at serious wounds ('you took your last real walk on the Falklands, Robert', a doctor says) [235, p. 45] was compounded by his betrayal by his girlfriend, his regiment and his country. He says of the war 'it wasn't worth it', [235, p. 36] which in his autobiography is put in a different context. In his own story, Lawrence admitted that 'I had, and still have, this white-hot pride. The kind of pride that the Army trains young soldiers to build up. The kind of pride that enables them to go off to war and fight and kill for what they are taught to believe in; principles like freedom of choice and of speech'. [137, p. 192] It was the contrast between these principles – which he still adhered to – and his desire to 'beat the realities of the modern world' that Lawrence claimed inspired his recovery: the desire to overcome 'the small-mindedness which stops us changing as a society or race'. It was this small-mindedness that could render the war 'not worth it'. [137, p. 193]

Wood's version of Lawrence's retaining his loyalties shifted the emphasis, though it also crystallised Lawrence's experience. The last scene shows Lawrence saluting his Lieutenant-Colonel, Bill Kirke, wearing a panama hat: and saluting him correctly ('I looked it up, sir'). [137, pp. 72–3] This was a military gesture with a most unmilitary headgear, which makes the point that Robert, though still not divested of his military traditions, is no longer an insider, but a semi-civilian: perhaps the worst fate of all for this thoughtless, and thoughtlessly brave, young man.

Lawrence focused on the effect on one individual of the trauma of battle, and left the scene to speak for itself: there was no attempt to fit it into the wider context of how men in battle can face the most powerful fears, but recover and endure. But the debate over the play was wider than the depiction of the stress of war. For, as its director, Richard Eyre, put it, he wanted to make a 'deeply political point'. [207, 1 June 1988] This was perhaps most tellingly made in the scene where Robert Lawrence is shown being mugged, and fighting back, but falling over because of his injured leg. His attackers kick at his head, shaven for his operations. [235, p. 72] This was the ultimate symbol of the England that Robert fought for; he was a victim of its own violence, as well as that of the Falklands War.

Critics of the play alleged that it was seeking to 'undermine the sacrifices and heroism which enabled us to repossess the Falkland Islands'. The BBC was 'stabbing the nation in the back', the play was 'confused and ugly', and calculated to 'demoralise the public'. [207, 1 June 1988] On 9 June Ian Hislop in *The Listener* took up the director's point that he wanted to make a 'deeply political' play. It was, Hislop wrote, 'political in the widest sense, but "political" in this country is now a word which means "critical of the present Conservative government" when applied to television programmes'. 'Tumbledown' was not a 'rabid left-wing attack on the Government of the Day but a dramatic reconstruction of one man's experience of war'. He pointed out that the play showed Lawrence's 'arrogance and pride'; and therefore when Lawrence said, 'It wasn't worth it', he had to be taken seriously. 'This is the phrase that clearly sparked off the hysterical reaction'.

Hislop's focusing on these vital words contrasts with Lawrence's insistence in his autobiography that, 'I still believe that what I did in the Falklands War was worth doing. I still believe that what I did had to be done'. In a letter to *The Times* on 27 May Lawrence insisted that he was aggrieved because he 'was not allowed to take part in the victory parade in London'; he was 'really proud' that he took part in the Falklands campaign: 'I'm just sad they didn't admit there were serious problems after the war'. The BBC play attacked the whole concept of war and character of army life, which Lawrence never did. The drama documentary style of the play was one perfectly entitled to alter words and scenes to suit the author's and director's message; but the controversy was one with a still wider significance.

For 1988 was a year that invited an attack on what was now known as 'Thatcher's Britain'. Her Government had recently won a third term of office. The Labour Opposition was deemed to be even less electable than it was in 1984. The Falklands War had, it was alleged, spawned a kind of 'khaki election', and Thatcher was still garnering the fruits of victory. Critics of the Conservatives spoke of the heartlessness and even brutality of what was called 'Thatcherism'. This was defined in 1982 by Anthony Barnett as 'the ruthlessness of her dedication to the destruction of many of the gains that have been made in Britain since the (Second World) war, both economically and in the quality of life ...Her "authoritarian populism" strikes a chord, while Foot's Labour patriotism is ill-dressed and unconvincing'. [9, p. 80] Thatcherism could be regarded as a new variant, if a more extreme one, of 'mind-set that has held all British politicians in its grip since 1945. For if the crippling aspects of Churchillism were to be summed up in one sentence, it is that British politicians have been unable to articulate a programme of reform for the UK as a minor industrial power except in terms that seek to reassert Britain's world greatness'. [9, p. 83] This 'self-punishing ambition' was expressed above all 'in terms of excessive military expenditure...The celebration of coercion which accompanied the Falklands Armada shows every sign of returning to the United Kingdom. It is the theme that Thatcher sought from the beginning of her leadership of the Conservative party...she has gained the belligerent nationalist colours that her policies always needed to appear to succeed...Militarisation might well become domesticated in a way that has been missing from Britain hitherto...Now the military may be projected as one of the few agencies that can "get things done"'. [9, p. 85] Thatcherism, Barnett concluded, offered an 'authoritarian populism, a celebrant militarism, a pitiful nostalgia, the export of capital, fewer jobs for lower real wages, non-existent "princes of industry", and, oh yes, the Falklands'. [9, p. 86]

Now, six years later, the forces opposed to the Falklands War, and to the 'Thatcherism' that (it was alleged) both inspired it and was inspired by it, gathered momentum. The City Art Galleries in Manchester mounted an exhibition between 10 December 1988 and 22 January

1989 entitled 'The Falklands factor: Representations of a Conflict'. It was subsequently transferred to the Righton Gallery, Manchester Polytechnic from 4 February to 17 March, and then to the Wolverhampton Art Galleries between 31 March until 20 May. The exhibition was organised by the Manchester City Galleries in association with the History of Art and Design department of Manchester Polytechnic. Howard Smith, Keeper of Exhibitions, wrote in his foreword to the catalogue that it was now over six years since the end of the war 'and time to reflect on some of the issues it raised'. 'The phrase "The Falklands Factor" which became a catch phrase during and immediately after the conflict, referring specifically to the war resulted in a significant rise to popularity for Mrs Thatcher's government, but we have used it to refer to how the conflict has affected the consciousness of the people of this country as a whole and to how this has been described or expressed through usual means'. [76, p. 3]

Tim Wilcox of the Manchester Galleries put the exhibition in context. He began by describing a story which appeared around the world, and which 'points to the strange and complex nature of the conflict'. During 2 Para's advance from Darwin to Fitzroy and Bluff Cove under the command of Brigadier Tony Wilson, Wilson was reported to have found a working telephone box at Swan Inlet and used it to contact Reg Binney, the farm manager at Fitzroy. 'Any Argies around?', he asked. 'There were but they've gone', Binney replied. 'Then I think I'll join you' said Wilson. This (highly inaccurate) anecdote epitomised notions of Britishness: an improvising nonchalance in time of conflict recalled the camaraderie of World War Two, the characterisation of the enemy as the 'other' (for 'Argies' read 'Huns'), the bond between defender islander and liberating soldier, and all importantly the image of the bright red phone box and the farming village. 'Yes', Wilcox concluded, 'we really are "All Falklanders Now", as *The Times* had it, and they were "us", British subjects through and through. However, the story is a complete invention since the very first red telephone box was sent off to the Falklands for use by the troops in September 1988'. [76, p. 4]

Wilcox described the conflict as 'one of the most under reported and mis-reported wars of modern times'. Delay and censorship made the 'truth' as 'tangled and as slippery as the great fringe of kelp which covers the Islands' complex coastline'. The 'complexity' of the ideological terrain of image and text 'involved a struggle for the high moral ground – for the abstractions of nationhood, British justice and the "natural" order of sovereignty'. Thus representations of previous wars and especially the Second World War were revoked to affirm the national cause. [76, p. 5]

The exhibition focused mainly, though not exclusively, on contrasts, such as that between the 'gleaming' HMS *Ardent* and photographs of the 'mangled stern and rear deck with acrid smoke pouring from it; of HMS *Coventry* in black and white image with 'blue sky, cotton wool clouds and a radiant sun...in the centre an ugly black lightening strike cuts through this world and on the right of the ship becomes a black silhouette surrounded by clouds filled with question marks'. Images of marriage break-up and drink problems were juxtaposed with newspaper reports of 'happy returns and reunions'. [76, p. 5] The exhibition showed the way in which, in a 'patriarchal system', war and its preparations are 'disguised in the apparently innocent game of soldiers'. Mrs Thatcher's 'Rejoice, rejoice' cry, is returned to her 'with interest' in a collage which brings together photographs of limbs and then builds into the shape of a Union Flag which is then crudely coloured in red and blue. 'Underneath each of the three panels of the vertically arranged triptych the phrase "Next of Kin will be Informed" in tones relentlessly, driving home the cost of bellicose nationalism in human lives'. The 'authenticisation' of war is illustrated in a photograph of HMS *Antelope*, silhouetted against a plume of flame, one 'that could be used to fit in with the narrative played out in the press where seemingly nobody got hurt'. A commemorative medal showed the *Belgrano* surrounded by drowning figures. [76, p. 6] A work by the artist David Cobb, who received assistance from the Admiralty was shown; the 'technically competent' work was described as re-imposing 'order on conflict both through artistic and ideological means. While purporting to represent the truth of battle it removes the possibility of suffering and death and returns it to the fantasy realm of Boys Own comics...'. [76, p. 7] In an essay on photography John Taylor traced the way in which the exclusion of the horrors of war, pictures of the dead and mutilated held together national unity: 'Most of the 202 photographs were of the patriotic flag-waving variety: none was blood-and-guts photo reportage'. MOD 'ploys' of silence, delay and deception 'increased tension and anticipation, but they also gave space for patriotism and resolution'. British soldiers were shown as 'extremely tough'; Argentine prisoners as showing 'defeat in their faces'. A photograph of a British soldier having a cup of tea across a garden fence combined 'the restorative drink with the English idea of home as a castle'. [76, pp. 10–11]

James Aulich wrote an incisive essay on cartoons under the heading 'Government Health Warning: Cartoons can damage your health', in which he explained that the cartoonist, able to visualise and comment on any given news situation in satirical and humorous ways, as succinctly as possible with a minimum of words. [76, p. 13] Cartoons supported the war, showing for example, Mrs Thatcher as organiser and controller of events. [76, p. 36] But a cartoon by Gerald Scarfe, a poster design for Bradford City Art Gallery in 1984, showing Mrs Thatcher in bed surrounded by the skeletal accusing fingers of the dead was judged to be too critical of the Government by the leader of the City Council and too sensitive for a poster design. [76, pp. 13, 22] The image of the Prime Minister as a Britannia figure contrasted with Scarfe's cartoon, but, as Aulich pointed out, both were resonant of the 'symbolic vocabulary of Empire, nation, endeavour and sacrifice'. [76, p. 14] The paucity of photograph and film images of the war meant that the 'dominant populist rhetoric of the new right filled the gap with its cries for the national heritage of empire, deference for national heroes and the commemoration of great national events within a framework of authority and freedom to provide a common language the cartoonist could either question or confirm'. [76, p. 16]

The attack on the nationalistic mood and (apparent) national consensus on the Falklands War was renewed in the early 1990s through the Open University's 'Framing the Falklands War: Nationhood, Culture and Identity'. The film director Paul Greengrass wrote a foreword drawing 'a line of sorts, however loose, between the Paras yomping their way across the Falklands to the lager louts of today, laying waste to European cities in the name of football'. [7, p. x] James Aulich in his introduction noted how what Mrs Thatcher called 'the spirit of Britain at its best', a 'fervent new age rhetoric' evaded the issues of 'economic recession, high unemployment, unpopular government policies and personalities', yet 'found concrete historical expression in the events of the Falklands conflict', expressing a 'moral idea of England that is confident and steeped with evangelical fervour'. [7, p. 2] John Taylor traced what he saw as the Government's desire to 'effect' (sic) the media from 1982, beginning in May with the Conservative Party's media committee criticising the BBC for its unpatriotic attitude, and continuing through 1986 when the Conservative Central office charged the BBC with biased coverage of the American raid on Libya. [7, p. 29] Jeffrey Walsh pointed out that the Thatcher decade represented a kind of fight back, with its emphasis on the Falklands War's symbolic value: 'to challenge it in any way was to invite the kind of official criticism levelled at Charles Wood's "Tumbledown", [220, pp. 37–8] which, while displaying the patriotism that motivated Robert Lawrence, attacked those who were "unworthy custodians of his political beliefs"'. [220, p. 42] Likewise, Paul Greengrass's 'Resurrected', which told the story of a Scots Guardsman who went missing during the fighting and who was revered as a hero and then reviled as a coward, also depicted a 'harsh, inconsiderate society, over-influenced by a scandal-mongering press and underpinned by a military culture whose behaviour is little different from the violent tribalism of football hooligans'. [220, p. 43] Martin Stellman's 'For Queen and Country' likewise presented social violence as 'an integral condition of life for many British citizens, especially those of ethnic minorities'. [220, pp. 44–5] The volume presented 'Thatcher's England' as a 'divided culture and a polarised society'. [220, p. 49] All this built upon Jack McFadyen's 'With Singing Hearts…Throaty Roarings' (1983) which portrayed an 'ugly assemblage of bull-necked nationalists swelling the foreground', though the authors of 'Framing the Falklands War' felt that the cartoon failed to penetrate 'the deeper working of the ideological system which creates such spectacular events'. [7, pp. 64–5]

Framing the Falklands noted that novelists had nothing to say about the war, but the theatre, television and even a children's writer filled the gap. Steve Berkoff's play 'Sink the Belgrano!' was first performed at the Half Moon Theatre on 2 September 1986. The dramatis personae's names made Berkoff's point: Margaret Thatcher became 'Maggot Scratcher'; John Nott was 'Nit'; Francis Pym was 'Pimp'. The stage was divided into three areas: upstage, on a rostrum was the 'political arena', with a desk, and behind it a large screen for projecting images. Downstage, on the main playing area, was drawn the outline of a huge submarine. Stage left was a pub area which represented 'the voice of England'. In his preface 'Why I wrote it', Berkoff set out his reasons for attacking the 'pack of fakes' who authorised the attack on the *Belgrano*, following which 'all havoc broke loose'. [18, p. 1]

Berkoff's Britain was

Worn out with strikes and dazed social strife.
Numb with queues of unemployed that add
Their groaning weight to the nation's back…
But once aroused, oh ho! Old Albion snorts
The Bulldog, start-eyed, drools for Argy blood… [18, p. 3]

'Maggot' asked 'Pimp', 'by the way…where is the Falklands?'. Falklands farmers described their island as 'this pisspot, this dreary rock' where they lay under the threat of the 'bloody bleedin' FIC' (Falklands Islands Company). [18, p. 5] Maggot needed a war to 'Establish once again our might and strength'. 'Sailor 1' on the *Conqueror* orders his mates to 'to kill/Go Fido, fetch'. 'Command' enlightens his men: 'Don't look for principles in politics/It's just a game they play, you're Whitehall's toys'. Maggot despises the 'lazy sods' in Britain who won't work and who are spoiled by the welfare state. [18, pp. 7, 9, 11, 12–15] 'Reason' pleads in vain that 'Surely, before we shed young blood/We must seek an ointment for the wound' (a plea met by 'appeaser' and 'coward'). Meanwhile the sailors on *Conqueror* think of football, killing, or not killing, while Command longs to 'get some juicy Argy ship'. Maggot dismisses Pimp's peace plans: Britain was not going to war for the Islanders, but for 'us', 'Great bloody Britain, mate'. If Britain accepted a compromise 'then, farewell/ England falls to Socialist claws/Who will tear our land apart'. A peaceful resolution of the conflict would mean the troops returning with 'drooping flags/No "knees up, Mother Brown" in pubs'. [18, pp. 25, 26, 27, 28–9]

Maggot is not without some qualms over sinking a ship and killing 'hundreds of young boys, they could be ours', but she is easily persuaded when her reputation as the 'Iron Lady' is at stake. [18, pp. 34–5] The *Belgrano* is sunk; and a British sailor has the last word: 'Somebody threw the first stone/When the *Belgrano* was going home'. [18, p. 38] On screen is an image; 'I would do it again'…Margaret Thatcher. Blackout.

For Ian McEwan Thatcher's war epitomised the emptiness and heartlessness of Thatcher's Britain. In his preface to his 'The Ploughman's Lunch' (1985) he explained that he had originally conceived of the film in 1981, when he wanted to explore 'the uses we make of the past, and the dangers, to an individual as well as to a nation, of living without a sense of history'. The title was inspired by an item McEwan heard on the radio programme, 'Woman's Hour', which revealed that the 'ploughman's lunch' was not 'an English tradition' but the invention of an advertising campaign to persuade people to eat in public houses: thus it became a 'controlling metaphor for self-serving fabrication of the past'. One of the most significant of such fabrications was the Suez crisis in which 'the liberal consensus and political idealism' found itself 'generally in retreat'. And so McEwan considered how an ambitious writer might set out to rewrite the crisis in terms of the 'steely pragmatism being promoted by the Government of Mrs Thatcher. The past would be re-interpreted while the amateur historian unconsciously acted out in his private life a sequence of betrayals and deceits which would parallel the events he was distorting in his history'. The first draft of the script was completed by the time the Falklands crisis began to break; the second when the Task Force sailed. The Suez and Falklands affairs were, McEwan acknowledged, not the same: the Egyptians had a legitimate claim to the canal; Argentina had only an 'emotional claim'; to the Falklands. Nevertheless, in 1982, 'A large Task Force was to be despatched and lives were to be risked to regain territory which successive British Government had been trying quietly to unload on the Argentinians'. Moreover, 'It was not clear then, and is even less clear now, that the Government conducted negotiations in good faith to avoid armed conflict'. [140, p. v]

The eruption of jingoism, the thunderous Churchillian rhetoric which was so readily available to politicians of all persuasions showed that this was less a matter of real territorial ambition, or a desire to protect 'our own'; but, like Suez, was more an affair of the heart, of 'who we thought we were, of who we wanted to be'. [140, p. vi] Thus the journalist whose ambition was to rewrite Suez to show that Britain was right was himself rewriting his own history. To disguise his humble origins James Penfold found it convenient to claim that his parents were dead. His search for a place in a false society parallels that in the Conservative party Conference which James attends: Francis Pym is heard intoning 'we were seen to be fighting to defend principles which are fundamental to free nations everywhere, and our reputation has been enhanced as a result'. Mrs Thatcher proclaims that the 'spirit of the South Atlantic was the spirit of Britain at her best'. [140, pp. 10, 32, 33] The theme of false values is explored in James' publisher, Gold, who sees the market for James' rewritten history of Suez ('It gives us direct access to literally hundreds of American colleges. Twentieth century history is a growth area out there, don't ask me why'); [140, p. 6] and in the BBC news editor who shows scant regard for anything other than the immediate demands of 'news values'. [140, p. 23] 'Woman's Hour' is featuring an historian telling how 'the governments of Eastern Europe distort their recent past in history books to suit their present policies and allegiances'. [140, p. 2] The characters in 'The Ploughman's Lunch' are as false to themselves and to others, as is the advertising ploy that inspired the pub gimmick.

While McEwan's 'The Ploughman's Lunch' focuses on the aspirations of a journalist who longed to make his way in metropolitan society, thus illustrating the sickness of the Thatcher era, Nick Perry's 'Arrevederchi Millwall' exposed what he defined as the violent undertones that made patriotism a dangerous sentiment. The play revealed the restless, unpredictable relationships between several Millwall football fans, whose aggression reflected that of the nation at war. But this nationhood was an ephemeral structure: for while one of the characters boasts that 'Argies start at Calais', he adds that 'civilisation ends at Watford'; [180, p. 5] and his aggression towards his fellow fans is only matched by that towards, for example, a Spanish waiter. The shallow jingoism induced by the Falklands war is satirised by placing it alongside speeches from the House of Commons debate on the Argentine invasion; and the nationalism released by the crisis is akin to that of the Millwall fan who when he heard 'dago bastards' chanting 'Argentina, Argentina' admits now that 'I never thought in a million years I'd have warm feelings for Aston Villa. But I did that night'. [180, p. 39] Victory in football sits beside victory in war. But the difference – that in war men are killed – soon surfaces. A Royal navy chaplain calls to tell Billy Jones that his brother has been killed in the Falklands, and that Billy should be proud of him. His brother's ghost appears, plaintively telling his Falklands story:

> It was murder that day, murder:
> Johnny gaucho caught us napping,
> Diving from the clear blue sky…
> We met our doom in burning water… [180, p. 53]

The Great War poem, 'They shall not grow old' provokes Billy to respond, 'We will not break faith with ye'. [180, p. 55]

What is this faith not to be broken? Not by an act of remembrance, but by Billy and his friends embarking on a drunken violent spree in Spain. There they meet a former paratrooper who says their behaviour makes him 'ashamed to be an Englishman'. Real soldiering is all about 'Foot patrol: scared shitless. Back to barracks: bored shitless. Get the idea?… It's good crack scraping your oppo off the pavement. It's a reet laugh getting shot at by twelve-year-old-micks. You like blood, do you? You should join the fucking Professionals, son'. The revenge for Billy's brother's death is an encounter with the Spanish police who try to get the English fans to sing 'Malvinas son Argentinas'. [180, pp. 71–3] The fans are defiant: they respond with 'Rule Britannia', and violence is elevated into an historical tableau in which the Ghost calls 'Sons of England, Arise!', but this contrasts with the paratrooper's description of his own, less than heroic, almost commonplace death:

> ...up on Wireless Ridge,
> bending to dimp my cigarette –
> he picked picked me out in infra-red,
> the sniper up on Wireless Ridge,
> the Argie with the Russian rifle. [180, p. 82]

In the historical tableau the King, 'A Warry Bastard, I am!' dismisses (in Mrs Thatcher's words) defeat: 'The possibility does not exist'. [180, p. 85] The peasant is sentenced to die, while the Queen shouts 'rejoice', and compares Elizabeth I's speech before Drake's attack on the Spanish Armada with Mrs Thatcher's rhetoric on her election victory in 1979: 'Where there is hatred, let us sow love'. [180, p. 86] Beneath the 'Gloriana gear' there lies a 'Bulldog Billy T-shirt'. For Billy Jones, the fight with the Spanish police awakens his sense of nationhood: 'we wasn't Millwall no more...we was English'. [180, p. 87] But being English, like being Millwall, is an ephemeral sentiment, and the play ends with a domesticated Billy, and no football on Saturday any more.

None of these works explored the causes that were, or might be, advanced for the Falklands War. This was done by the children's writer, Raymond Briggs, in his cartoon style *The Tin Pot General and the Old Woman*, published in 1984. Briggs found Britain and Argentina equally guilty. General Galtieri was portrayed as an iron-clad, menacing figure, Argentine flag in one hand, bloody dagger in the other, who 'wanted to do something Historical, so that his name would be printed in all the big History Books'. Mrs Thatcher, the Old Iron Woman, was depicted as a monstrous figure, with teeth bared and guns and mines stacked up beside her. When she heard that the Tin Pot General had 'baggsied' the 'sad little island' she screamed 'MINE! MINE! MINE! I baggsied it AGES ago! I baggsied it FIRST! DID! DID! DID!'. It was 'so exciting to have a real crisis!'. Briggs's use of child-like language in the context of bloody conflict both undermined the causes of war and pointed up its malevolence.

The text then changes, from cartoon to realism. Dead soldiers are shown ('Some men were shot'; 'some men were drowned'; 'Some men were buried alive'; 'Some men were blown to bits'). Men are shown in bandages and wheelchairs, 'only half blown to bits and came home with parts of their bodies missing'. The next illustration shows rows of crosses: 'Hundreds of brave men were killed. And they were real men, made of flesh and blood' and not 'made of Tin or Iron'. Then the style reverts to cartoon drawings, showing the Old Iron Woman calling for people to rejoice; but the 'sad little island' is shown littered with dead sheep, bombs, crosses, and with as many (or more) soldiers on it now as there are shepherds, surrounded by barbed wire with a sign saying 'Danger! Keep Out!'. Finally, the book reverts to a monochrome realistic style. Soldiers get a 'special medal' and there is a grand victory parade, and 'everyone went to Church and Thanked God'. A man and his family are watching television, with the Old Iron Lady's face, large, purpled, on the screen. A closer look reveals that he has lost a leg; an artificial limb stands beside him. The soldiers 'with bits of their bodies missing were not invited to take part in the Grand Parade, in case the sight of them spoiled the rejoicing. Some watched from a grandstand and others stayed at home with their memories and their medals'. The last frame continues in realistic mode: women and children gather round a gravestone, and 'the families of the dead tended the graves'.

Brigg's savage indignation is, like Berkoff's, in the classic tradition of satirical use of the English language, supported by powerful visual images. Berkoff's scatological play, Briggs's use of the children's story format, were powerful and effective attacks on the Falklands War, and contrast strongly with the misconceived attempt to test the weight of intellectual opinion in *Writers Take Sides on the Falklands*, which was compiled between the despatch of the Task Force and the Argentine surrender at Stanley. Those approached to give their opinion were asked if they were for or against the Government's response to the Argentine 'annexation' of the Falklands; and how in their view the dispute should be settled. The reasoning behind the enterprise was the feeling that the Government was attempting to stifle debate, and that the book would represent 'minority views'. [238, p. 8] Out of about 150 authors approached, about 100 responded, out of which 39 were for the Government's response, 59 against, and 'eight appeared to be neutral'. [238, p. 10] The writers ranged from A (Paul Ableman) to, if not Z, then at least to W (Aubernon Waugh). Those who held that intellectuals had little to contribute to contemporary political debate in Britain could have felt vindicated by the exercise. Few authors had anything useful or important to say (some replied that Argentine aggression was wrong, but so was the 'jingoistic' response it provoked), [238, pp. 10–12, 15–18, 67–8] and this attempt to revive the style of debate aroused by the Spanish Civil War in the 1930s failed to excite any interest, or exert any impact. Perhaps Frank Muir had the last word when he replied that 'my political views on the Falklands are about as worth reading as General Galtieri's views on eighteenth century humorous novels'. [238, p. 81]

This contrasts with the powerful and sustained indictment of the British Government and indeed the Argentine Junta developed by writers such as McEwan, Perry, Berkoff and Briggs. The weakness in these writers' case – and in that of the other critics of the war – was inseparable from their strength: that to attack their target they had to adopt a simplified version of the crisis. They took the politics out of what was, after all, a deeply political affair; the war itself was inseparable from the politics of war. They ignored what Trevor Wilson in his book on the Great War called the 'terrible constraints facing politicians', who 'often had only dreadful evils to choose between – and were not always free to choose the lesser evil'. [232, pp. 677–8] It was essential for some critics to reduce the Falkland Islands' inhabitants to the dimension of 'sad' people eating mutton for 'breakfast…for dinner and…for tea' (Briggs), their home to a 'pisspot,…dreary rock' (Berkoff) and a place

Where the sound of sheep
will make you weep
and the *drizzle comes*
right behind the rain. [17, p. 150]

By the same token it would be possible to reduce the 1914 'Gallant Little Belgium' to a sad, dreary little Belgium. Though, by the same token also, it could indeed be argued, and with great truth, that gallant little Belgium was the occasion, not the cause, of a British declaration of war on Germany, and of her determination to assert her role as a great power (or in 1982 a declining one) with Belgium/The Falklands as the (unlikely) piece of earth that offered an excuse for going to war.

David Monaghan's *The Falklands War* (1998) and Kevin Foster's *Fighting Fictions*: *War, Narrative and National Identity* (1999) can be said to bring the characterisation of the war as expressing all that was bad in 'Thatcher's Britain' full circle. Monaghan saw the war as an exercise in manipulation by the 'British establishment'; the Falklands War was a short one, but one that 'lasted long enough for Margaret Thatcher to transform the struggle for the Falklands into a myth of national rebirth in which feats of arms would open up the way for a simultaneous retrieval of pre-Welfare State verities and radical change along monetarist economic lines'. [154. p. xi] Moreover the 'ideological agenda that Thatcher promoted through the medium of the Falklands War continues to flourish', nurtured by a Labour Party under Tony Blair, 'a man who has expressed admiration for Thatcher, who seems embarrassed by the term socialism…'. For Monaghan, the post-war literature of the conflict 'seems to remind us that there are alternatives to the reductive and savagely dehumanising monetarist and entrepreneurial agenda that was given credibility by Thatcher's skilful manipulation of her war with Argentina and that continues to this day to dominate the political and social landscape in Britain and other countries'. [154, p. xvii]

Monaghan argued that Mrs Thatcher's Conservatism combined the idea of an 'ancient nation' imbued with eternal values, transcending

> actual time and space with an exclusion of 'enemies' who threatened this vision, enemies who 'included more than socialists': black immigrants 'could easily be turned into a group whose exclusion was a matter not of ideological contestation by of self-evident necessity'. To this end the Task Force comprised 'the most honourable and brave members of Her Majesty's services', used the vocabulary of the Second World War, and identified the 'authentic Britain' with the Falkland Islands and their inhabitants, enabling her to continue the struggle after the war against the 'enemies within'. [154, pp. 5, 13, 25]

Monaghan's polemic exaggerated both the strength of Mrs Thatcher's position in the Falklands crisis – her War Cabinet was by no means unanimously supportive – and the uniqueness of her vocabulary. As Professor Lawrence Freedman points out, political leaders rarely offer cynical explanations for their political behaviour, but instead seek to develop them through the forms of moral reasoning, appealing to values which they believe are shared by the community. [89, p. 106] Mrs Thatcher both created and dipped into the moral climate of Falklands War Britain; she both exploited and satisfied it.

For Kevin Foster, the Falklands War was portrayed as a last-ditch stand against political oblivion, not as an improvised response to unexpected events, but 'as an expression of the essential national character, last evident with equivalent clarity during the Second World War at Dunkirk and the Blitz'. The war was a struggle between British and Argentine 'sacred myths'. [82, pp. 3, 6] He endorsed the view of those who claimed that the conflict took place in a Britain whose society was 'more polarised than at any time since 1939'; [82, p. 9] and the archaic language employed at the time only made British social divisions more prominent and obvious. Foster pointed out what he saw as the contrast between the media's presentation of the Falklands as a 'green and pleasant land' and the 'reality' of its dour inhabitants, often hostile to the troops who came to liberate them [82, pp. 28, 62–8] (though the mother of Sergeant Ian McKay, who was killed at Mount Longdon, said that the Islanders had an 'immense feeling of gratitude…for what our men did'). [57] Foster's account of troops stealing and otherwise misbehaving [82, pp. 70–2] is consistent with other evidence, but implies that soldiers should indeed always behave impeccably – which would only have the effect of giving them a share in the 'romance' that the media presented as the Falklands War.

Foster's book offered a sustained critique of 'Thatcher's Britain' – a state 'where the measures undertaken in the South Atlantic ostensibly to preserve social and cultural coherence were by the mid 1980s employed more and more often at home, at Orgreave, Wapping and at picket lines and demonstrations across the country to enforce the dissolution of any such coherence and the fragmentation of any sense of a genuinely collective society'. Thus the 1980s saw a 'dramatic rolling back of the government's commitment to those institutions dedicated to the provision, defence and promotion of the family and the community, the shrinking of the welfare state, the starving of the National Health Service, the emasculation of trade unions, and a full-scale retreat from the principle of public ownership of collective assets culminating in Margaret Thatcher's infamous assertion that "there is no such thing as society"'. [82, p. 151] This picture of the making of 'Thatcher's Britain' might, or might not, be endorsed by historians of her premiership; but it helped create another myth, that of a Britain dragged along from the progressive, all-inclusive, caring, collectivist society that Labour had created in 1945 and that successive Labour governments had defended to the last.

Those who attacked Thatcher over the Falklands War depicted her as standing, not for what she thought she stood for – the best of what was British – but the worst: an uncaring, brutal society, in which even the physical bravery of its soldiers was but an extension of the violence displayed by its football supporters (Alan Clark held that the two were, thankfully, inseparable). Her critics and enemies saw her as standing for a kind of bastard Churchillism, in which the values of 1939–40 were now repackaged in a perverted and reprehensible form.

This was the 'Thatcher's Britain' that the left-wing playwright, Edward Bond, predicted in 1981 would emerge from the Conservative victory in the general election of 1979, one looking both backwards and forwards to a time when

> England owned half the world
> And Englishmen were free

Thus,

> ...so the generations go
> Into the fire and into the woe
> Into the trenches and into the blood
> Bellowing shouts of brotherhood! [24, pp. 76–7]

In 2002 Ian Curteis's 'Falklands Play' was at long last broadcast on BBC radio. A BBC spokesman explained that 'there is a big difference between doing something like this very close to the event and after a twenty-year gap. The situation has changed'. [56, 29 Nov. 2001] What had changed was not the question of the war and its morality, but the burial of 'Thatcher's Britain' and the birth of 'Cool Britannia'.

The significance of the cultural war on the Falklands war was not that it gripped the public mind – there was no retreat from the idea that the war was justified – but that it marked the emergence of its critics into a public and political commitment that had last only appeared in the 1930s. It took another war, in Iraq in 2003, to mark the end of the intellectual's belief in the Labour Party, which now experienced the cultural attack in plays like 'Stuff happens' which Mrs Thatcher had endured in her ascendancy.

10

War and the Falklands

The shadow of Wilfred Owen and the other Great War poets hangs over narratives of war in British history. Kevin Foster, in his *Fighting Fictions*, confessed that, though no poet, his purpose was to take up the torch lit by Owen and his fellow poets, and to write a narrative 'no less admonitory'. [82, pp. 155–6] But in a review of a collection of books about the First World War in the *Times Literary Supplement* of 16–22 September 1988 Nicholas Hiley wrote that:

> It is often forgotten that war is an abstract concept which can only be understood through other abstractions such as nationality, honour and duty. Because the concept of war has to be taught to each succeeding generation it has been reduced to a few simple ideas which can fit easily within the dominant ideology. This naturally produces a wonderful unity of purpose during wartime…

But because war was an abstraction, people can carry different and conflicting images of it in their mind at the same time: 'An image of war as destructive and barbaric can easily exist alongside another of war as noble, just and heroic'.

Most people today, he added, 'prefer to see war not as an abstraction, but as tangible and concrete about which there can be no doubt; an affair of fighting and suffering which must be seen in terms of mud, blood and death'. Fighting and suffering had become 'the reality of war' to which civilians were blind and ignorant 'while the whole range of wartime expressions and emotions has to be measured'. But what was the reality of war? 'Why, if the soldier and his wife are parted by war, must we imagine that the "reality" goes with the husband?' When families of servicemen went to the Falklands on a visit arranged by the Ministry of Defence in April 1983, some rarely left their cabins, 'unable to share their grief. Others found it comforting to do so…'. Some were grateful for the opportunity to show their children where their fathers died; others disapproved of the 'occasional high spirits' of young widows, who had been briefly married before their husbands were killed, and of those who rushed on to the sun-deck in their bikinis on the return voyage. Marion McKay, widow of Sergeant McKay who was awarded a posthumous VC, was not bitter, but sometimes angry that this 'colonial' war took place: the days were long gone when 'people living on the other side of the world, calling themselves British, could expect their mother country to take care of them'. Moreover, 'a dead hero is soon forgotten by the public. In twenty years' time it won't mean a thing except to the regiment, where it has already become just another part of their history'. [40, pp. 144, 148–9]

In the Falklands War, the whole range of experience must include the crowds who cheered the Task Force as it set out for the South Atlantic; the politicians who watched its progress anxiously; the families who waited for news, good or bad, at home; the soldiers who fought and died at Goose Green or Tumbledown, at San Carlos or on the *Sheffield*. War – even a 'small war' like the Falklands – can tell much about these realities of war, and help explore this enduring human experience.

Two very contrasting images of war emerge from the Falklands. One is that of a Scots Guardsman who followed his officer up the slopes of Mount Tumbledown. The following exchange took place when the officer asked the Guardsman 'How long have you been without ammunition?':

> 'Since the bottom of the hill, Sir'
> 'Did you know that?
> 'Yes, Sir'
> 'Well, why did you come on up with me if you had no bloody ammunition?'
> 'You asked me to, Sir'.

And when this same officer had asked his men before their advance, '15 Platoon, are you with me?' and got no reply, and asked again, 'this voice right beside me said, "aye, Sir, I'm with you" and it was MacKenzie, who had no ammunition! Amazing boy'. [5, p. 298]

This scene, which would no doubt set some nerves on edge with its portrayal of the bond between an officer and his faithful soldier, can then be set beside Robert Lawrence's account of the aftermath of Tumbledown. Here a young man who thought that war was fun – a phrase that should have been his epiphany, but instead became his epitaph – complained that, 'What I didn't realise, until like so many others, I came back crippled after doing my best for my country, was the extent to which we had been conned…We had been "their boys" fighting in the Falklands, and when the fighting was over, nobody wanted to know'. [137, p. 192] But the fighting, while not seen as 'fun' by a Commando officer, Lieutenant Colonel Andrew Whitehead, nevertheless, he believed, tested his men: 'Young boys have grown up. Our confidence has blossomed. Our pride has swelled justifiably. We have fought and won…' [201, 24, March 2002] Lieutenant Colonel Crispian Black, of the Welsh Guards, who was on board the *Sir Galahad* when it was struck by an Argentine missile, maintained that 'looking back, although it was tragic and awful, I'm afraid it was still exciting. It was probably the most vivid thing I've done in my life'. [57, 30 March 2002]

War throws up several archetypes: the hero; the tragic but courageous wounded soldier; and the figure who epitomises the futility of the whole business. Colonel H. Jones was the first, but he was perhaps too readily elevated into heroic status, and was therefore vulnerable to the kind of criticism that a Channel 4 documentary made in a programme screened in 1996: that he had been killed doing 'comic book stuff'; that the Argentines described him as 'crazy'; that he might have been killed by bullets from his own side; that fellow soldiers described his actions as 'a death before dishonour effort which wouldn't have passed the lance corporal's tactics course'. [57, 30 March 2002] His widow, Sara, believed that, while the Channel 4 programme was 'very hurtful for the family…thankfully a lot of people said H's reputation came out of it stronger than before because so many people said, "this is outrageous".' When asked if she thought her husband, 'given his time again', would have done the same thing, she replied 'I'm sure he would, yes. I think he still would have felt it was a cause worth dying for and certainly the Falklands were worth fighting for'. [201, 17 March 2002]

The soldier who fitted the second category was the Welsh Guardsman, Simon Weston, who was badly burned in the *Sir Galahad* incident. Weston spoke frankly about the nature of the military profession: 'we were always under pressure to be…aggressive. They took innocent sixteen year olds and turned them into homicidal maniacs. But then again, you can't have innocent youngsters going to war, or on the streets of Northern Ireland; you've got to have people who can be nice when they have to be, but bone-crushers when they need to be'. [225, p. 39] Weston admitted that he and his comrades had one desire as they sailed south: to see action, and not to end up as 'the brass-collecting team...Picking up all the spent cartridges...' They were anxious to tell the Argentine bully to 'pick on someone his own size'. [225, pp. 1, 2]

Weston did not blame his commanding officer for the decision to retain the Guardsmen on the *Sir Galahad*: it was 'military regulation that men and ammunition do not travel in the same boat'. His description of the consequences are vivid: men were mutilated and burning, 'screaming like pigs', but comradeship prevailed: there were 'unsung acts of heroism'; they 'played as a team'; 'I have no complaints'. [225, pp. 3–6] Weston showed his remarkable strength of character in making a recovery: he overcame depression, learned to fly, and the Army did not neglect him, but helped him retrieve his life: 'The Welsh Guards couldn't have responded more quickly'. [225, p. 9]

Weston's stoicism and loyalty to his regiment provoked some into epitomising him as part of a healing process that the country needed to have constructed for it after the war; his recovery, his lack of bitterness, was criticised by those who felt that he was fulfilling a role designed for him by those with an agenda: that of showing the British Army and the nation it represented in the best possible light: as a story of 'triumph over tragedy', thus shifting the Falklands campaign 'from misery to exultation'. [7, p. 30] But there was another, darker side to his story. Simon Weston's family felt isolated and even spurned by the Army. They had to telephone the Welsh Guards each time they needed travel expenses to visit him in hospital. Simon was furious with his mother who was not at home when his fingers could not cope with opening a bottle of whisky for her husband, who was feeling unwell. When Simon Weston's mother met his platoon commander he asked her if there was anything they could do for the family. 'She told him: "you are too late"'. [40, pp. 136–9] But it could be argued that the third figure – the serviceman who discovered, alas too late, the futility of war – also fitted into a category that, in this case, was needed by critics of this war, and war in general.

David Tinker was a young man serving on HMS *Glamorgan* when it was attacked and damaged by an Exocet missile on 12 June; Tinker was killed. His father wrote that a 'vein of poetry and gentle fantasy' pervaded his son's life, [208, p. 10] and he linked David Tinker's doubts about the war to those of Wilfred Owen 'who also died just as pointlessly, in the final days of a war'. Owen too spoke 'with the voice of sanity when almost all eminent, and those who take it upon themselves to pronounce on public matters, seem (temporarily, let us hope) to have lost all sense of reality, all sense of proportion, and all thought for the future in the South Atlantic'. [208, p. 12] There was, as in the case of many of the soldier-poets of the Great War, a transition from enthusiasm for the cause, to disillusionment. Tinker set off 'light hearted', eager to 'bash the Argentinians'. It was 'great fun and very much like Maggie Thatcher to stick up for our few remaining colonies with a show of force!'. This really was 'like the days of 1914 and great fun'. [208, pp. 161, 164–5] On 7 April he was still sure that there would be no war; the Argentines would be frightened by the large British fleet. And if it came to fighting, 'our submarines can take out the aircraft carrier and type 42s…and we can take care of the rest'. [208, pp. 162–8] By 10 April he acknowledged that 'we must do our job well to defeat the Argentinians and survive'. But there was also a sceptical note: 'At times the situation seems so absolutely silly; here we are, in 1982, fighting a colonial war on the other side of the world: 28,000 men going to fight over a fairly dreadful piece of land inhabited by 1,800 people'. [208, pp. 169–70]

The next part of Tinker's letter is one of the most significant texts to emerge from the Falklands War: the almost fatalistic acceptance it was the duty of each generation to confront warfare: 'I personally do not want to kill any Argentinians, or anybody else. However, I always felt that it is something one is bound to do at some stage. With a grandfather in France, 1915–18, his brother going on to the Archangel campaign in Russia and winning an MC, grandfather McKenzie in the Sudan, Elizabeth's brother in the RAF…Hugh in Burma: Tinkers and relatives have covered quite a few wars in the last hundred years!' He added – still in lighthearted vein – 'I shall be happy if we call it a day after this one'. [208, p. 170]

The sinking of the *General Belgrano* and the *Sheffield* were for Tinker the turning point in his war. He wrote on 6 May that he wished the politicians would 'see sense and stop the war. What is happening here is barbaric and totally unnecessary'. This was a war for a flag: 'I think that Maggie Thatcher sees herself as a Churchill'. World pressure and economic sanctions were 'quite enough for solving the dispute over a rock with a village population'. Now Tinker began to see the war in a different light: the alternative to war as a kind of national destiny was now replaced by war as a lesson which must be learned: 'I cannot believe that Britain, after the experience of the First World War, can be starting another'. [208, pp. 179–82] But war was 'an experience we should go through if only to drive home for each generation how stupid war is'. His chosen epitaph was Rupert Brooke's 'Fragment written during the voyage to Gallipoli, April 1915':

> He wears
> The ungathered blossom of quiet; stiller he
> Than a deep well at noon, or lovers met,
> Than sleep, or the heart after wrath. He is
> The silence following great words of peace. [208, pp. 193–4]

Tinker did not represent his comrades' emotions – or certainly not all of them – any more than did the Great War poets speak for all their soldiers. He himself remarked on the Royal Marines' reaction to an Argentine air attack on the *Glamorgan*, when one of the soldiers shouted 'Come here and let me get you, you so and so'. [208, p. 196] But his legacy to the Falklands War was, if not as lasting as that of the Great War poets he loved, one that carried on their tradition.

There was something here that war itself seemed to demand; some response that is, at least, unsurprising. The Falklands War also elicited familiar responses in other respects. In his *Nine Battles to Stanley*, Nicholas van der Bijl wrote angrily,

> Although President Menem (the Argentine President who replaced the disgraced General Galtieri) had the graciousness to attend a remembrance service during his state visit in 1998, to their shame the Falkland Islanders, defying the forgiveness due for soldiers killed on active service, refused to allow Argentine families to visit the graves of their husbands, sons and friends. This is not what I and others who fought the war want. [215, p. 231]

Here again the writing of the Falklands War was almost predictable. It comes as no surprise to read in one of the anthologies of the war that soldiers did not risk their lives for Queen and Country, the Government, or even the Falkland Islands; 'it was for their comrades, who depended upon them'. [5, p. 1] Major Michael Norman, one of the Royal Marine garrison on the Falklands when the Argentines invaded was expecting the Islanders to help: 'We were disappointed that they didn't. There are over 1,000 people in Stanley and we could have used the men, but it was clear that the Governor quite rightly wanted to avoid endangering the civilian population as far as possible. But I still thought people would come out on the streets'. [5, p. 11] Another soldier was in a pub 'in company with a number of very wise, appreciative civilians…urging us to go down to the airport and machine-gun the prisoners'. [5, p. 289] An injured soldier put it more bluntly: 'Two dead…two fucking dead. All for some pimple on the arse-end of the world'. [20, p. 132]

These responses were consistent with earlier British wars; as Niall Ferguson put it, the soldiers probably cared as little for 'Bloody Belgium' as their descendants did for the Bloody Falklands. [207, 26 Oct. 1998] There was also the inevitable guying of politicians. It is true that one officer praised the Prime Minister who had sent the army to the Falklands ('Thank Christ we had Maggie, because she proved that you can't hold this country to ransom'); [5, p. 227] but a corporal possibly expressed the rank and file perception more accurately: 'The only thing I remember about the boat journey southwards was being pissed off with politicians. I can't stand the way they leap about trying to make decisions…Here we were thinking, "Let's get on with it. Let's do it". We wanted to go straight down and blast the Argies before they had time to do anything. I don't believe soldiers fight for political reasons; we do it because that's what we're paid for and that's what we wanna do – that's why I do it and because I get a kick out of it'. [5, p. 255]

'Getting a kick out of it' involved, for the Royal Marines, writing a song during their stay on Ascension Island, which ran

> We're all going to the Malvinas,
> We're all going to kill a spic or two,
> We're all going on a pusser's holiday,
> For a month or two…
> Or three or four. [141, p. 63]

But this has to be put in context of the nature of war. Soldiers on their way to fight were engaged in several tasks: preparing their weapons and their skills; maintaining fitness; preparing themselves for violence, wounds and death; and denigrating the enemy (especially one whose national character was summed up in their description as 'Argies'). The padre of 45 Commando edited the 'Oily Rag' as a ship's newspaper on the way to the South Atlantic. A Marine officer contributed a column in which he invented a 'comic-opera hierarchy of Argentine military characters and chronicling their rise and fall as fearful news of the approaching Task Force reached them'. But, he asked 'what can you say about the enemy? It was psychologically better for us – and more civilised – to ridicule them than to portray them as odious'. [144, pp. 62–3]

Witnesses to war did not shrink from describing what they saw in battle: A lance-corporal who had lost a leg and suffered wounds to the other one 'was absolutely grey because he'd lost so much blood'; [5, p. 218] a medical lance-corporal who had to partially amputate a soldier's leg with a clasp knife; [5, p. 172] perhaps worst of all, the scenes on the Sir *Galahad* when it was hit by a missile:

> The sound was the first thing: the sound of horribly mutilated and frightened, disorientated men – a noise from a different world…The first thing I saw was a man running through a wall of flame from the fore stern on the ship. He was on fire from head to foot and was begging his fellow Guardsmen to shoot him and put him out of his misery…What he must have seen on the other side of the wall of flame I shudder to think. [5, p. 98]

Such descriptions are hardly novel and certainly not surprising. The face of battle is an ugly one, and a 'neat little war' [52, p. 350] like the Falklands was no exception. But there was also the anticipation of battle, keenly felt by soldiers of elite units. 40 Commando was left behind at San Carlos to defend the beachhead; they were disappointed at missing the chance to 'go east'. [213, p. 40] A corporal from 42 Commando on Mount Harriet recalled that 'Once we got into the fighting, we all switched to "auto" and got stuck in… The guys worked fantastically. We were literally knocking their weapons from the hands and going on'. [213, p. 59] A colour sergeant of the Parachute Regiment on Mount Longdon confronted 20 or 30 Argentine soldiers: 'We just opened fire on them. I don't know how many we killed, but they got what they deserved, because none of them were left standing when we'd finished. That was satisfactory'. [5, p. 220] Officers, as they were expected to, showed coolness under fire. A sergeant of the Parachute Regiment recalled seeing Major Neame, 'cool as a cucumber' who 'walked up past where I was and I said, "Sod off, Sir, you're attracting bullets wherever you go". So he went off and had a chat to the Platoon Commander and then walked back to the rest of the company… He was all on his own; he was amazing, great guts. He really helped the lads' morale, they were saying, "look at that crazy sod up there"'. [5, p. 211]

The experience of fighting – and especially of the close order combat of the Falklands War – produced not only horror but also caused soldiers to respond with a kind of callous – or perhaps gallows – humour. The sight of an Argentine soldier's body dismembered by shell-fire inspired the joke, 'Hey, look at the Isle-of-Man sign – three legs, all which way'. [226, p. 163] Near the end of the battle for Mount Longdon, 'a young Para corporal was hit by artillery shrapnel, and went down in agony. "Christ, I've lost my leg" he moaned. His mate crouched beside him and using a humour he knew his injured oppos would understand, he said, "No you haven't mate. It's over there"'. [141, p. 241]

Soldiers responded by stressing what they called their 'professionalism', 'just doing a job', 'getting on with it'. [213, pp. 98, 121] A father from Wales quoted from his son's letter from the Falklands: 'he said he did not want to go out and kill people, but he realised he had to do it. It was his duty.' Some of his comrades were 'looking forward' to action: 'a chance to do some real soldiering'. [207, 15 June 1982] One officer spoke of the 'dogged qualities' of the British; [213, p. 62] another referred to the training which 'showed that the young men of today, if trained properly and disciplined, will be magnificent'. [213, p. 46]

There was also the rediscovery of the experience of previous generations of soldiers. In May 2002 Dave Brown of 2 Para spoke in a radio interview of the men fixing bayonets and advancing down the slope at Goose Green as the soldiers did in the First World War. He had, he said, 'no personal feelings of hate or anger' towards the enemy. He admitted that 'hard men do cry, do suffer'. He wept when he heard the tune 'Flowers of the Forest' (at this point the programme interpolated Mrs Thatcher's sound-bite, that the war was a 'chapter of pride for our country'). Brown spoke of the difficulty of coming to terms with his experience. The Paras were not given time to adjust; people who were not there would not understand what it was like. Brown took to climbing to forget. His father said he had 'changed completely'. Dave Brown felt that the experience of war was one 'we could not share'. [30]

But some wanted to share it, in what might be called the mood of Coleridge's *Ancient Mariner*, who was determined to stop one of the wedding guests and tell his harrowing, but cathartic, tale. Vincent Bramley's *Two Sides of Hell* published in 1994, aimed to tell the 'truth about the way we treat our heroes'. [27, p. x] Like Dave Brown, he almost at once recalled the seminal British experience of conflict, the Great War, quoting Laurence Binyon's poem, 'At the going down of the sun and in the morning/ We will remember them'. [27, p. xviii]

His account of the Falklands memorial service at St Paul's reflected almost exactly the response of Siegfried Sassoon, who in 1933 wrote:

> I can't repress ironic thoughts about
> The 'representatives' who're here to-day.
> The man they wear silk hats for has meanwhile
> Entered his unmolestable immunity:
> And can afford, as dead men do, to smile
> Serenely at this G.H.Q. community. [192, pp. 168–9]

Bramley found the Falklands memorial service ('which TV crews were filming for national posterity') disillusioning. He and a coach load of soldiers from 3 Para had warm beer and cucumber sandwiches on the terrace of the House of Commons: 'One of the MPs came up to us. Well done chaps, good show, but it was easy, eh? All young conscripts, seventeen years old. No match for us pros! This was his message to us. They were young, but so were our boys…'. 'Forget whose side you're on. It's the soldier and his loved ones who suffer'. [27, pp. 267–8]

From cucumber sandwiches to battle: Bramley strove to convey to those who did not know what battle was like: when 'killing seemed easy, but the overwhelming memory was the smell. It was overpowering.… It was like rotten onions, damp and smelly clothes, human shit and blood all mixed together in one big bag. Add to that the smell of fear and the stench of body sweat coming from your enemy in his last seconds of life and it is nauseating'. [27, p. 149] And in a scene which has been shown in many war films (most recently in 'Saving Private Ryan'), Bramley described in detail the killing of an enemy soldier: 'He screamed in English: "I like the pop group Queen…I want to see my grandmother…I want my grandmother". It must have been the only English he knew. He was screaming it as my bayonet struck him in the throat and chest…I was in a rage, doing my job, knowing that if I didn't kill him it would be me dead. I was reacting to my military training to kill.' [27, p. 153]

This terrible image was not new, but stands in the tradition of the soldier's resolve to explain to any non-combatant what battle was really like. It conveys what the French historian Stephanie Audoin-Reugeau called the 'horrified fascination' of an encounter with death in the Great War, described by a soldier who could 'see those men who just now were two living beings and now, one is nothing but a mass of mud and blood, the other this long stiff body, with blackened face…'.

[6, p. 78] And there was another tradition in war writing that Bramley revived: that of the 'thin red line', doted on in wartime, only to be ignored thereafter. One Paratroop soldier suffered from depression after he lost a leg, but was determined to get on with his life, even though the Army 'didn't help much'. [27, p. 220] Another soldier who was mentioned in despatches claimed that 'after all the glory, all the bullshit, the Army doesn't want us any more'. [27, p. 239] Another paratrooper, who underwent 19 operations on his injured arm, found common cause with his Argentine counterpart, who sent his best wishes to 'the boys in England'. 'Now that I have met British soldiers I realise we are the same in many ways…'. [27, pp. 243, 253–4] Bramley set the seal on his story: 'Looking back, I think it was a pointless war, a war that should never have happened'. [27, p. 263]

Ken Lukowiak's *A Soldier's Story: True Stories from the Falklands* (1993) was written in a more ironic tone, with a series of flashbacks to his youth. Significantly, one of these was when 'we were taking turns to read aloud from a book called *All Quiet on the Western Front*.' He was to remember it 'many times over the next few weeks. My few weeks of war'. [139, pp. 3–4] Lukowiak's story showed soldiers coping with the brutality of war, obscenities, fear, anger and hatred, all of which were part of the tradition of war-writing since (at least) 1918. He described one soldier picking up a dead Argentine and supporting the corpse's weight underneath his arm, putting a cigarette in the dead man's mouth, then one in his own, and then holding a lighter under the Argentine soldier's cigarette while a friend took a photograph: 'They both laughed….This was foolish – smoking can kill'. [139, Frontispiece] It was important for a soldier to show that he was 'a man', and to do so he kicked a wounded Argentine on his injured leg. [139, p. 49] When a television crew filmed him and he later saw his image, he was pleased that he 'looked very warrie'. [139, p. 74] He and his comrades laughed when the *Belgrano* was sunk, [139, p. 12] but despised *The Sun* for its 'Gotcha' headline: no one 8,000 miles from the war should write such a thing, because they were risking nothing. [139, p. 127] The tape of the return home, the bands, the cheering crowds, made him cry, not only because it reminded him of the homecoming, but also because 'I feel we were robbed'. [139, p. 170]

This phrase, 'we were robbed', is of profound importance. Lukowiak's book, laconic, tough, at times obscene, could not of course be called a lament for a lost generation; casualties in the Falklands War were few; the conflict was brief. But in a sense it was a lament for lost generations, because of its connections, surely deliberate, he made with previous war literature, especially with *All Quiet on the Western Front*. Philip Williams' *Summer Soldier* made another kind of connection, this time with the depiction of war as farce: and of the anti-hero who is hailed as a hero, before his true status is revealed. Williams was a young Scots Guardsman who went missing on Mount Tumbledown, and who was believed to have died, only to emerge after the war was over. His experience contrasted strongly with that of Robert Lawrence, from whom he differed in social background, rank, character and aspiration. Williams drifted into the Army after a number of dead-end jobs, interspersed with periods of unemployment. His story is notable for its lack of bitterness or self-pity – at least when he was telling his own story (his book was written in collaboration with a novelist, M. S. Power, who took an interest in William's story when he read about it in the press). Thus, although his preface strikes an awkward, artificial note (the books is dedicated to 'the few who have freed their minds from the institutions of power and authority which demand war as a civilised policy'), the text is marked by an ironic, at times self-mocking style: when he sat in the Army Recruitment Office he saw posters on the wall 'explaining the advantages of an army career to morons like me'. [230, p. 4] He described his photograph in uniform as showing 'the face of a young fascist'. [230, p. 16]

This disposition serves him well when he describes his experience after being knocked senseless by a shell at Tumbledown. He wandered around, lost for several weeks in what he called a 'desolate bloody place', [230, p. 40] and found a farmhouse where the owners told him that 'the Brits had won'. When the Army discovered Williams' whereabouts, they arrived so quickly that his suspicions were aroused: 'They were shit scared I might tell someone else about what happened to me before they got what they wanted out of me'. [230, p. 57] The Army seemed to want to make him into a hero. Photo-opportunities followed; Military public relations men handled the press. He was welcomed home as a hero by local people in Lancaster, and although he was irritated by a letter from the Scots Guards' Commander on 22 June which claimed that a 'thorough search' had been made for him, [230, p. 77] and complained about examples of what he saw as 'official indifference', he was struck by the different status he held when he was believed to be dead, but was then found alive. The Mayor of Lancaster had spoken of 'sacrifice', 'loss' and 'grief'; but when he turned up alive, 'it made them look like right wallies, and they hated that'. He quoted from a letter written to his parents by Major-General Langley stating that Williams had died 'in the service of his country'; his life was 'in no sense a waste', for he was fighting in a just cause and was doing his duty, and he died alongside his comrades in a famous regiment taking part in a 'historic and victorious campaign'. The most ironic touch was when he learned that 300 people had attended his memorial service, of which his mother (in words that could have come from Alan Bennett's 'Talking Heads') remarked, 'It was lovely, Phil'.

Williams' difficulties began when the press began to rewrite the story of the 'Teenager who died for Britain'. [230, pp. 82–6] The *Manchester Evening News* on 11 August headlined the story 'A deserter? Not me, says soldier'. [230, p. 101] The result was a flow of hate mail and telephone calls. People in his village became 'edgy'. When he returned to his regiment ('Soldier back from the dead returns to his first love') he was verbally abused by Guardsmen ('a shitty English coward') [230, pp. 106–12] and then attacked several times. His officers refused to investigate, and Williams went absent without leave, though even now 'Somewhere inside me, I think, there was some dumb sense of duty'. [230, pp. 122–3]

It was at this point that his story crossed with that of Robert Lawrence. The Scots Guards were 'getting some flak from other sources. There was a lieutenant called Lawrence who was stirring up a lot of shit of his own, and he had quite some clout which made them very nervous: you can't just dismiss what an officer says the way you can someone from the ranks'. [230, p. 135] Williams was put in hospital and then discharged from the Army with – a final ironic touch – a medal, the citation for which certified that 'Guardsman Philip Williams took part in the battle for Mount Tumbledown. Well Done. Best wishes, your commanding officer…'. [230, p. 148] Williams' ability to stand back and, so to say, observe himself engaging in the follies of military life are matched by his ability to apply the same tests to those who tried to use his story for their own ends. Paul Greengrass produced a film of his experience, 'Resurrected'. Williams believed the motive was 'just riding on the back of the Falklands euphoria, and hoping the film would get the same publicity as Tumbledown did, having a right go at the Army, and the Scots Guards in particular, without fretting about the truth too much'. 'I could just picture them', he added, 'sitting around a table saying "Shit, is that all they did to him? That wouldn't make anyone talk about our film. Let's make this and that happen. Really give the Army some stick"'. [230, p. 186] His verdict on the film was that 'it seemed to have very little to do with me', and 'was just another war film, and, Christ knows, we've seen enough of them'. [230, p. 206]

And, as Williams noted, 'they didn't seem to understand that I'd be blamed. And I was'. [230, p. 187]

Williams' final word of advice was given in characteristic style: 'if you want them to love you, if you really want to be called a hero, make sure you come back dead. It's far simpler. Far tidier for everyone in the long run. And especially for yourself'. His co-author claimed that Williams' experience 'ruined his life'. [230, pp. 209–10] But the strength of his book lies in Williams' portrayal of himself as an unlikely victim of war, in that the crisis of his life arose, not from wounds or trauma arising from combat, but from the way in which his status as a dead hero was transformed into the man who, by stubbornly staying alive, betrayed his heroic status. And, if he was not after all a hero, then he must be the opposite: a coward. His failure to join (for good) the glorious dead caused his downfall: he simply was all too much alive.

Hugh McManners' *Falklands Commando* has a different tone, though he too adopted (and adapted) the role of Coleridge's *Ancient Mariner*, inviting the reader to '"Pull up a sandbag, cross the white line, swing the lantern" and listen to my story'. [144, p. 299] He was a very different story-teller from Bramley and the other chroniclers. McManners was from a comfortable background and enjoyed a good education (his father was Regius Professor of Ecclesiastical History at All Souls College, Oxford). He joined the army in 1972, leaving in 1989. The cover of his book, showing the author in full battle order, moustachioed and tense, might suggest its contents would conform to the 'eye deep in hell' category of war writing. But McManners' story is told in measured, thoughtful words. He frankly admits that he and his comrades were unwilling to believe that the crisis would end in fighting; but, once home, he would not exchange his '1982 break' with anyone. [144, pp. 27, 30] He criticised those who showed 'glee' at hearing of the sinking of the *Belgrano*; [144, p. 109] he recalled how shooting to kill made him and his men feel 'like butchers'. [144, p. 145] His description of wounded soldiers, though not of the 'butcher's shop' style, is perhaps the most harrowing of all the Falkland stories:

> We had eight casualties brought on board – two were left on the wardroom floor for most of the afternoon. They were the worst, bullet wounds in the head and both thought likely to die. One had a fractured skull and was haemorrhaging into his face. His head and face were slowly swelling up. He had a drip (intravenous drip) and his eyes opened occasionally, but blankly.... The other was worse, with another bullet in the head. His eyes were open and kept darting

> about, even seeming to follow what was going on, but there was that very disturbing blankness of expression that all serious head wounds have. They were both very pale and still, their heads swathed in blood-soaked first field dressings with bits of mud and heather where their mates had patched them up. [144, p. 157]

McManners' book perhaps lacks the literary art to make it a classic in war writing. But he conveys the physical and mental impact of conflict, where a 'sort of weariness envelops everyone....Clear moral distinctions become blurred and people move with tired resolution through one sad and violent crisis to the next....Strangely there are also unique moments of clarity, of comradeship and joy of living, which can only exist in contrast with the discomfort and danger'. [144, p. 29] What McManners called 'optimistic fatalism' was the only way for the soldier to avoid becoming convinced of the inevitability of death, or worse, mutilation. Above all 'motivation when we were doing the fighting was very much simpler than the arguments that raged at the time....We did it for each other'. [144, p. 298] This war was 'basic and brutal. Despite a huge array of modern technology, the war was won by exhausted soldiers with soaking wet clothing and bad feet, who walked across East Falkland to use bomb and bayonet on their enemy'. [144, p. 17]

Veterans of the Falklands War bore witness to the destructive impact of war on their personal and family lives. Hugh McManners described the decline of Des Nixon, whose catch phrase was 'I'm a rubber duck, you won't crack me'. His marriage collapsed; he suffered sporadic bouts of depression. He remarried, only to see his second wife leave him and ('his legendary resilience gone'), one day he went into the New Forest and took his own life. [144, p. 302]

But not all servicemen – not all pilots – had the same experience. Commander 'Sharky' Ward of the Royal Navy's Fleet Air Arm, acknowledged that for some the war 'was a shock: for others it was a dream come true'. [222, p. 4] He welcomed the news: 'in my heart of hearts, I wanted a fight'. [222, p. 807] Peacetime flying was 'not the real McCoy'. His account is that of an officer whose technical grasp of his airplane and its performance is impressive. His account of the atmosphere in his squadron was, like that of the Royal Marines, optimistic and even aggressive: 'the song "Don't Cry for me, Argentina", was adapted to the forthcoming battles:

> You don't frighten me Argentina,
> The truth is we will defeat you;

We'll sink your carrier with our Sea Harrier
And with our Sea Kings subs'll [submarines] be sinking. [222, pp. 85–6]

Ward enjoyed air combat. Even after the exhilaration of duelling in the sky had evaporated he regretted that his 'head-on pass and initial turn against the Daggers (Argentine aircraft) had not developed unto a real dog-fight'. What made this even more disappointing was that 'logically, the Daggers could have made a decent fight of it because it had been at least a three-to-one situation'. [222, p. 272]

But Sharkey Ward was repelled by the request of *The Sun*'s reporter that names and messages be written on the missiles and bombs being prepared for action (with the named party being awarded a cash prize for the first missile so inscribed and delivered), [222, p. 168] and he was critical of the assertion that a pilot who had shot down an Argentine Mirage fighter in a 'ball of flame' was showing 'a lack of moral fibre' because he had 'reacted badly'. [222, p. 207] And despite his squadron's song which promised to 'throw you out / to Buenos Aires, you bloody fairies', [222, p. 86] Ward described the Argentine pilots as 'gentlemen' who 'lacked nothing in guts and moral fibre'. [222, pp. 270–1] This combination of respect for the enemy, the exhilaration of combat, and regret – but not bitterness or depression – at the loss of comrades is without a false note; and it is as authentic a view of war, at least of war in the air, as any that lingers on the horror and brutality of military conflict.

There were many servicemen in the Falklands War, and they all have their own individual experience and story to tell. The official war artist, Linda Kitson, sought to capture these (or some of these) experiences in her sketches and drawings of the campaign. She published her 'visual diary' in 1982, dedicating it to the 'X2 Tonys' (Commanders of 5 Infantry Brigade (Tony Wilson) and 4 Field Regiment Royal Artillery (Tony Hart)). Kitson's collection did not, however, fulfil what Dame Elizabeth Frink, RA, claimed in her Introduction: that 'only an artist can portray in such a personal way the sadness and horror of war'. [134, p. 7] Linda Kitson herself noted that at Goose Green she 'had to make a decision about what aspects of war I should record. My brief was to record the sights that might be recognised as common experiences. I decided that the horrifying sight of parts of human bodies, a helmet with a head still in it – pictorially sensational and relevant though they were – were not part of my brief; neither were the war graves, which were recorded in news film and in photographs'.

She reflected that 'I still question my decision', and asked 'would it have been a stronger, cautionary record if I had used such shock tactics?'. [134, p. 65]

This is not to say that the drawings lack integrity or a strong sense of purpose. They encapsulate both. But essentially they show the busy nature of a military campaign, its range of activities, and especially the way in which it absorbs the concentration and energies of those engaged in it. Her work depicts the conditions in which, for example, the Air Force and helicopter pilots operated, and the complexity of their operations. Naval Air Defence units are drawn 'all tripping over each other on the bridge wings, to assemble the Brownings (machine guns)'; [134, p. 29] after each day's flying the flight deck of the carrier was repainted, patched, repaired and re-marked out. Soldiers were equally absorbed in their professional tasks. Gurkha units' rifles were 'being loaded, unloaded, dismantled and put together again'; [134, p. 27] sappers 'with every sort of expertise – Army, Navy and Air Force – were present at Goose Green: bomb disposal, explosive experts, engineers…They all liked a good big bang'. [134, p. 58] The collection neither reflects the alienation shown in paintings of the Great War, nor the subversion of illustrations of the 1991 Gulf War. This might be taken as a criticism that Kitson had missed the essentially horrific heart of war: that it is about killing, wounding, fear, suffering and death. But war, as Professor Trevor Wilson has pointed out, had indeed 'myriad faces'; even a 'small war' like the Falklands bears out the truth of his description of this field of human activity.

11
Retrospect

The Falklands War can all too easily be dismissed as a 'colonial war': a throwback to the wars of the Victorian age and the early twentieth century that were the means by which the British acquired and retained their empire. It seemed too short and marginal to effect the great changes in British society that the First and Second World Wars did (though its critics alleged that its part in raising Mrs Thatcher's popularity and establishing a firm hold on the machinery of government facilitated the monetarist policies that were the hallmark of her Downing Street years). [174, p. 247] It was the subject of hard-hitting, but ephemeral plays and films; but it produced no poetry of lasting significance, such as Wilfred Owen's or Siegfried Sassoon's. Personal accounts by soldiers were in some cases impressive, but not original, perhaps because this war, unlike the great watershed in wartime experiences, Vietnam, did not provoke disillusionment and alienation among those who fought it. The novels that it inspired were 'superficial thrillers'. [138, Ch. 6]

There was a significant aftermath for the armed forces, with the predictions that the centrality and performance of the Royal Navy and the Royal Air Force in the campaign would call a halt to the run down of the more expensive high technology branches of the armed forces. Just over a month after the war ended John Nott wrote in *The Times* 'After the Falklands, let's not go overboard in navy spending'. Britain did not need more ships, but ships with the best equipment. It was important not to increase naval expenditure at the expense of the other services. 'Usually in our history we have our forces, already deployed in the right place – that is good both for deterrence and for the defence of the United Kingdom itself'. He defended the maintenance of the Army in Germany, to the 'forward land/air defence of Europe; for the forward defence of Germany is the forward defence of Great Britain itself'. Nott claimed that last year's 'broad strategic decisions...will probably produce the best balanced and more effective force structure to meet the prime threat from the Soviet Union and its allies into the 1990s and beyond'. [207, 22 July 1982]

Nonetheless, the Falklands War gave the Navy the chance to re-fight the bureaucratic battles with the Ministry of Defence. Some cuts were restored before December 1982. Four ships were to be built to replace those lost in the war, and three old destroyers were retained in service. HMS *Endurance* was to resume its South Atlantic patrolling. The anti-submarine warfare carrier, *Invincible*, was not sold to Australia; two more carriers joined *Illustrious*, so that two would always be on patrol. In order to sustain patrols around the Falklands the total number of destroyers and frigates was to be 55, not the 50 of the 1981 Defence Review. All of this contrasted with the Government's insistence that its main defence focus was against the Soviet threat to Europe, which reflected traditional British defence preoccupations. [91, p. 81] Britain must look towards Europe and the NATO alliance, and she must also cultivate the American alliance – which had been threatened, rather than strengthened, by the Falklands crisis. There was as yet no Bosnian crisis, for the resolution of which the United States could reasonably ask the European states to take the lead. The Army was to be reduced, with one divisional headquarters of the British Army of the Rhine removed. [91, p. 84] Other lessons were drawn from the conflict, such as the unexpectedly high ammunition expenditure. [91, pp. 86–7]

This was of great importance in the land campaign where the battle was dominated by close quarter infantry fighting. The defence of ships against missiles fired from enemy airplanes was another 'lesson', though this was one whose importance was evident in the Second World War, now given greater urgency because of the refinement of missiles by modern technology. The need to modify equipment and improvise its use was, not for the first time, imperative. Submarines showed their destructive power in the sinking of the Balgrano, and also their potential to deter further naval activity by the enemy. Helicopters, though not used in an attacking role, proved vital for carrying and supplying front line soldiers; their depletion as a result of the loss of the Atlantic Conveyor was keenly felt. The taking up of ships as troop carriers, carriers of fuel, helicopters, Harrier planes and stores, and as hospital and repair ships was a major success of the campaign.

The presentation of the campaign was the subject of a report of a study group commissioned by the Ministry of Defence. It concluded that the vetting of war correspondents both in the field and at home was too heavily applied. The public would not tolerate the unnecessary witholding of news, and though it was prepared, 'in certain circumstances' to accept this if it contributed to the success of the campaign, this principle must not be taken too far, for 'as one editor put it to us, all wars are "people's wars"'; (153a, pp. 7, 99). The MOD offered a cautious response to this report, but it did accept that 'double vetting' was undesirable. The overall lesson was one already learned in Northern Ireland: that military commanders needed to be trained in handling the media, and that failure to do so, while it would not lose wars, would render them more difficult to fight, and perhaps even to win. The practice of 'embedding' journalists in fighting units was used with great success in the Iraq war of 2003; media people, exposed to at least some of the dangers faced by serving soldiers, came to identify more closely with them; it could be said that this was, informally, foreshadowed in the Falklands War.

These lessons were in one sense familiar: the importance of logistics in any campaign is self-evident. But what gave them their peculiar dimension in the Falklands was the theatre of war itself: the distance of the islands was of greater significance for the British than for Argentina, though Argentina's airplanes were operating from the extreme edge of their capability. The climate took its toll even of the best trained troops, and the open nature of the terrain, together with its exposed rocky ridges, made it a most demanding one for the attacking forces, and a distinctly uncomfortable one for the defenders. Intelligence about Argentine dispositions and numbers was not always accurate, which was to have serious consequences at Goose Green. But at least the war was fought in as humane a way as possible. Prisoners were well treated, and although there were accusations of British soldiers shooting prisoners (made long after the war ended) they came to no significant conclusion. Above all, for the servicemen, medical treatment was of the highest standard and was applied to British and Argentine soldier alike. It is therefore not difficult to see why this war was regarded by the victors, and even to some extent by the vanquished, as a 'good war'.

The Falklands War was in many respects a classic 'limited war'. Limited War has been a notable aspect of the Cold War era after 1945, from Korea to Vietnam. It is usually defined as one confined to a particular area, with no extension beyond that area. Ideologies and self-interest of the combatants drive it, but they do not draw in a wide range of states, nor do they involve the committed states in deploying all their military might (such as nuclear weapons). In Korea, the period of almost static warfare from about the middle of 1951 was accompanied by diplomacy, with the fighting acting as a kind of lever on the negotiating parties, when they realised total victory was impossible. The Falklands War exhibited many of these characteristics. The war was not extended to the South American mainland, and there was never of course any possibility of the British using their nuclear weapons. The diplomatic dimension was ever present, at least until the British, for their part, felt assured of victory in the last stages of the campaign. But there was the difference that both Britain and Argentina sent forces substantial enough to win the war, not merely to exert diplomatic pressure. This again reflects the geographical area where war was waged. With winter fast approaching the British could not afford to hold back their Task Force in the South Atlantic to facilitate an open-ended negotiation process. 'Withdrawal' of the antagonists, which was often cited as a pre-requisite of a negotiated settlement, might have been acceptable for Argentina (though national pride would have been wounded by the sight of an army evacuating the beloved Malvinas); but for the British the distance already covered by the Task Force in getting to the area precluded, or at least rendered very difficult, withdrawal of their forces. Moreover, Argentina had already 'won' her war in invading the islands; her diplomacy was naturally deeply influenced by this consideration: why should she surrender the fruits of her fine military success? For the British, the more successful was the Army's advance, the harder it was to contemplate a settlement that fell short of the principle of reasserting British sovereignty over the Falklands, though they did make considerable concessions on the administration of the islands, pending a negotiated final settlement.

But the Falklands War raised, and left unanswered, a great central question about warfare in the modern world (or at least in the European democratic world): was it a just war? The idea of the just war arose in the Middle Ages, when it was essential to establish a set of rules that would enable Christians to take the lives of other Christians, at the behest of their states. Canon law distinguished between the *jus in bello* (justice in the course of war) from the *jus ad bellum* (a just cause of war). A just cause could be pursued by unjust means, such as the killing of non-combatants. Thomas Aquinas held that a war was just only if there was sufficient authority in the party waging it; that there was a just cause of offence; and that there was an intention to wage war solely for the sake of peace, or to suppress the wicked and sustain the good. [194, p. 244] This raised many questions, such as the concept of authority invoked (did the Boer leaders who in 1899 led the fight against the British to maintain their freedoms have 'authority'?); and the incorporation into the condition that war must be waged for the sake of peace or to sustain the good (who were the wicked and who the good?). In the Falklands War the Argentines claimed that they were only recovering their land that had been forcibly taken from them by the British in the early nineteenth century. The British victory in the war did not lead unambiguously to 'peace', for the British had to settle a considerable garrison on the Falklands to deter Argentina; and Argentina's claims to the Islands were as legitimate in her eyes under her democratic government that replaced the junta as they had been before.

The unease in Britain over the war did not surface to any significant degree until its end. It arose in particular form from the service of thanksgiving that was conducted on 26 July 1982. The form of that service itself occasioned controversy, with the Prime Minister and the Archbishop of Canterbury finding themselves in disagreement; and with disagreement within the ranks of the Church of England as well. In his sermon, the Archbishop praised the courage of men in battle, an experience which (unlike the Prime Minister) he had himself undergone. War, the Archbishop declared, occurred when love which should be given to God was given to some 'God substitute' – and one of the most dangerous of these was nationalism. People were mourning on both sides of the Falklands conflict, and the congregation remembered the bereaved of our own country and also the Argentine bereaved. But they did not just 'mouth opinions and thanksgiving which the fashion of the moment judges acceptable'. 'The parent who comes mourning the loss of a son may find the consolation, but also a spirit which enlarges our compassion to include all those Argentine parents who have lost sons'. [207, 27 July 1982]

The Archbishop had earlier engaged in controversy with the Prime Minister when he made what *The Times* called the 'felicitous proposal' of reading the Lord's Prayer in Spanish as well as English at the service. [207, 3 July 1982] But his sermon, and that of other preachers – Mrs Rosalind Goodfellow, Moderator of the United Reform Church, and Dr Kenneth Greer, Moderator of the Free Church Federal Council – sparked off a new and heated debate. This arose because, as *The Times'* reporter put it, the Archbishop's thanks were for 'the end of hostilities, for which the Archbishop of Canterbury summed up as "Thank God it's stopped"'. Indeed, Dr Runcie reserved his sharpest criticism for those 'spectators who remained at home', but who continued 'to be the most violent in their attitudes, and untouched in their deeper selves'. [207, 27 July 1982]

The Archbishop's critics fell upon this message. John Gummer MP, a prominent Conservative churchman, eschewed the notion that 'God was an Englishman', but remarked that

> It did seem surprising that at no point in the prayers were the bereaved given the comfort of knowing that the fallen had died to some good purpose. Nowhere were we allowed to thank God that their deaths had secured freedom for others and ensured that armed aggression did not succeed.

He referred to the 'slightly self-righteous feelings' that came over in the service 'to many whose simple desire was to thank God, honour the fallen, and pray for a better world'. [207, 29 July 1982] Enoch Powell drew attention to a *Times'* leader of 28 July. Which urged the 'duty to be reconciled to one's enemies' as 'logically…equivalent to a duty of unconditional surrender'. [207, 29 July 1982]

It was not only politicians from the Right who found the Archbishop's words displeasing. Commander R. N. E. Payne, RN, argued that the Christian ethic recognised the idea of the 'just war', and claimed that the Falklands War fitted into this category: 'It follows that they should recognise the success of the Task Force as being God's will'. Thanksgiving for freeing the Islanders should predominate; after all, there was still a service of thanksgiving for the victory granted in the Battle of Britain of 1940. [207, 29 July 1982]

Anglican clergy contributed to the debate. The Reverend Dr A. R. Winnett of Southampton thought that the service had gone too far in its attempt to avoid military triumphalism. It maintained an 'almost complete silence concerning the objects for which the Falklands campaign was waged – the defeat of armed aggression and the deliverance of the Islanders from the threat of alien rule'. The language of the service must have left servicemen wondering 'for what cause, and with what result, the Falklands War was fought'. [207, 30 July 1982] Another clergyman complained that the nation was being made to feel ashamed of thanking God for victory in the war, and that 'those who were unable to prevent the military expedition are turning their hands to the creation of a sense of guilt in its backers'. Either the war was just, or it was not: 'either we were right, or we were wrong, to engage in it. If it was just, if those who gave their lives to repossess the Islands, died in a righteous cause, then God be thanked'. But if the war was considered unjust, prosecuted to gain a victory that was undeserved, then it was not thanksgiving but 'humiliation and repentance' that should sound from the cathedral. 'What real comfort can it be to the bereaved', he asked, 'to tell them that their sons and their husbands have died gaining a victory for which we cannot thank God?'. [207, 30 July 1982]

These, and similar objections to the service of thanksgiving caused Canon Paul Ostreicher, Secretary of the Division of International Affairs of the British Council of Churches, to write a stern and unapologetic reply. He claimed that it was not the task of church leaders to reflect public opinion or to bless political decisions, but as far as they were able 'to reflect the mind of Christ'. The 'de facto worship of the state' was one of the Church's greatest temptations since the conversion of Rome to Christianity. The state's wish for a 'Falkland's celebration laid on the Church of England' highlighted the problem in the British context: 'it was recognised and wisely tackled by the Churches together'.

The Church had the duty to serve the nation in the only way in which it was authorised to serve it: 'Those who mourned were comforted. Many others were discomfited'. The service was 'pastoral and prophetic at the same time'. 'Prophecy' meant to 'speak the truth in love and not just to individuals but to the community. It is an expression of critical solidarity with the nation' and 'angry reactions' to it were proof that the message was heard. That message, Canon Ostreicher urged, for the Church to serve the state on its (the state's) own terms was not service but servility. 'What is the point of churches which reflect the class divisions, the racism, and the sexism of society? And its violence? Despite Christ's teaching the churches have blessed every kind of violence from long before the crusades to Hiroshima and beyond'. Whatever the rights and wrongs of the Falklands War ('and they were far from obvious') the question was 'could a Falklands service do more than comfort the bereaved, thank God for an end to the conflict and pray for a peace that would last? It is salutary to reflect why the state made no moves for such a service after the disastrous Suez adventure of a generation ago'. 'But how better still if state pressure had been fully resisted, and Argentine Christians, perhaps a bereaved father and mother, had been invited to pray with us, in their own tongue: "Father, forgive us, as we forgive them who sin against us"'. [207, 31 July 1982]

The service of thanksgiving raised in its own way the question of whether or not the Falklands War was a just one. Simon Jenkins suggested that many people, including politicians and civil servants, had pondered on the reverse of T. S. Eliot's notion of 'doing the right deed for the wrong reason'. 'They wonder if Britain did the wrong deed for the right reason'. [207, 9 June 1982]

One of the most controversial of these deeds was the sinking of the *Belgrano*, an act that might fall into the category of 'war waged unjustly'. This would not go away; and it was raised again when the *Conqueror* flew the 'Jolly Roger' (skull and crossbones) flag on its return to base. The Government's explanation was that this was a 'lighthearted' use of the flag which began during the First World War when submarines were regarded almost as pirates by other branches of the Service. [207, 5 July 1982] In 1986 Christopher Wain wrote in the *Listener* an article entitled 'The *Belgrano* Incident will not go away', concluding that 'there is some reason for sympathising with the Argentine's belief that its ships were safe from attack until they crossed into the danger zone'. [218, 25 Oct. 1984] Clive Ponting, a senior civil servant in the Ministry of Defence, raised the issue again when he revealed documents that, he claimed, showed that the Government was on doubtful legal grounds in ordering the sinking of the *Belgrano*, that it misled parliament when it refused to give further information about the incident on the grounds that it was classified and that it was engaged in blocking a Parliamentary Select Committee inquiry. [181, Chs. 3–5]

The broader question of the just war was whether or not nations had an 'automatic right' to be defended. Underlying the talk of 'political sovereignty' was the truth that authentic political processes, whereby people actually shape their laws and institutions, might be of great value; but they were not necessarily protected by keeping a nation immune from outside intervention. Thus, one philosophical argument ran, 'The possible justification for war has to be a matter of judgements about how important these things are, how they are threatened and how they can be secured or defended in a particular case, and whether or not they are of sufficiently good value to override the very strong moral presumption against the destruction of human lives'. What way the decision should go was 'the great moral dilemma', but it 'cannot be resolved by invoking rights to territorial integrity and political sovereignty'. [169, p. 153]

The need to weigh up the justice of the Falklands War involved two particular questions. One was proportionality. The war cost 255 British and 625 Argentine lives. They died to save 1,800 islanders. This was not an argument that could easily be resolved. What kind of figure would be acceptable as justifying war? Could a sliding scale of casualties as against those who they died to protect be devised? Yet proportionality cannot be set aside. In a letter to *The Times* on 8 May the Archbishop of Canterbury noted that it was a cardinal principle of the just war theory that the cost of every action should be counted: 'It is possible for a war to be waged at such a high cost as to entail so much suffering that this would out-weigh any attainable good'. [207, 8 May 1982] It was this consideration that Francis Pym mused on when (to Mrs Thatcher's disgust) he asked if the Falkland Islanders would desire to be liberated by means of a destructive war.

The second was the modern version of *jus ad bellum*. In the Middle Ages the church was the organisation that could speak with authority on the question of whether or not it was just to enter into armed conflict; in the post 1945 world it was the United Nations. Here the British Government was in safe grounds in securing the UN Security Council resolution 502 of 3 April 1982, calling for Argentine withdrawal from the Falklands. Yet this did not offer a definitive justification for the war. The UN Charter licensed member states to take individual or collective self-defence if armed attack should occur; but Article 2(4) of the Charter outlawed the use of force in absolute terms against the territorial integrity or political independence of any state: and Argentina claimed that Britain was ignoring Article 2(4) since the Falklands were rightfully part of the Argentine state. [23, pp. 39–48]

This claim was, of course, the nub of the dispute, and was based on Argentina's partial reading of history; but the British reading of history was also one-sided: the British claim to sovereignty was 'at best open to debate'. And there was for the British the embarrassment of Resolution 2065 of 1965 which set out the need to end colonialism in all its forms 'one of which covers the case of the Falkland Islands (Malvinas)'. [133, p. 9] The balance of the argument seemed to be tilted towards the British by the forcible Argentine occupation of the Islands: the classical terms for waging a just war did not sanction an offensive war to correct an injustice, and the Argentine invasion was hardly 'defensive'. [227, p. 40] But Argentina could claim that her use of war was a last resort, since all peaceful alternatives had been exhausted. It is arguable that, whatever way the objective case fell, the Falklands War was 'subjectively just' on both sides. [111, pp. 146–82]

There can be no definitive answer to this question, for circumstances alter cases: there could have been no possibility that a premature Chinese incursion into Hong Kong, had it occurred, would have led to the despatch of a task Force to assert British sovereignty. In the field of diplomatic relations, the Falklands War produced little change.

British relations with the European Community might have been expected to deepen, given its support, with a few exceptions, to the United Kingdom; the French response was especially positive. Likewise the American 'tilt' towards Britain suggested that Anglo-American relations would remain on a firm and friendly basis. Certainly Mrs Thatcher and President Reagan enjoyed a fruitful and genuinely affectionate relationship. But the United States tilted towards Germany as the most prosperous and significant core member of the Community; and Anglo-French relations did not long retain their warm Falklands glow. There was no international re-alignment as a result of the war, though there was admiration of the British military success (coupled with some bafflement at the cause) which might be said to have laid the ground for the British taking a leading part in the military campaigns in Bosnia and Kosovo, and the Iraq war of 1991.

The cost of the war for the British – estimated at some £700 million – must be supplemented by the estimated cost of replacing material, such as ammunition and fuel, which some put at £970 million. The cost of post-war protection of the Falkland Islands was estimated at about £250 million for 1982–83, £424 million for 1983–84 and in multiples of a hundred million pounds for some time thereafter. But the silent acquiescence with which the British public met this confirmed that this was not a war of costs and benefits, of proportionality in response, or even whether or not this was a just war. The British response to the Falklands crisis, and to the military campaign and its aftermath, revealed that this was a war of ideologies, and, as such, transcended domestic politics and international law alike.

The Falklands War was, for the British, a very personal war. It was laced with what Professor Keith Jeffery (referring to the Great War) called 'big words': [124, p. 210] in the Falklands these were duty, democracy, self-determination, the defeat of aggression and national honour. There were words which exercised a genuine motivating power; however they might become entangled in the web of personal and political survival, and tested by the reality of the battlefield. The historian and biographer Edward Pearce was so moved by the conjunction of history and identity that he asked if 'it' would 'ever be quite the same again?'. A lot of 'old-fashioned' items were 'dusted off and seem to shine bright'. [178, p. 34] The crisis seemed to bear out the truth of the claim that the British are 'mesmerised' by war. [123, p. xi] But war, once over, is soon forgotten. The historian T. D. Devine in his *The Scottish Nation, 1700–2000* (1999) made no mention of the war at all, referring only to Mrs Thatcher's 'nationalism'. [62, index] National unity ('British nationalism'?) soon crumbled. Patrick Cosgrave wrote of Enoch Powell that he realised 'the portentiousness of this for Ulster: if you fight for the Falklands, you can scarcely fail to fight for Ulster'. [207, 14 June, 1982] But the Anglo-Irish Agreement, giving the Irish Republic a consultative role in the government of Northern Ireland, was only a few years away.

Those who experienced conflict directly had to come to terms with the war. Two hundred and sixty veterans have committed suicide since the war. [56, 14 Oct. 2003] One former Welsh Guardsman brought a case before the High Court claiming that he and his comrades had been taken off ceremonial duties and were 'sent to be sitting targets' with 'no appreciation of what they were going in to'. [197, 13 March, 2002] But Hugh McManners probably spoke for many, perhaps most, of the serving soldiers when he wrote that 'Now that I'm back home, I would not have missed any of it, but I'm sorry it had to happen and so very glad to be home'. [144, p. 297] The journalist and historian Kevin Myers explained the paradox of war: that war, 'serious fighting', which the British Army had not experienced since the Falklands, tested soldiers' training and resilience; there was of course apprehension: but 'War is the only time when soldiers feel truly cherished'. [201, 26 Jan. 2003]

The question of who was to blame for the war was investigated by a Committee of Inquiry which took written and oral evidence; but its self-denying ordinance was expressed in its concern that it must 'avoid the exercise of hindsight in reaching judgements on the development of policy and on the actions of Ministers and officials'. The Committee, its chairman Lord Franks wrote, 'sought to judge on each important issue whether the views expressed and the action taken by those concerned were reasonable in the light of the information available to them and the circumstances prevailing at the time, and not to substitute our judgement of what we might have done in those circumstances'. For good measure the Committee also bore in mind 'that our task required us to focus exclusively on the Government's responsibilities for the Falklands Islands and the Dependencies, whereas those concerned, both Ministers and officials, had to deal with many other major and pressing preoccupations'. [77, paras. 13, 14]

The result was that the report was greeted with the dismissal that it was a 'whitewash' – the first of many such accusations about such reports since then. John Cole in the Listener on 27 January 1983 wrote that the Franks report's 'bottom line' – that Buenos Aires 'rather than London was responsible for the invasion of 2 April 1982' – 'reads rather as if Neville Chamberlain at the time of the Norway debate in 1940 had proclaimed that Britain's defeat was Herr Hitler's fault rather than his. True, but it would not have saved Chamberlain's premiership'. [50, 27 Jan. 1983] This and similar accusations were met by one member of the Committee later claiming that the scope of the inquiry did not include 'the general deterrence of Argentina from invasion'. [58a, p. 144] The Committee refused to indulge in virtual history – it was it said impossible to judge how Argentina would have reacted had the British Government acted differently – and in so doing sought to turn politics into history. John Cole saw that history as part of the difficulty 'our constitutional system has in adopting to the "melancholy long withdrawing roar" of empire'. [50, 27 Jan. 1983] But it could be said that the war was not a withdrawal from empire affair, but a return to the nineteenth century assertion made by Lord Palmerston of 'Civis Brittanicus Sum': that British people anywhere were entitled to the full protection of the British state. And that this was now reinforced with the modern doctrine of the right to self-determination. Paul Kennedy's prediction in 1977 that Britain would act only as a member of a 'fixed alliance system' was premature. [131, p. 16] British Governments in the 1990s seem to have worked on the assumption that Britain's role in the international world was naturally a military one, of which the second Gulf War, 2003, was the apotheosis. But although Britain did engage in further conflicts after 1982 – the Gulf Wars of 1990 and 2003, the Balkan crises of the 1990s – she would only do so as part of a multi-national force, on behalf of the United Nations, NATO, or a 'coalition of the willing'.

None of these crises would reach as deeply into the British way of thinking about their history and their moral values as did the Falklands War. None would reproduce the remarkable spectacle such as that of the Task Force embarking for the South Atlantic in April 1982. The people to whose rescue the British came were the chief beneficiaries of the war. In 1982 the population of the Falklands was 1,800, and falling. The 2001 census revealed that it had risen to 2,379 people, of whom 79 per cent were aged 55 years and under. This figure excluded the 1,700 military and civilian personnel based in the Mount Pleasant complex, where an international airport was constructed and military installations based. The islands by this time were economically self-sufficient in all areas except defence, the cost of which amounted to 0.5 per cent of the total United Kingdom defence budget. The British gave financial aid for reconstruction and development. But these were mixed blessings. The way of life that the islanders claimed in 1982 was especially their own was changed by the war; if isolation was their preference, it was no longer an option: for victory in war and a reversion to the pre-1982 life were, as it turned out, incompatible.

The consequences of the war for Argentina were, of course, less comfortable. Military defeat in the Falklands brought down General Galtieri; but as Jimmy Burns has pointed out, it was the Army High Command that removed Galtieri from his presidency, and a military regime lasted for a further 16 months. [32, pp. 398–400] The transition to democracy was not easy. The man who replaced the military rulers, Raul Alfonsin, was a lawyer with a record of defending human rights. He shrewdly built up his popular support in 1982 and emerged as Argentina's new hope with the message that 'We must fight to make sure that the armed forces not only leave government but that they never return'. [32, p. 418] The military still felt that it was its duty to assess the performance of the new President, who was elected in October 1983. But it would take a crisis even greater than that of the 1970s before the military would again risk its reputation and exchange the barracks for the *palacio*.

But the original objective of the disgraced military junta – the recovery of the Malvinas – did not disappear with the generals. On the contrary President Alfonsin held that the coming of democracy to Argentina rendered the claim to the Malvinas more authentic and legitimate. [32, p. 467] Mrs Thatcher once again suspected that the Foreign Office was in the business of necessary ambiguity over the issue of sovereignty, which, as she put it in November 1985, was 'of course not negotiable'. [32, p. 473] By the 1990s Argentina declared herself ready to convince the Falkland Islanders that they need not harbour suspicions about Argentina's intentions. A visit by the Argentine President Menem to Britain in October 1998 – the first by a President since the Falklands War – was carefully choreographed, with the tabloid press being taken, in particular, by the 'oriental beauty' of Menem's first lady, his daughter Zulemita. [32, p. 514] If 'war war' had not been replaced by 'jaw jaw', then it had certainly been replaced by spin spin.

Conclusion

The Falklands War, Sir John Keegan has said, marked the point at which Britain's 'late twentieth century renaissance as an international power may be dated' (231, p. xiii). If this is so, it is in one sense hard to understand. It was a small war fought at a great distance from the European Continent, whose proximity to the British Isles obliged the United Kingdom to engage in two world wars. It can be seen as an aberration, a diversion from the real needs of British defence policy, or even as a re-enactment of the colonial wars that should have disappeared with the dissolution of the British Empire. But its importance lay not in the theatre of war, nor even in its cause, the clash of sovereign claims, but in its political control and operational techniques. It was the first British campaign since the Second World War in which all her armed forces combined against a regular, if not especially effective, enemy: airplanes, ships and soldiers met in formal combat, so different from the wars of imperial retreat or the political complexities and murky killings of counter-insurgency and counter-terrorist operations. The relationship between politicians and public, civil servants and ministers, soldiers and civilians were tested in real war conditions. The services fired their weapons, old and new, against an enemy equally well armed, and in some respects using superior arms. Small wonder, then that the war resulted a whole series of analyses and hypotheses about what its lessons really were. How well did British political control of the campaign work, and why did it prove more effective than the apparently less complicated management by a military junta? Why did the Royal Navy lose ships, and why did it not lose more than it did? How effective was this or that weapon? What influence did the climactic and physical conditions of the Falklands have on the service personnel? What weapon or military machine was a key instrument of victory?

The British won the war because they worked out effective political control, with their small but well chosen War Cabinet, ably supported by civil servants and diplomats and willing (with the exception of the decision to attack Goose Green) to let the professionals in the armed forces work out their own way to wage war. Argentina seemed to lack this kind of well integrated and purposeful control, and no single member of the Junta seemed able to take and keep responsibility for the conduct of military and diplomatic policies. Differences within the British War Cabinet did not spill over into public dispute or paralysing deadlock. British diplomacy, which failed in the run-up to the Argentine invasion of the Falklands, rarely put a foot wrong in the ensuing two months of crisis, and the gradual tilt of the United States towards the British, while not of course engineered by the Foreign Office, was neatly facilitated by it. Argentina made intelligent use of her role as a South American state among her neighbours, calling upon their sympathy, which (with the exception of Chile) she obtained; but this was less significant than her loss of the United States as an 'honest broker', and more than that had the 'Latinos' had their way.

The British Armed Forces revealed an impressive ability to improvise, down to the Parachute regiment's use of the Milan weapon in its hard fight at Goose Green. The war in the air was not won by the British, but if their pilots could not gain air mastery, they did deny that to the excellent Argentine flyers, whose tactics did not match up to their skills, for example in their failure to attack the more vulnerable supply ships in San Carlos Bay. British public opinion remained supportive of the war, and genuinely saw it as a fight for cherished values, however open their sentiments were to accusations of jingoism. Argentine opinion was likewise thoroughly behind the recovery of the Malvinas, but was misled by the easy initial victory, when the Junta invaded the islands. Junta, armed forces, and people alike seem to have believed that the war was over almost as soon as it had begun. The British seemed to be following their time honoured tradition of losing the first battle (when Argentina captured the Falklands) but winning the rest, and especially the last one. Had the Royal Navy lost an aircraft carrier, or Goose Green been a signal catastrophe, then the mood might have changed. But the element of luck did not desert the war effort; or perhaps the British made their own luck, for example in obliging Argentine attacking aircraft to release their bombs prematurely.

Above all, it was the spectacle of a British Task Force sailing thousands of miles in a large combined operation and fighting the kind of war that NATO had been designed to fight, but never did, that provokes such fascination with this small war. From high command to the lowest tactical level, from sophisticated missiles to the soldier in the trench, this was 'real war' as the service trained for it. Battles on sea, land and in the air were open contests between regular armed forces, contrasting with the easy victories over a weak Iraqi land forces, the bitter and murderous civil conflicts in Bosnia or Kosovo, or the complexities of the 'war on terrorism' and the security crisis in Iraq after regime change. Yet it is dangerous to dismiss the Falklands War as what one journalist called 'a dotty fantasy of history'. [86, p. 2] It did happen. It is never wise to draw lessons from one war and apply them to other conflicts, and it may be that the military lessons of the Falklands War have a limited application, especially after '9/11'. But it is not to deny the uniqueness of an historical event to say that the variables of warfare, political, military and moral, are ever-present, and were exemplified, in their own way, in the Falklands War of 1982.

Guide to Further Reading

Full details of the books listed below are provided in the bibliography which follows.

General histories

The starting point for any study of the Falklands War is Freedman and Gambia-Stonehouse, *Signals of War: the Falklands conflict of 1982*, which is indispensable for its meticulous scholarship, accuracy of detail and reliable analysis. I have struggled in vain for independence. The Strategic and Combat Studies Institute Occasional Paper No. 46 'The Falklands Witness Seminar', records the recollections of key political, diplomatic and service personnel, with only minor quibbles about who said what to whom and when. Moro's *The History of the South Atlantic Conflict*: *the war for the Malvinas* is a full account from the Argentine perspective. Likewise, Jimmy Burns' *The Land that lost its Heroes*: *how Argentina lost the Falklands War* is notable for the author's first-hand knowledge of Argentine politics and society. Journalists who went to war wrote their accounts quickly, but with their ability to convey vividly the experience of crisis and conflict. The best of these are Patrick Bishop and John Witherow, *The Winter War: the Falklands*; Brian Hanrahan and Robert Fox, *'I counted them all out and I counted them all back': the battle for the Falklands*; Max Hastings and Simon Jenkins, *The Battle for the Falklands*; and the Sunday Times Insight Team, *The Falklands War: the full story. The Falklands Islands Review: Report of a Committee of the Privy Councillors chaired by Lord Franks* (the 'Franks Report') collects and scrutinises much evidence, but with conclusions that hardly seem to bear out its own labours.

Diplomacy

Peter Calvert, *The Falklands Conflict: the rights and the wrongs* is a careful and balanced inquiry into the diplomatic origins and justifications of the conflict. Douglas Kinney's *National Interest/National Honour: the diplomacy of the crisis* is a thorough description and analysis of key aspects of the diplomacy of the crisis, especially authoritative on the 'Peruvian initiative'. Peter Beck, *The Falkland Islands as an International Problem* sums up his valuable contribution to the debate. For Anglo-American relations see Louise Richardson, *When Allies Differ: Anglo-American relations during the Falklands crisis*; for European reactions see Stelious Stavridis and Christopher Hill (eds) *Domestic Sources of Foreign Policy: Western European reactions to the Falklands conflict*. Virginia Gambia's *The Falklands/Malvinas War: a model for North-South co-operation* is important for the Argentine side. Michael Charlton (ed.) *The Little Platoon: diplomacy and the Falklands crisis* contains much valuable information from the normally reticent mouths of diplomats themselves.

The fighting

For the Royal Navy see David Brown, *The Royal Navy and the Falklands War*. The best account of the infantry war is Nick van der Bijl, *Nine Battles to Stanley*. For the air war see Jeffrey Ethell and Alfred Price, *Air War South Atlantic*. The weapons used by both sides are discussed in Bryan Perrett, *Weapons of the Falklands Conflict*. Indispensable individual accounts are Admiral Sandy Woodward, *One Hundred Days: the memoirs of the Falklands Battle Group Commander*; Brigadier Julian Thompson, *No Picnic: 3 Commando Brigade in the South Atlantic, 1982*; Michael Clapp and Ewen Southby-Tailyour, *Amphibious Assault Falklands: the battle for San Carlos Wate*r, which is wider than its title suggests, and contains many important original documents. Martin Middlebrook, *The Argentine Forces in the Falklands War* is based on extensive research, including interviews with Argentine servicemen.

Personal histories

The most vivid of these, because the most committed, is Lady Thatcher's *The Downing Street Years*. The best, because of its detail and also its engaging style is John Nott's *Here Today, Gone Tomorrow*. At the soldierly level see Ken Lukowiak's *A Soldier's Song; true stories from the Falklands*; Michael Bilton and Peter Kosminsky (eds), *Speaking Out: untold stories from the Falklands War*; 'Sharky' Ward, *Sea Harrier over the Falklands*; Hugh McManners, *Falklands Commando*. The tragic consequences of war are conveyed in David Tinker's *A Message from the Falklands*; Simon Weston, *Walking Tall: an autobiography*; and John and Robert Lawrence, *When the Fighting is Over*.

The media war

Valerie Adams *The Media and the Falklands Campaign* is indispensable, as is Derrick Mercer, Geoff Munngham and Kevin Williams (eds) *The Fog of War: the media on the battlefield*. The Glasgow University Media Group's *War and Peace News* is written from a particular point of view, but contains important material and impressive argument. Susan L. Carruthers, *The Media at War: communication and conflict in the twentieth century* gives a general survey, with a detailed examination of the Falklands War. Robert Harris, *Gotcha! The Media, the Government and the Falklands Crisis* is a vigorous analysis of the wilder shores of media reporting of the war. The House of Commons: *Final Report of the Defence Committee, session 1982–83* does not sound exciting, but is, as media people give an account of themselves.

Culture and war

The best surveys (all of them critical of the Falklands mood of the time) are James Aulich (ed.), *Framing the Falklands War: nationhood, culture and identity*; Kevin Foster, *Fighting Fictions: war, narrative and national identity*; and David Monaghan, *The Falklands War*.

Postscript

The official history of the Falklands crisis is being compiled by Professor Lawrence Freedman. It will contain much hitherto undisclosed information, but has not, at the time of writing, cleared its official pre-publication vetting.

Bibliography

Please note that items are numbered in accordance with the numbers appearing in square brackets in the body of the text.

1. ADAMS, V., 'Logistical support for the Falklands Campaign', *Royal United Services Institution Journal*, 129, 3 (1984), pp. 43–9.
2. ADAMS, V., *The Media and the Falklands Campaign* (London, 1986).
3. ADKIN, M., *Goose Green: a battle is fought to be won* (London, 4th ed., 1997).
4. ALDEA, D., 'Blood and Mud at Goose Green', *Military History* (April, 2000), 42–9.
5. ARTHUR, M., *Above all Courage: the Falklands front line: first hand accounts* (London, 1985).
6. AUDOIN-REUGEAU, S., *Men at War, 1914–1918* (Oxford, 1992).
7. AULICH, J., *Framing the Falklands War: Nationhood, Culture and Identity* (Milton Keynes, 1992).
8. BARKER, N., *Beyond Endurance: an epic of Whitehall and the South Atlantic* (London, 1997).
9. BARNETT, A., *Iron Britannia* (London, 1982).
10. BARTE, E., 'The external dimension: Spain', in Stavridis, S. and Hill, C. (eds), *Domestic Sources of Foreign Policy: Western European reactions to the Falklands Conflict* (Oxford and Washington, 1996), Ch. 8
11. BAYLIS, J., et al., *Strategy in the Contemporary World: an introduction to Strategic Studies* (Oxford, 2002).
12. BECK, P., 'The Anglo-Argentine dispute over title to the Falkland Islands: changing British perceptions of sovereignty since 1910', in *Millenium: Journal of International Studies*, 12, 1 (1983), pp. 6–24.

13. BECK, P., 'Britain's Antarctic Dimension', in *International Affairs*, 59, 3 (1983), pp. 429–44.
14. BECK, P., 'The Future of the Falkland Islands: a solution made in Hong Kong?', in *International Affairs*, 61, 4 (1985), pp. 643–60.
15. BECK, P., *The Falkland Islands as an International Problem* (London, 1988).
16. BELGRANO ACTION GROUP, *The Unnecessary War: the Belgrano Inquiry* (Nottingham, 1988).
17. BELL, S., *The IF Chronicles* (London, 1983).
18. BERKOFF, S., *Sink the Belgrano* (London, 1987).
19. BILTON, M. and KOSMINSKY, P. (eds), *Speaking Out: untold stories from the Falklands War* (London, 1989).
20. BISHOP, P. and WITHEROW, J., *The Winter War: the Falklands* (London, 1982).
21. BLACK, J., *European Warfare, 1453–1815* (London, 1994).
22. BLAKEWAY, D., *The Falklands War* (London, for Channel 4, 1992).
23. BOLOGNA, A. B., 'Argentine Claim to the Malvinas under International Law', in *Journal of International Studies*, 12, 1 (1983), pp. 39–48.
24. BOND, E., *Restoration: a Pastoral* (London, 1982).
25. BOND, G. C., *The Great Expedition: the British invasion of Holland in 1809* (Glasgow, 1979).
26. BRAMALL, FIELD MARSHAL THE LORD, 'The Task Force Falklands', in Washington, L. (ed.), *Ten Years On: the British Army in the Falklands War* (London, 1992), pp. 5–18.
27. BRAMLEY, V., *Two Sides of Hell* (London, 1994).
28. BRAYBROOK, R., *Battle for the Falklands: 3, Air Forces* (London, 1982).
29. BRIGGS, R., *The Tin Pot General and the Old Woman* (London, 1984).
30. BROWN, D., in BBC Radio 4, 'Falklands Families' (4 May, 2002).
31. BROWN, D., *The Royal Navy and the Falklands War* (London, 1987).
32. BURNS, J., *The Land that lost its Heroes: how Argentina lost the Falklands War* (London, 2002 ed.).
33. BURNS, R. A., *Diplomacy, War and Parliamentary Democracy: further lessons from the Falklands War, or Advice from Academe* (New York, 1985).

34. CABLE, Sir J., 'The Diffusion of Maritime Power', in *International Relations*, 7 (1982–3), pp. 2139–57.
35. CABLE, Sir J., 'Surprise and the Single Scenario', in *Royal United Services Institution Journal*, 28 (1983), pp. 33–38.
36. CALVERT, P., *The Falklands Crisis: the rights and the wrongs* (London, 1982).
37. CALVERT, P., 'Latin America and the United States during and after the Falklands Crisis', in *Millenium: Journal of International Studies*, 12, 1 (1983), pp. 69–78.
38. CALVERT, P., 'Sovereignty and the Falklands Crisis', in *International Affairs*, 59, 3 (1983), pp. 405–13.
39. CALVOCORESSI, P., 'The Future of International Conflict', in *International Relations*, 7 (1981–3), pp. 1103–16.
40. CARR, J., *Another Story: women and the Falklands War* (London, 1984).
41. CARRINGTON, LORD, *Reflections on Things Past: the memoirs of Lord Carrington* (London, 1989).
42. CARRUTHERS, S., *The Media and the Falklands War: communication and conflict in the twentieth century* (London, 2000).
43. CEADEL, M., *Thinking about Peace and War* (Oxford, 1987).
44. CHANNEL 4, 'When Britain went to War' (30 March 2003).
45. CHARLTON, M., *The Little Platoon: Diplomacy and the Falklands Crisis* (Oxford, 1989).
46. CLAPP, M. and SOUTHBY-TAILYOUR, E., *Amphibious Assault Falklands: the battle of San Carlos Water* (London, 1997 ed.).
47. CLARKE, P., 'The Rise and Fall of Thatcher', in *Historical Record*, lxxii, 177 (1999), pp. 301–22.
48. *Clausewitz: On War* (ed. M. Howard, Oxford, 1983).
49. COCKERILL, M., 'Whitehall and the Media War', in *The Listener*, 21 Oct. 1982.
50. COLE, JOHN, 'The Franks Report', in *The Listener*, 27 Jan. 1983.
51. COLL, A. and AREND, A. C., *The Falklands War: lessons for strategy, diplomacy and international law* (Boston, 1985).
52. CORDESMAN, A. H. and WAGNER, A. R., *The Lessons of Modern War: Vol. III, The Afghan and Falklands Conflicts* (Colorado, 1990).
53. CURTEIS, I., *The Falklands Play* (London, 1987).
54. CURTIS, M., *Close Quarter Battle* (London, 1998).

55. DABAT, A. and LORENZANO, L., *Argentina: the Malvinas and the end of Military Rule* (London, 1984).
56. *Daily Telegraph*, 17 Jan. 2002.
57. *Daily Telegraph*, 'The Falklands War: a commemorative supplement', 30 March 2002.
58. DALYELL, T., *One Man's Falklands* (London, 1982).
58a. DANCHEV, A. (ed.) International Perspectives on the Falklands Conflict: a matter of life and death (London, 1992).
59. DARTFORD, M. (ed.), *Falklands Aftermath: Forces '85* (London, 1984).
60. de la BILLIERE, MAJOR GENERAL P. E., 'The Falkland Islands: the strategic and military aspects', in *Royal United Services Institution Journal*, 131 (1986), p. 13–16.
61. del SOLAX, L. G., *Argentina and the United Kingdom: from war to peace* (Southampton, 1990).
62. DEVINE, T., *The Scottish Nation, 1700–2000* (London, 1999).
63. DILLON, G. M., *The Falklands, Politics and War* (London, 1989).
64. DOBSON, C., MILLER, J. and PAYNE, R., *The Falklands Conflict* (London, 1982).
65. DUNNETT, D., 'Self Determination and the Falklands', in *International Affairs*, 39, 3 (1983), pp. 415–28.
66. *Economist*, Opinion Poll, 1 May 1982.
67. *Economist*, Opinion Poll, 8 May 1982.
68. *Economist*, Opinion Poll, 15 May 1982.
69. *Economist*, Opinion Poll, 29 May 1982.
70. *Economist*, Opinion Poll, 5 June 1982.
71. *Economist*, 12 Nov. 1982, pp. 49–60.
72. EDWARDS, G., 'Europe and the Falkland Islands crisis, 1982', in *Journal of Common Market Studies*, xxii, 4 (1984), pp. 295–313.
73. EDWARDS, G., 'Europe and the Falkland Islands Conflict', in Stavridis, S. and Hill, C. (eds), *Domestic Sources of Foreign Policy: Western European reactions to the Falklands Conflict* (Oxford, 1996), pp. 40–56.
74. ENGLISH, A. and WATTS, A., *Battle for the Falklands: 2, Naval Forces* (London, 1982).
75. ETHELL, J. and PRICE, A., *Air War South Atlantic* (London, 1983).
76. *Falklands Factor: Representations of a Conflict: Catalogue of an Exhibition at Manchester City Art Gallery* (Manchester, 1989).

77. *Falkland Islands Review: Report of a Committee of Privy Counsellors* (London, 1983).
78. FEMENIA, N. A., *National Identity in time of crisis: the Scripts of the Falklands-Malvinas War* (New York, 1996).
79. FERGUSON, N., 'From the Somme to Port Stanley', *The Times*, 26 Oct. 1998.
80. FINLAN, A., 'British Special Forces in the Falklands War of 1982', in *Small Wars and Insurgencies*, 13, 3 (2002), pp. 75–96.
81. FOSTER, K., 'The Falklands War: a critical view of Information Policy', in YOUNG, P. (ed.), *Defence and the Media in Time of Limited War* (London, 1992), pp. 155–67.
82. FOSTER, K., *Fighting Fictions: war, narrative and national identity* (Cambridge, 1999).
83. FOSTER, S., *Hit the Beach! Amphibious Warfare from the Plains of Abraham to San Carlos Water* (London, 1995).
84. FOWLER, W., *Battle for the Falklands: 1, Land Forces* (London, 1982).
85. FOX, R. and HANRAHAN, B., 'I counted them all out and I counted them all back': *The Battle for the Falklands* (London, 1982).
86. FOX, R., *Eyewitness Falklands: a personal account of the Falklands Campaign* (London, 1982).
87. FREEDMAN, L., 'The War of the Falkland Islands, 1982', in *Foreign Affairs*, 61 (1982–3), pp. 196–210.
88. FREEDMAN, L., 'Intelligence Operations in the Falklands', in *Intelligence and National Security*, 1, 3 (1986), pp. 299–335.
89. FREEDMAN, L., *Britain and the Falklands War* (London, 1988).
90. FREEDMAN, L. and GAMBIA-STONEHOUSE, V., *Signals of War: the Falklands Conflict of 1982* (London, 1990).
91. FREEDMAN, L., *The Politics of British Defence Policy, 1979–1998* (London, 1999).
92. FRIEDMAN, N., 'The Falklands War: lessons learned and mislearned', in *Orbis*, 26, 4 (1983), pp. 907–40.
93. FROST, MAJOR GENERAL J., *2 Para Falklands* (London, 1984).
94. GAMBIA, V., *The Falklands/Malvinas War: a model for North-South Crisis Prevention* (London, 1987).
95. GAVSHON, A. and RICE, D., *The Sinking of the Belgrano* (Sevenoaks, 1984 ed.).

96. GIBRAN, D. K., *Britain versus the Past in the South Atlantic* (Jefferson, North Carolina, 1998).
97. Glasgow University Media group, *War and Peace News* (Milton Keynes, 1985).
98. GOMPERT, D., 'American Diplomacy and the Haig Mission: an insider's perspective' in Coll. A. P. and Arend, A., *The Falklands War: lessons for strategy, diplomacy and international law* (London, 1985), Ch. 8.
99. GORTON, S., 'Thoughts on the Falkland Islands War', in *United States Naval Institute Proceedings* (Sept., 1982), pp. 105–7.
100. GRAINGER, J. D., *The Royal Navy and the River Plate*, 1806–7 (London, 1996).
101. GRAY, C. S., 'Inescapable Geography' in *Journal of Strategic Studies*, 22, 2–3 (1999), pp. 161–77.
102. GUERTNER, G. L., 'The 74 Day war: new technology and old tactics' in *Military Review*, 2 (1982), pp. 65–72.
103. HAIG, A., *Caveat* (London, 1984).
104. HARRIS, R., *Gotcha! The Media, the Government and the Falklands Crisis* (London, 1983).
105. HASTINGS, M. and JENKINS, S., *The Battle for the Falklands* (London, 1983).
106. HEALEY, D., *The Time of my Life* (London, 1989).
107. HEFFER, E., in *The Listener*, 9 April 1984.
108. HENDERSON, Sir N., 'America and the Falklands: case study in the behaviour of an ally', in *Economist*, 12 Nov. 1983, pp. 49–60.
109. HOFFMAN, M., 'Third Party mediation and conflict resolution in the post-war world', in Baylis, J. and Rengger, N. J. (eds), *Dilemmas of World Politics: International issues in a changing world* (Oxford, 1992), pp. 261–86.
110. HOLMES, R., *The Western Front* (London, 1999).
111. HOLMES, R. L., *On Wars and Morality* (Princeton, 1989).
112. HOPE, A. F. J., 'Sovereignty and Decolonisation of the Malvinas (Falkland) Islands', in *Boston College International and Comparative Law Review*, 6, 2 (1983), pp. 391–446.
113. HOPPLE, G. W., 'Intelligence and Warning: Implications and Lessons of the Falkland Islands War', in *World Politics* 36, 8 (1984), pp. 339–61.
114. House of Commons *Debates*, 6th Series.
115. House of Commons: *Final report of the Defence Committee, Session 1982–83: The Handling of Press and Public Informa-*

tion during the Falklands Conflict: Vol. II, Minutes of Evidence (London, 1982).

116. House of Commons: *Foreign Affairs Committee: Minutes of Proceedings, Session 1982–83*, HC 31 (iii), 1983.
117. House of Lords : *Debates*, 5th Series.
118. HUGHES-WILSON, Colonel J., *Military Intelligence Blunders* (London, 1999).
119. HUNT, Sir R., 'The Falkland Islands: the political and economic aspects', in *Royal United Services Institution Journal*, 131, 1 (1986), pp. 10–13.
120. HUNT, Sir R., 'Falklands Families: the Governor's Story', BBC Radio 4, 23 Sept. 2002.
121. HURRELL, A., 'The Politics of South Atlantic Security: a survey of proposals for a South Atlantic Treaty Organisation', in *International Affairs*, 59, 2 (1983), pp. 179–93.
122. JACKSON, Sir W., *Withdrawal from Empire: a military view* (London, 1986).
123. JAMES, L. *Warrior Race: a history of the British at War* (London, 2001).
124. JEFFERY, K., *Ireland and the Great War* (Cambridge 2000).
125. JENKINS, S., 'Britain's Pearl Harbour', Part I, *Sunday Times*, 22 March 1987.
126. JENKINS, S., 'Britain's Pearl Harbour', Part II, *Sunday Times*, 29 March 1987.
127. JENNINGS, C. and WEALE, A., *Green Eyed Boys: 3 Para and the battle for Mount Longdon* (London, 1996).
128. JOLLY, SURGEON R., in 'Falklands Families', BBC Radio 4, 14 Oct. 2002.
129. JONES, M., *Michael Foot* (London, 1994).
130. KEEGAN, J., *Intelligence in War* (London, 2003).
131. KENNEDY, P., 'British Defence Policy, Part II: a historian's view' in *Royal United Services Institution Journal*, 122, 4 (1977), pp. 14–17.
132. KINNEY, D., 'Anglo-American Diplomacy and the Falklands Crisis, in Coll., A. R. and Arend, A. C., *The Falklands War: lessons for Strategy, Diplomacy and International Law* (London, 1985) Ch. 7.
133. KINNEY, D., *National Interest/National Honour; the diplomacy of the Falklands Crisis* (New York, 1989).
134. KITSON, L., *The Falklands War: a visual diary* (London, 1982).

135. LAFFAN, J., *Fight for the Falklands*! (London, 1982).
136. Latin America Bureau, *Falklands/Malvinas: whose crisis?* (London, 1982).
137. LAWRENCE, J. and LAWRENCE, R., *When the Fighting is Over: a personal story of the battle for Tumbledown Mountain and its aftermath* (London, 1988).
138. LEIGH, N., 'A Limited Engagement: Falklands Fictions and the English Novel', in Aulich, J., *Framing the Falklands War* (Milton Keynes, 1992), Ch. 6.
139. LUKOWIAK, K., *A Soldier's Song: true stories from the Falklands* (London, 2002 ed.).
140. McEWEN, I., *The Ploughman's Lunch* (London, 1985).
141. McGOWAN, R. and HANDS, J., *Don't Cry for me, Sergeant-Major* (London, 1991).
142. McGRUTHER, COMMANDER K. R., 'When Deterrence Fails: the nasty little war for the Falkland Islands', in *Naval War College Review*, (March–April, 1983), pp. 47–56.
143. McKEARNEY, LIEUT-COMMANDER T. J., 'An Old-Fashioned modern War', in *United States Naval Institute Proceedings* (1982), pp. 117–20.
144. McMANNERS, H., *Falklands Commando* (London, 2002).
145. MAKIN, G. A., 'The Military in Argentine Politics, 1880–1982', in *Millenium: Journal of International Studies*, 12, 1 (1983), pp. 49–68.
146. MAKIN, G. A., 'Argentine Approaches to the Falklands/Malvinas: was the resort to violence foreseeable?', in *International Affairs*, 59, 3 (1983), pp. 391–403.
147. MARCELLA, G., '*The Malvinas/Falklands War of 1982: lessons for the United States and Latin America*', Strategic Studies Institute: United States Army War College (Pennsylvania, 1983).
148. MERCER, D., 'Is Press Freedom a threat during National Crisis?', in *Royal United Services Institution Journal*, 129, iii (1984), pp. 38–42.
149. MERCER, D., MUNGHAN, G. and WILLIAMS, K. (eds), *The Fog of War: the media and the battlefield* (London, 1987).
150. METFORD, J. C. J., 'Falklands or Malvinas? The background to the conflict', in *International Affairs*, 44, 3 (1968), pp. 463–81.
151. MIDDLEBROOK, M., *Operation Corporate: the story of the Falklands War*, 1982 (London, 1985).

152. MIDDLEBROOK, M., *The Fight for the 'Malvinas': the Argentine Forces in the Falklands War* (London, 1989).
153. MILLER, W. L., *Testing the Power of a media Consensus: a comparison of Scots and English treatment of the Falklands Campaign* (Strathclyde, 1983).
153a. MINISTRY of DEFENCE. The Protection of Military Information: Report of the study group on censorship. CMND 9122, December, 1983.
153b. MINISTRY of DEFENCE. The protection of Military Information: Government Response to the Report of the Study Group on Censorship.CMND 9499, April, 1985.
154. MONAGHAN, D., *The Falklands War* (London, 1988).
155. MOORE, MAJOR GENERAL Sir J. and WOODWORD, ADMIRAL Sir JOHN, 'The Falklands Experience', in *Royal United Services Institution Journal*, 128, 1 (1983), pp. 25–32.
156. MOORE, MAJOR GENERAL Sir J., 'The Falklands War: a commander's view of the defence/media interface', in Young, P. R. (ed.), *Defence and the Media in time of limited war* (London, 1994), pp. 142–54.
157. MORAN, D., 'Strategic Theory and the History of War', in Baylis, J. et al., *Strategy in the Contemporary World: an Introduction to Strategic Studies* (Oxford, 2002), Ch. 1.
158. MORO, COMMANDORO R. O., *The History of the South Atlantic Conflict: the war for the Malvinas* (New York 1989).
159. MORRISON, D. E. and TUMBLER, H., *Journalists at War: the dynamics of media reporting during the Falklands Conflict* (London, 1988).
160. MOULTON, J. L. 'British Maritime Strategy in the 1970s', *Royal United Services Institution Publications* (London, 1969).
161. MURRAY, W., 'Some Thoughts on War and Geography', in *Journal of Strategic Studies*, 22, 2–3 (1999), pp. 201–17.
162. MYERS, K., 'War is Hell: for soldiers who don't fight', in *Sunday Telegraph* 26 Jan. 2003.
163. MYHRE, J. D., 'Title to the Falklands/Malvinas under International Law', in *Journal of International Studies*, 12, 1 (1983), pp. 28–38.
164. NAILOR, P., 'Lessons of the Falklands Crisis?', in *International Relations*, 7 (1981–83), pp. 2158–66.
165. NEF, J. and HALLMAN, F., 'Reflections on the Anglo-Argentine War', in *International Perspectives* (1982), pp. 6–10.

166. NEILLANDS, R., *In the Combat Zone: special forces since 1945* (London, 1998 ed.).
167. NOAKES, L., *War and the British: gender, memory and national identity* (London, 1998).
168. NORMAN, R., *Ethics, Killing and War* (Cambridge, 1995).
169. NOTT, J., *Here Today, Gone Tomorrow: Recollections of an errant politician* (London, 2002).
170. NOTT, J., *Daily Telegraph*, 12 March 2002.
171. NOTT, J., *Daily Telegraph*, 13 March 2002.
172. NOTT, J., *Daily Telegraph*, 14 March 2002.
173. OWEN, C., *No More Heroes: the Royal Navy in the twentieth century: anatomy of a legend* (London, 1975).
174. PARIS, M., *Warrior Nation* (London, 2001).
175. PARKER, J., *SBS: the inside story of the Special Boat Service* (London, 1997).
176. PARSONS, Sir A., 'The Falklands crisis in the United Nations, 31 March–14 June 1982', in *International Affairs*, 59, 2 (1983), pp. 169–78.
177. PAYNE, K. B. and WALTON, C. D., 'Deterrence in the Post Cold War World', in Baylis, J. et al. (eds), *Strategy in the Contemporary World: an introduction to strategic studies* (Oxford, 2002), Ch. 7.
178. PEARCE, E., 'After the Falklands', in Encounter, 59, 3–4, June–Dec 1982, pp. 34–7.
179. PERRETT, B., *Weapons of the Falklands Conflict* (Poole, 1982).
180. PERRY, N., *Arrevederchi Millwall* (Boston, 1987).
181. PONTING, CLIVE, *The Right to Know: the inside story of the Belgrano Affair* (London, 1985).
182. PYM, F., 'British Foreign Policy: constraints and opportunities', in *International Affairs*, 59, 1 (1982–3), pp. 1–6.
183. PYM, F., *The Politics of Consent* (London, 1989).
184. RATCLIFFE, P., *Eye of the Storm: twenty-five years in action with the SAS* (London, 2000).
185. REGELSBERGER, E., 'The Converging National reaction: I, the Big States: France and Germany' in Stavridis, S. and Hill, C. (eds), *Domestic sources of Foreign policy: Western European reactions to the Falklands Conflict* (Oxford, 1996), Ch. 3.
186. RICHARDSON, L., *When Allies Differ: Anglo-American relations during the Suez and Falklands Crises* (London, 1996).

187. ROCK, D., *Argentina, 1516–1987* (London, 1987).
188. ROUQUIÉ A., 'Argentina: the departure of the military – end of a political cycle or just another episode?', in *International Affairs* 59, 4 (1983), pp. 575–86.
189. ROYLE, T., *War Report: the war correspondents' view of battle from the Crimea to the Falklands* (London, 1989).
190. RUBIN, A. P., 'Historical and legal background to the Falklands/Malvinas dispute', in Coll, A. R. and Arend, A. C., *The Falklands War: lessons for strategy, diplomacy and international law* (London, 1985), pp. 9–21.
191. SANDERS, D., WOOD, H. and MARSH, D. (with Tony Fletcher), *Government Popularity and the Falklands War* (Essex, 1986).
192. SASSOON, S., *Collected Poems, 1908–1956* (London, 1984 ed.).
193. SCOTT, L., *World Famous SAS and Elite forces* (London, 1994).
194. SCRUTON, R., *A Dictionary of Political Thought* (London, 1983).
195. SMARTT, I., 'British Defence Policy: Part II: an international view', in *Royal United Services Institution Journal*, 122 (1977), pp. 8–14.
196. SMITH, G., *Battles of the Falklands War* (London, 1989).
197. SOUTH WALES EVENING POST.
198. SPEED, K., *Sea change: the battle for the Falklands and the future of Britain's navy* (Bath, 1982).
199. STAVRIDIS, S. and HILL, C. (eds), *Domestic Sources of Foreign Policy: Western European reactions to the Falklands Conflict* (Oxford, 1996).
200. Strategic and Combat Studies Institute, Occasional Paper No. 46, *The Falklands Witness Seminar* (Swindon, Wiltshire, 2002).
201. *Daily Telegraph*.
202. Sunday Times Insight team, *The Falklands War: the full story* (London, 1982).
203. THATCHER, M., *The Downing Street Years* (London, 1993).
204. THOMAS, G., *Mr Speaker: the memoirs of Viscount Tonypandy* (London, 1985).
205. THOMPSON, BRIGADIER J., *No Picnic: 3 Commando Brigade in the South Atlantic*, 1982 (London, 1985 ed.).
206. THOMPSON, BRIGADIER J., *The Royal Marines: from sea sailors to special force* (London, 2000).

207. *The Times*.
208. TINKER, D., *A message from the Falklands: the life and gallant death of David Tinker, RN, from his letters and poems* (Harmondsworth, 1982).
209. TOMA, B., 'The International Dimension, II: Ireland', in Stavridis, S. and Hill, C. (eds), Domestic Sources of Foreign Policy: *Western European reactions to the Falklands Conflict* (Oxford and Washington, 1975).
210. TOWNSHEND, C., *The British Campaign in Ireland, 1919–21: the development of political and military policies* (Oxford, 1975).
211. TRICKETT, P., *U.K. Rep. and the Falklands Conflict: driving the machine* (Leicester, 1999).
212. TUSTIN, MAJOR W. J., 'The Logistics of the Falklands War, Part I', in *The Army Quarterly and Defence Journal*, 114, 3 (1984), pp. 195–330.
213. UNDERWOOD, G., *Our Falklands War: the men of the Task Force tell their story* (Liskeard, 1983).
214. VAN DER BIJL, N., 'There's None Better', in *Military Illustrated: Past and Present*, 56 (1993), pp. 21–4.
215. VAN DER BIJL, N., *Nine Battles to Stanley* (London, 1999).
216. VAUX, N., *March to the South Atlantic: 42 Commando Royal Marines in the Falklands War* (London, 1986).
217. WAIN, C., *The Listener*, 3 March 1983.
218. WAIN, C., *The Listener*, 25 October 1984.
219. WALLACE, W., 'How frank was Franks?', in *International Affairs*, 59, 3 (1983), pp. 453–8.
220. WALSH, J., 'There'll always be an England: the Falklands War on Film' in Aulich, J. (ed.), *Framing the Falklands War: nationhood, culture and identity* (Milton Keynes, 1992), pp. 33–49.
221. *War in the Falklands, 1982: The Sunday Express volume* (London, 1982).
222. WARD, COMMANDER S., *Sea Harrier over the Falklands* (London, 2000 ed.).
223. WASHINGTON, L., *Ten Years on: The British Army in the Falklands War* (London, 1992).
224. WEST, N., *The Secret War for the Falklands: the SAS, M16, and the war Whitehall nearly lost* (London, 1997).
225. WESTON, S., *Walking Tall: an autobiography* (London, 1989).

226. WESTON, S., *Going Back* (Bath, 1993).
227. WHITELEY, MAJOR G., 'The "Just War" tradition and the Falklands Conflict', in *Royal United Services Institution Journal*, 131 (1986) pp. 33–40.
228. WILLIAMS, G. A., 'When was Wales?', in Woolfe, S. (ed.), *Nationalism in Europe: 1815 to the present* (London, 1996), pp. 192–204.
229. WILLIAMS, P., 'Miscalculation, crisis management and the Falklands Conflict' in *World Today*, 38 (1983), pp. 144–9.
230. WILLIAMS, P. (with Power, M. S.), *Summer Soldier* (London, 1990).
231. WILSEY, J., *H. Jones VC: the life and death of an unusual hero* (London, 2002).
232. WILSON, T., *The Myriad Faces of War* (Cambridge, 1986).
233. WINDSOR, P., 'Diplomatic Dimensions of the Falklands crisis', in *Millenium: Journal of International Studies*, 12, 1 (1983), pp. 88–96.
234. WINTON, J., *Signals from the Falklands: the Navy in the Falklands Conflict: an anthology of personal experience* (London, 1995).
235. WOOD, C., *Tumbledown* (Harmondsworth, 1988).
236. WOODWARD, ADMIRAL S. (with ROBINSON, P.), *One Hundred Days: the Memoirs of the Falklands Battle Group Commander* (London, 1992).
237. WOODWARD, ADMIRAL S., Interview in BBC2 'War at Sea' 15 February 2004.
238. WOOLFE, C. and WILSON, J. M., *Authors take sides on the Falklands* (London, 1982).
239. WOOLFE, S. (ed.), *Nationalism in Europe: 1815 to the present* (London, 1996).
240. YOUNG, P. R. (ed.), *Defence and the Media in time of Limited War* (London, 1992).
241. ZAKHEIM, D., 'The South Atlantic Conflict: Strategic, Military and Technological Lessons', in Coll. A. and Arend A. C. (eds), *The Falklands War: lessons for strategy, diplomacy and international law* (London, 1985), Ch. 11.

Index

Active, H.M.S, 145
Alacrity, H.M.S., 118
Alfonsin, Raul, 220
Allara, Rear-Admiral Gualter, 32
Amery, Julian, 47
Andrew, Prince, 159
Antelope, H.M.S., 77, 125, 152, 179
Antrim, H.M.S., 122, 125
Appeasement, 47, 51–2
Archer, Peter, 151
Ardent, H.M.S., 123, 125, 179
Argentina, 1,6,9. Claim to Falklands, 10, 11, 12; military junta in, 10, 15, 22, 23, 40; plan to invade Falklands, 17, 30–33, 38; dispute with Chile, 19–20; public opinion and Falklands, 6, 10, 27–8, 32, 56, 59; relations with USA, 57, 134; response to first Haig mediation, 86; gets support from Organisation of American States, 89; and second Haig mediation, 90–91; and UN peace proposals, 113–14, 115; consequences of defeat for, 220
Argentina, armed forces. Land forces, 19–20, 61, 63–8, 72–3, 73–4, 76; in battle of Darwin/Goose Green, 128–9, 130–31; defence of Stanley, 142–3, 146. Air Force, 19–20, 73–5, 123. Navy, 72–3. *See also* General Belgrano
Argonaut, H.M.S., 122, 123, 125
Arrow, H.M.S., 100, 125
Ascension Islands, 75, 91, 96, 116
Atkins, Hunphrey, 35, 43, 44, 49
Atlantic Conveyor, 75, 116, 123, 125, 127, 137, 141
Aulich, James, 180
Avenger, H.M.S., 140, 145

Bailey, Sergeant Ian, 62
Barker, Nicholas, 88
Barnett, Anthony, 177
Belaunde Terry, President Fernando, 107
Berkoff, Steve, 181–2, 186, 187
Binyon, Laurence, 199
Bishop, Sam, 77
Beetham, Air Chief Marshal, 50
Benn Tony, 52
Bevan, Ernest, 3
Biffen, John, 44
Bishop, Patrick, 62, 164, 166
Black, Lt. Col. Crispian, 193
Black, Jeremy, 1
Blair, Tony, 188
Blakeway, Denis, 66
Bluff Cove, 69, 137, 138, 139, 140
Bond, Edward, 190
Bonzo, Captain Hector, 102
Bosnia, 217, 223
Braine, Sir Bernard, 47
Bramley, Vincent, 199–201
Bramall, Field Marshal Sir Edwin, 50, 111, 125, 126–7
Brazil, 134
Briggs, Raymond, 185, 187
Brilliant, H.M.S., 122
Britain, and Korean War, 4; and 'imperial retreat', 3–4; claim to Falklands, 9, 10–11, 216–17; negotiations with Argentina, 12–13, 17–18, 19, 21–3; communications agreement with Argentina, 13; Shackleton Report, 14, 23–4; and occupation of Southern

Thule, 16–17; and lend-lease scheme, 18–19, 20–21; House of Lords debate on Falklands, 23–5; withdrawal of H.M.S. Endurance, 27; and South Georgia incursion, 29–31; Intelligence operations, 34–5, 38; and invasion of Falklands, 33–6; preparation and sending of Task Force, 42–44, 45; direction of the campaign, 50; and appeasement, 51–2; and E.E.C., 58, 93–4, 106, 217; and Haig mediation, 83–5, 90–91, 94; sinking of General Belgrano, 103–6; and Peruvian Peace Plan, 111–15, 133–4, 135; relations with USA, 92–3, 107, 133, 134, 217; public opinion and the war, 167–9; reasons for victory, 221–3, criticism of after the war, 172–90
British Broadcasting Corporation, 129–30, 157, 159, 169; dispute with Government over war reporting, 160–62; and 'Tumbledown' play, 174; and 'The Falklands Play', 174–5, 190
British Land Forces, character and traditions, 61–2; relations with journalists, 163–6; 3 Commando Brigade, 125, 136, 138; 40 Commando, 62, 80, 198; 42 Commando, 62, 77, 142, 143, 144, 147, 163, 198; 45 Commando, 136, 142, 143, 145–6, 147, 163; 7th Gurkhas, 63, 95, 145; 2 Para, 126, 127, 128, 130–31, 136, 137, 138, 139, 142, 144, 145, 146, 147; 3 Para, 62, 142, 143–4, 147; Royal Artillery, 62; Royal Engineers, 62, 80; Horse and Life Guards, 62–3, 80; Special Air Service, 68, 69, 87, 88, 99, 120, 121, 136–7, 164; Special Boat Service, 68, 88, 99, 121; 5th Brigade, 95–6, 137–41; Scots Guards, 69, 136, 137, 139, 140, 144–5, 192, 203; Welsh Gaurds, 69, 136, 137, 139, 140, 141, 142, 143, 145–6, 193, 194, 218
Broadsword, H.M.S., 122
Brooke, Rupert, 196
Brown, Dave, 199
Brown, David, 70
Burns, Jimmy, 64, 65, 220
Busser, Rear Admiral Carlos, 39, 40

Callaghan, James, 15, 17, 18
Calvert, Peter, 4
Camilion, Dr Oscar, 21, 22, 57
Canberra, 72, 122, 136
Carey, George, 162
Carrington, Lord, 19, and leaseback scheme, 20, 22; meeting with Argentine Foreign Minister, 21; and withdrawal of Endurance, 27; reviews Falkland Islands problem, 1981, 28–9; and South Georgia crisis, 30, 33–4; and Argentine invasion, 43; resigns, 48, 49, 79
Central Intelligence Agency, 17
Chalfont, Lord, 10, 17
Chamberlain, Neville, 219
Chile, 19, 27, 63, 72, 73
Church of England, attitude to Falklands war, 212–14
Clapp, Commodore Michael, 78, 94, 95, 97; planning landing on Falklands, 99, 117, 118–19, 120, 121, 122, 146; and Sir Galahad disaster, 136, 137, 138, 139, 140
Clark, Alan, 45, 52, 189
Clarke, Peter, 171
Clausewitz, Carl von, 5–6, 77–8
Cobb, David, 179
Cole, John, 218–19
Colombo, Jorge, 74
Conqueror, H.M.S., 101, 102, 103–4, 106, 159, 215
Conservative Party, British, 13, 18, 19, 20, 41, 44, 48–9, 113, 135, 162, 167, 171, 177
Cook, Robin, 105
Cooper, Sir Frank, 41, 50, 154, 155, 156, 158, 164
Cormack, Patrick, 47
Cosgrave, Patrick, 218
Costa Mendez, Dr. Nicanor, calls for UN intervention in Falklands dispute, 28; and South Georgia incursion, 30; and invasion plans, 33, 34; and UN resolution, 50, 56; and possibility of reaching settlement, 59; and Peruvian peace plan, 107

Coventry, H.M.S., 122, 123, 124, 125, 127, 179
Crouch, David, 161
Curteis, Ian, 174–5, 190

Daily Express, 132
Daily Mirror, 163, 166–7
Daily Record, 170
Dalyell, Tam, 46, 161
Darwin/Goose Green, 99, 119, 120, 121, 122, 126; battle of, 127–32, 135, 136, 137, 145, 157, 165, 199
Davidoff, Constantino, 29, 33
De Cuellar, Perez, 112–13, 114, 115, 135
Defence Policy, British, 4, 26–7, 71–2, 208–9, 221
Delves, Major Cedric, 88
Devine, T.D., 217
Di Tella, Guido, 11, 32
Dowling, Major Patrick, 172
Du Cann, Edward, 47
Dunphie, Brigadier Christopher, 127
Dytor, Lieutenant Clive, 63

Economist, 152, 153, 167
Eden, Sir Anthony, 3
Emery, Sir Peter, 47
Empire, British, 3, 4, 221
Enders, Thomas, 28, 58, 107
Endurance, H.M.S., 16, 23, 24, 25, 27, 29, 30, 31, 43, 44, 88, 209
European Community, 41, 58, 93–4, 106, 124
Exclusion Zone, Argentine, 81
Exclusion Zone, British, 81; Total Exclusion Zone, 90, 96–7, 98, 100, 102, 103, 105, 109, 110, 112
Eyre, Richard, 176

Falkland Islands, cost of war, 217; consequences for islanders, 219–20
Falkland Islands Executive Council, 12, 14, 21
Fanning Head, 121
Farrer-Hockley, Major Dair, 130–31
Fenn, Nicholas, 158
Ferguson, Niall, 197
Fieldhouse, Admiral Sir John, 42, 50, 88, 94, 96, 97, 103, 110, 127, 159
Fitzroy, 136, 138, 140, 142
Foot, Michael, 46, 47, 106
Foster, Kevin, 187, 188–9, 191
Foulkes, George, 45, 161
Fox, Robert, 165
France, 58, 93, 106, 134, 217
Franks Report, 33, 37, 38, 69, 218–19
Freedman, Sir Lawrence, 38, 188

Galtieri, General Leopoldo, takes power, 22; and USA, 27, 42, 56; and South Georgia incursion, 33; invasion of Falklands, 35, 41; reinforces garrison, 65, 68; desires to 'avoid conflict', 84; and Peruvian peace plan, 107, 108, 109, 196; and defence of Stanley, 142; fall of, 220
Gambia, Virginia, 23, 28, 33
Gardiner, Captain Ian, 136
Gavshon, Arthur, 108
General Belgrano, 2, 73, 101, 102, 103, 104, 105–6, 107, 108, 109, 116, 134, 159, 160, 167–8, 179, 195, 204, 215; Argentine response to sinking, 109–18, 124
Germany, 93, 106, 208, 217
Gilbert, Dr. John, 155
Gilmour Sir Ian, 18
Glamorgan, H.M.S., 100, 194
Glasgow, H.M.S., 116, 125
Glasgow University Media Group, 160, 169–70
Gompert, David, 57
Goodchild, Ian, 174
Goodfellow, Mrs Rosalind, 212
Goose Green *see* Darwin and Goose Green
Gould, Chief Petty Officer, 71
Gray, Colin S., 6–7
Greengrass, Paul, 180, 181
Greer, Dr Kenneth, 212
Grytviken, 30, 31, 33, 35, 40, 87, 88, 89, 172
Guardian, 5, 47, 164, 166, 170
Gulf War, 1991, 1, 2, 219; 2003, 1, 55, 219
Gummer, John, 213

Haig, Alexander, 28, 52, 53, 57–8, 59, 81, 85, 92, 96, 107, 109, 124, 133, 134; first mediation, 89, 90, 94, 98; second mediation, 89, 90, 94, 98; and sinking of Belgrano, 105

Haig, Field Marshal Sir Douglas, 67
Hanrahan, Brian, 152, 160, 163–4, 165, 171–2
Harris, Robert, 158
Hastings, Max, 69, 164
Haughey, Charles, 93
Healey, Dennis, 49, 54, 56
Heath, Edward, 53–4
Henderson, Sir Nicholas, 58, 134
Hermes, H.M.S., 71, 72, 98, 107, 122, 131, 149, 151, 159, 163
Hiley, Nicholas, 191–2
Hill-Norton, Lord, 24
Hislop, Ian, 176
Hitler, Adolf, 219
Hong Kong, 216
Hunt, Sir Rex, 21, 29–30, 39–40, 53

Independent Television News, 163, 169
Ingham, Bernard, 150, 158
Intelligence Services, British, 14, 16, 17, 19, 22, 28, 34–5, 38, 43, 158
Invincible, H.M.S., 63, 72, 98, 209
Ireland, Republic of, 93, 106, 124, 134
Irish Republican Army, 2, 132, 163, 166
Israel, 38
Italy, 124

Jackling, Sir Roger, 44
Jay, Peter, 47
Jeffery, Keith, 217
Jenkins, Simon, 214
Joffre, General Oscar, 64, 67, 68
Johnson, Russell, 47
Jolly, Surgeon Rick, 141
Jones, Colonel 'H', 128–31, 193
Jones, Mervyn, 46
Jones, Sara, 132
Just War idea, 1, 211–12, 215–16

Keeble, Major Christopher, 132
Kee, Robert, 161–2
Keegan, Sir John, 221
Kennedy, Paul M., 25–6, 219
Kinney, Douglas, 108
Kirkpatrick, Jeanne, 56, 57, 92
Kiszely, Major John, 145
Kitson, Linda, 206–7
Korean War, 1, 4, 210
Kosovo, 217, 223

Labour Party, British, 18, 20, 41, 46, 54, 177, 188, 189, 190
Lawrence, Lieutenant Robert, 145, 172–4, 175–6, 177, 192–3, 203
Le Page, John, 150
Leach, Admiral Sir Henry, 26, 42, 43, 50
Leith, 29, 30, 33, 87, 88
Lewin, Vice Admiral Sir Terence, 49, 50, 53, 79, 103, 106, 158
Limited War, 210–11
Listener, 54, 176, 215
Lombardo, Rear Admiral Jose, 142
Luce, Richard, 21, 35, 49
Lukowiak, Ken, 201–2

MacDonald, Ian, 150, 156–7, 158, 162
McEwen, Ian, 182–4
McFadyen, John, 181
McKay, Sergeant Ian, 143, 144, 189, 192
McKay, Marion, 192
McManners, Hugh, 204–5, 218
MacMillan, Maurice, 48–9
McQueen, Alaistair, 163
Makin, G.A., 14
Manchester Art Galleries, 178–80
Manchester Evening News, 203
Mason, Roy, 4, 15, 16
Mass Observation, 169
Massera, Admiral Emilio, 73
Mates, Michael, 49, 161
Menem, President Carlitos, 196, 220
Menem, Zulemita, 220
Menendez, General Mario, 64, 66, 67, 68–9, 142
Meyer, Sir Anthony, 161
Middle East, 3
Middlebrook, Martin, 66
Middleton, Captain Linley, 159
Mill, John Stuart, 8–9
Mills, Lieutenant Keith, 40
Ministry of Defence, British, 95; anxiety about media in the Falklands War, 148, 149, 151, 153; restrictions on media, 154, 155, 159, 160, 163, 164, 170; Press Conferences, 156–7, 158; Study Group on the media, 209–10
Mitterand, President, 74
Monaghan, David, 187–8
Montes, Rear Admiral Oscar, 72
Montgomery, Lord, 24

Moore, Major General Jeremy, 87, 125, 127, 137–8, 139–40, 145–6, 151
Moro, Rubin O., 30, 31, 55, 108–9
Morris, Lord, 23–4, 25
Mottistone, Lord, 24
Mount Harriet, 66, 77; battle of, 143, 144
Mount Kent, 136, 137
Mount Longdon, battle of, 142, 143, 166
Mount William, 145
Mulley, Fred, 156
Myers, Kevin, 218

Neame, Major Philip, 130, 198
Nicholson, Michael, 150, 152, 159, 160
Norman, Major Mike, 39–40, 196
Norris, David, 165
North Atlantic Treaty Organisation, 26, 36, 37, 57, 65, 72, 209, 222
Northern Ireland, 2, 5, 20, 44, 51, 62, 77, 82, 132, 151, 164, 166, 167, 210, 218
Nott, John, review of British defence policy, 26; reaction to invasion of Falklands, 35, 41, 42, 43; speech in Commons, 49, 50; opinion of Mrs Thatcher, 54, 89; opinion of Argentine armed forces, 63–4; negotiations for settlement, 91, 124; sinking of General Belgrano, 103–4; suggests blockading of Falklands, 116; expects Royal Navy losses, 123; criticises delay in leaving beachead, 124–5; and BBC in war, 161, 162; defence review after war, 208–9

Observer, 164
Ogden Eric, 52
Oldfield, Maurice, 17
Operation Condor, 12
Organisation of American States, 89, 133
Ostreicher, Canon Paul, 214
Owen, David, 29, 85
Owen, Wilfred, 191, 208
Page, John, 153
Palmerston, Lord, 219
Panama, 133
Panorama programme, 161–2
Parkinson, Cecil, 50, 110, 158
Parry, Gareth, 164–5
Parsons, Sir Anthony, 56, 106, 113, 114, 115
Payne, Captain R.N.E., 213
Pedrozo, Air Vice-Commodoro, 67
Peron, President Juan, 10–11, 12, 14, 57
Perry, Nick, 184–5
Peruvian Peace Plan, 107–8, 109, 111; revised plan, 124
Plymouth, H.M.S., 122, 140
Ponting Clive, 104, 215
Powell, Enoch, 51, 112, 172, 213, 218
Press Association, 164
Prothero, Alan, 160
Public Opinion, British, 6, 12, 22, 30, 41, 56, 59–60; Government anxiety about, 149–50, 167–9
Pym, Francis, 49, 50, 51–2, 53, 55, 79, 100, 216; disagreements with Mrs Thatcher, 53, 109; and Haig mediations, 85, 86, 89, 102–3; and General Belgrano sinking, 104, 105, 109; describes USA as ally, 107, 108; and Peruvian peace plan, 109, 111; and UN initiative, 112, 113; and the media, 153

Reagan, Ronald, 4, 44; asked to mediate on Falklands dispute, 35, 42, 52, 56; response to invasion, 92; visits Europe, 33; hopes 'deal' can be struck, 135; relationship with Mrs Thatcher, 217
Rice, Desmond, 108
Ridley, Nicholas, 18, 19, 20, 21, 22
Rio Treaty, 108, 124
Rowlands, Ted, 18
Royal Air Force, 75–6, 222
Royal Navy, character and traditions, 70–73, 77; difficulty of defending Falklands, 16, 26; cuts in spending, 26–7, 71–2; submarine sent to Falklands, 31, 34; preparation of Task Force, 35, 42; decision to send to Falklands, 45, 47–8; rules of engagement, 81, 96–7, 100–101, 111; and Operation Parquet, 87–88, 98; uses US communication channels, 92; bombardment of Stanley, 99–100; attacks Belgrano,

101–104; vulnerable to air attack, 110, 116, 122, 125–6; defence of San Carlos, 118–21, 122–3, 125–6; relations with journalists, 150–53, 159; role of in Falklands War, 222
Rules of Engagement, British, 100, 102, 103, 104
Runcie, Dr Robert, Archbishop of Canterbury, 212–13, 216

San Carlos Bay, 69, 99, 115, 118, 119, 121–22, 124, 125, 135, 138, 139, 140
Sassoon, Seigfried, 200, 208
Scarfe, Gerald, 180
Scotland, 8, 17, 170
Scruton, Roger, 8
Self-determination, 8–10, 36
Shackleton, Lord, 15, 24
Shaw, Tony, 159
Sheffield, H.M.S., 71, 110, 111, 116, 125, 154, 157, 167, 168, 169, 170, 195
Sheridan, Major Guy, 87, 88
Shirley, John, 166
Shore, Peter, 20
Silkin, John, 43, 47
Sir Galahad, 69, 140, 141, 154, 160, 194, 198
Sir Tristram, 140, 141
Skelmersdale, Lord, 24–5
Smith, Ian, 4
Snow, Peter, 162–3
South Georgia, 29, 30, 31, 33, 40, 69; recapture of, 87–88, 91, 157
South Sandwich Islands, 16, 40
Southby-Tailyour, Major Ewen, 140
Southern Thule, 16, 24, 45
Sovereignty, 5, 8–9, 12–13, 14, 36, 52
Spain, 9, 44, 56, 133–4
Splendid, H.M.S., 101
Stanley, 16, 69, 118, 120, 126, 135, 136, 137; British attack airport, 99–100; British advance to, 137, 142, 144, 146
Steel, David, 49, 52
Stellman, Martin, 181
Stewart, Michael, 13
Suez Crisis, 1, 3, 47, 57, 91, 183
Sun, 92, 159, 166–7, 206
Superb, H.M.S., 31, 152–3
Swan Inlet, 137, 138, 178
Taylor, John, 179
Taylor, Neville, 158
Teal Inlet, 138, 139
Thatcher, Margaret, 2, 19, 35–6, 41, 46, 48, 49; reaction to South Georgia incursion, 33–4; decision to send Task Force, 35–6, 42–3, 79; debate in Commons, 45; assumes role of leader of the nation, 50–51; does not enjoy full support of own Government, 53; must pursue diplomatic response to invasion, 54; asks President Reagan to mediate, 56; disagreements with Francis Pym, 53, 109; and Haig mediations, 59, 83–4, 85; recapture of South Georgia, 89–90; and European Community, 94; and United Nations, 98, 112, 114, 115; agrees to change Rules of Engagement, 103; defends sinking of General Belgrano, 106–7; and Sheffield sinking, 110; and landings in San Carlos Bay, 123; anxiety about not moving from bridgehead, 125, 126; and Darwin/Goose Green battle, 132–3; doubts about US mediation, 135; and the media, 153, 161, 162; and public opinion, 167–8; disagrees with Archbishop of Canterbury on 'just war', 212; suspicious of Foreign Office intentions about future of Falklands, 220; effect of war on political career, 171; critics of 'Thatcher's Britain', 177–8, 180, 181–6, 188, 189, 208
Thomas, George, 45
Thompson, E.P., 172
Thompson, Brigadier Julian, 80, 88, 94, 137; praise for British army, 62; aware of difficulties of the campaign, 69–70; requests reinforcements, 96; plans for landing on Falklands, 117, 118, 120, 121; intentions after landing, 124–5, 126, 127; and attack on Darwin/Goose Green, 128; attack on Argentine forces at Stanley, 142–3; thoughts on the war, 146, 147
Till, Mike, 71

Times, The, 59–60, 75, 92–3, 148, 167, 178
Times Literary Supplement, 191
Tinker, Lieutenant David, 194–6
Townshend, Charles, 79
Two Sisters Mountain, battle at, 143
Tumbledown Mountain, battle at, 144, 181
'Tumbledown', TV Play, 174, 175–6

Ulloa, Manuel, 107
Union of Soviet Socialist Republics, 26, 41, 53, 56, 57
United Nations, Resolution 2065, 11, 16, 41, 43–4, 46, 53; Resolution 502, 55–6, 58, 79, 134; Resolution 505, 133–4; calls for settlement of dispute, 1973, 13, 14; peace initiatives, 111–12, 113, 124, 133–4
United States of America, 1, 3, 4, 19, 41, 54; relations with Argentina, 27, 57; relations with Latin American states, 58, 133; help for British war effort, 92; changes vote in UN, 134; relations with Britain and Europe after the war, 217

Van Der Bijl, Nicholas, 146, 196
Vaux, Lieutenant-Colonel Nick, 76–77, 144
Vieintecinco de Mayo, 100–101, 103, 104
Versailles Peace Conference, 9
Vietnam War, 148–9, 163, 210

Wain, Christopher, 80, 215
Wales, 8, 17, 199
Walsh, Jeffrey, 180–81
War Cabinet, British, 98, 110, 113, 124, 125; formation of, 50; declares Exclusion Zone, 81; anxiety about Haig mediation, 85; orders capture of South Georgia, 87; declares Total Exclusion Zone, 90; and European Community, 94; decision to change Rules of Engagement, 103; sinking of General Belgrano, 105–6, 109; and Peruvian Peace Plan, 107; and UN peace plan, 113; anxiety about forces not moving from San Carlos bridgehead, 124–5; and the media, 153, 158, 162; effectiveness of in the crisis, 221–22
Ward, Commander Nigel 'Sharky', 75, 205–6
Washington, Linda, 2
Watt, David, 168
Weinburger, Casper, 92
Weston, Simon, 193–4
Whitehead, Lieutenant Colonel Andrew, 193
Whitelaw, William, 44–5, 49, 125–6, 132
Whitney, Ray, 20
Wilcox, Tim, 178–9
Williams, Sir Anthony, 25, 30, 33, 37
Williams, Gwyn A., 11
Williams, Philip, 202–4
Wilson, Brigadier Anthony, 95, 138, 139, 178
Wilson, Harold, 4
Wilson, Trevor, 7, 187, 207
Wilson, Woodrow, 9
Winterton, Nicholas, 18
Winnett, Reverend R.A., 213
Wireless Ridge, 145
Wood, Charles, 174, 175, 176, 181
Woodward, Admiral 'Sandy', 71, 72, 73, 76, 81, 99; concerns about Haig mediation, 85; orders to him of 11 April, 86–7; and 'Operation Parquet', 87; concerns about negotiations, 98, 100; sinking of General Belgrano, 101–2, 103, 105, 106; sinking of Sheffield, 110; and San Carlos landings, 115; concerns about War Cabinet's slowness in decision making, 116–17; ordered to repossess Falklands, 120; anxiety about land forces not moving quickly, 122–3, 125; and Sir Galahad disaster, 137, 139, 140, 141; and the media, 151–2
World War II, 2
Wreford-Brown, Commander Christopher, 101, 102, 104

Yarmouth, H.M.S., 122
Young, Captain Brian, 98
Young, Hugo, 6